Nuclear Warfare: A Catastrophe

Nuclear Warfare : A Catastrophe

Capt. (Retd.) Prem Singh

Prashant Publishing House
DELHI - 110094 (INDIA)

PRASHANT PUBLISHING HOUSE
C-34, 28 Foota Road, Gali No. 3
West Karawal Nagar, Delhi-110094
Phone : 9810396373, 22963970

Nuclear Warfare : A Catastrophe

First Published : 2010

ISBN : 978-93-80565-07-1

PRINTED IN INDIA

Published by Mr. R. K. Jha M/s. Prashant Publishing House, Delhi and Printed at H.S. Offset Press, Delhi.

Preface

Nuclear warfare, or atomic warfare, is a military conflict or political strategy in which nuclear weapons are used. Compared to conventional warfare, nuclear warfare is vastly more destructive in range and extent of damage. A major nuclear exchange could have severe long-term effects, primarily from radiation release but also from possible atmospheric pollution leading to nuclear winter, that could last for decades, centuries, or even millennia after the initial attack. Nuclear war is considered to bear existential risk for civilization on Earth.

Even the most optimistic predictions of the effects of a major nuclear exchange foresee the death of a hundred million people within a very short amount of time; more pessimistic predictions argue that a full-scale nuclear war could bring about the extinction of the human race or its near extinction with a handful of survivors (mainly in remote areas) reduced quality of life and life expectancy for centuries after and cause permanent damage to most complex life on the planet, Earth's ecosystems, and the global climate, particularly if predictions of nuclear winter are accurate. It is in this latter mode that nuclear warfare is usually alluded to as a doomsday scenario. Such hypothesized civilization-ending nuclear wars have been a staple of the science fiction literature and film genre for decades. Today modern warfare constitutes aerial warfare, Asymmelric warfare, Battlespace, biological warfare, network-centric warfare, chemical warfare, electronic warfare, fourth generation warfare, Guerrilla warfare. Information Warfare, Naval Warfare, Nuclear Warfare, Psychological Warfare Propaganda, space warfare and total war.

The book is forward-looking as well, providing insight into what is surely the greatest challenge confronting security policymaking today: understanding the risks of current and future proliferation.

Contents

1

Introduction to Nuclear Warfare

Nuclear war, or atomic war, is war involving combatants deploying nuclear weapons. The United States is the only nation to have actually used nuclear weapons in war, having in 1945 dropped two of them on Japan—one on Hiroshima and another on Nagasaki. However, the term is used mainly to discuss the possibility of the use of nuclear weapons in a war involving two or more nuclear-armed parties. In general the discussion can be broken down further into subgroups. In the *limited nuclear war* (sometimes *attack* or *exchange*) only small numbers of weapons are used in a tactical exchange aimed primarily at opposing military forces. In the *full-scale nuclear war* large numbers of weapons are used in an attack aimed at an entire country, both military and civilian targets being "fair game". Soon after the first use of atomic weapons, a doomsday clock was instigated as a symbolic countdown to such full-scale nuclear war.

The Cold War

Before the development of a credible strategic missile force in the Soviet Union, much of the war-fighting doctrine on the part of the western nations revolved around the use a large numbers of smaller nuclear weapons used in the tactical role. It is arguable if such use could be considered "limited"; however, it was thought that the US would use their own strategic weapons (mainly bombers at the time) should the USSR use any sort of nuclear weapon against civilian targets.

Several scares over increasing ability of the USSR's strategic bomber forces surfaced during the 1950s. The defensive response on the part of the US was to deploy a fairly strong layered defence consisting of interceptor aircraft and anti-aircraft missiles and guns, like the Nike or Skysweeper, near larger cities. However this was a small response compared to the building of a huge fleet of nuclear bombers, the idea being that the USSR's huge area could not be defended against attack in any credible way, and they would "lose" any exchange.

This logic became ingrained in the US's way of thinking throughout the Cold War. As long as the *strategic* force of the US was larger than the USSR's forces in total, there was nothing to worry about. Moreover the USSR simply could not afford to build any reasonable counterforce, the US's economic output was such that they could never catch up.

Things changed with the introduction of the intercontinental ballistic missile (ICBM), which the USSR first tested successfully in the late 1950s. To get a warhead on target, a missile was far less expensive than a bomber that could do the same job. Moreover it was impossible to intercept them due to their high altitude and speed. The USSR could now afford to go head to head with the US in terms of raw numbers, although for a time they appeared to have chosen not to. Photos of Soviet missile sites set off a wave of panic in the US military, something the launch of Sputnik would do for the public a few years later. Politicians became obsessed with a percieved "missile gap" between the Soviets and the US. The US military gave missile development programs the highest national priority, and several spy aircraft and satellites were designed and deployed to check on Soviet progress.

Issues came to a head during the Cuban Missile Crisis in 1962. The USSR backed down from what could have been the spark for a nuclear war, and decided to institute a massive building program of their own. By the late 1960s numbers of ICBMS and warheads were so high on both sides that either the USA or USSR was capable of destroying the other country's infrastructure. Thus a balance of power system known as mutually assured destruction (*MAD*) came into being. It was thought that the possibility of a general thermonuclear war was so deadly neither power would risk initiating one. By the late 1970s people of both the US and USSR had been living with MAD for about a decade. It became ingrained into the popular psyche at a deep level. Such an exchange would have killed many millions of individuals directly and, it was thought, possibly induced a nuclear winter which could, in the worst-case scenario, have led to the death of a large portion of humanity and certainly the collapse of global civilization for decades, if not centuries. Many movies such as The Day After, Threads, WarGames, and Dr.Strangelove depict this scenario, as did the Planet of the Apes (1968-1973) and Mad Max (1979-1985) film series.

According to the 1980 United Nations report *General and Complete Disarmament: Comprehensive Study on Nuclear Weapons: Report of the Secretary-General*, it was estimated that in total there were approximately 40,000 nuclear warheads in existence at that time with a total yield of approximately 13,000 megatons of TNT. By comparison, when the volcano Tambora erupted in 1815 it exploded with a force of roughly 1000 megatons of TNT. Many people believed that a full-scale nuclear war could result in the extinction of the human species, but this was not based on any well-supported models. The idea that any nuclear conflict would eventually escalate into MAD was a challenge for military strategists. This challenge was particularly severe for the United States and its NATO allies because it was believed until the 1970s that a Soviet tank invasion of Western Europe would quickly overwhelm NATO conventional forces, leading to the necessity of escalating to theatre nuclear weapons.

A number of interesting concepts were developed. Early ICBMs were inaccurate which lead to the concept of counter-city strikes — attacks directly on the enemy population leading to a collapse of the enemy will to fight, although it appears that this was the American interpretation of the Soviet stance while the Soviet strategy was never clearly anti-population. During the cold war the USSR invested in extensive protected civilian infrastructure such as large nuclear proof bunkers and non-perishable food stores. In the US, by comparison, little to no preparations were made for civilians at all, except for the occaisonal backyard fallout shelter built by private individuals. This was part of a deliberate strategy on the Americans part that stressed the difference between first and second strike strategies. By leaving their population largely exposed, this gave the impression that the US had no intention of launching a first strike nuclear war, as their cities would clearly be decimated in the retaliation.

The US also made a point during this period of targeting their missiles on Russian population centres rather than military targets. This was intended to reinforce the second strike pose. If the Soviets attacked first, then there would be no point in destroying empty missile silos that had already launched; the only thing left to hit would be cities. By contrast, if America had gone to great lengths to protect their citizens and targeted the enemy's silos, that might have lead the Russians to believe the US was planning a first strike, where they would eliminate Soviet missiles while still in their silos and be able to survive a weakened counter attack in their reinforced bunkers. In this way, both sides were (theoretically) assured that the other would not strike first, and a war without a first strike will not occur.

As missile technology improved the emphasis moved to counter-force strikes: ones that directly attacked the enemy's means of waging war. This was the predominant doctrine from the late 1960s onwards. Additionally the development of warheads (at least in the US) moved towards delivering a small explosive force more accurately and with a "cleaner" blast, with fewer long-lasting radioactive isotopes). In any conflict therefore, damage would have been initially limited to military targets, there may well have been 'witholds' for targets near civilian areas. The argument was that the destruction of a city would be a military advantage to the *attacked*. The enemy had used up weapons and a threat in the destruction while the attacked was relieved of the need to defend the city and still had their entire military potential untouched.

Only if a nuclear conflict was extended into a number of 'spasm' strikes would direct strikes against civilians occur as the more accurate weapons would be expended early; if one side was 'losing', the potential for using less accurate submarine-launched missiles would occur. The fact remains that tactical usage of nuclear weapons against military targets would have caused death, destruction, and hardship on huge scales. Even comprehensive civil defence efforts to protect civilian populations would only partially mitigate the catastrophic effects of nuclear warfare.

Current Concerns

With the end of the Cold War and the collapse of the Soviet Union, conflict between the United States and Russia appears much less likely. Stockpiles of nuclear warheads are being reduced on both sides and tensions between the two countries have greatly reduced. The concern of political strategists have now shifted to other areas of the world. Current fears of nuclear war are mainly centred around India (first test May 18, 1974, the "Smiling Buddha" test) and Pakistan (first test May 1998), two nations whose majority religions and histories, as well as a territorial dispute in Kashmir and mutual possession of substantial (though probably numbered in dozens rather than thousands) nuclear arsenals makes many extremely nervous. In the case of Pakistan, their unstable government and the threat of radical Islamists seizing power and thus control over the nuclear arsenal has raised additional fears, compounded by the fact that a senior member of the development program, Sultan Bashiruddin Mahmood, is a strong Taliban sympathizer.

Another flashpoint which has analysts worried is a possible conflict between the United States and the People's Republic of China over Taiwan. Although economic forces have decreased the possibility of military conflict, there remains the worry that a move toward Taiwan independence could spin out of control.

A third potential flashpoint lies in the Middle East, where Israel is thought to possess on the order of one hundred nuclear warheads (although this has never been officially confirmed). Israel has been involved in wars with its neighbours on numerous occasions, and its small geographic size would mean that in the event of future wars the Israeli military might have very little time to react to a future invasion or other major threat; the situation could escalate to nuclear warfare very quickly in some scenarios.

In addition, there is the worry that so-called rogue states such as Iran, and North Korea may acquire nuclear weapons. Nuclear terrorism by non-state organisations could well be more likely, as states possessing nuclear weapons are susceptible to retaliation in kind. Geographically-dispersed and mobile terrorist organizations are not so easy to discourage by the threat of retaliation. Furthermore, while the collapse of the Soviet Union ended the

Cold War, it greatly increased the risk that former Soviet nuclear weapons might become available on the black market.

Glossary

- MIRV — Multiple Independent Re-entry Vehicless, nuclear devices carried, usually ten or twelve at a time on a single ICBM, allowing a single launched missile to strike a handful of targets, and allowing a few missiles to strike several targets redundantly.
- SALT I — Strategic Arms Limitation Treaty. A treaty signed by Richard Nixon and Leonid Brezhnev in 1972, limiting the growth of US and Soviet missile arsenals.
- SALT II — A treaty designed to further limit the growth of US and Soviet missile arsenals.
- START — Strategic Arms Reductions Treaty — A treaty proposed by Ronald Reagan to reduce the numbers of missiles and warheads.
- INF — Intermediate Nuclear Forces Treaty, signed in 1987, which eliminated tactical ("battlefield") nuclear devices and GLCMs from Europe.
- GLCM — Ground Launched Cruise Missile.
- ALCM — Air Launched Cruise Missile.
- ICBM —Intercontinental Ballistic Missile
- SLCM — Submarine Launched Cruise Missile.
- SLBM — Submarine Launched Ballistic Missile.
- Ballistic missile — A missile using a ballistic trajectory involving a significant ascent and descent including suborbital and partial orbital trajectories.
- Cruise missile — A missile using a low altitude trajectory intended to avoid detection by radar systems. Cruise missiles have shorter range and lower payloads than ballistic missiles, usually, and are not known to carry MIRVs.
- MAD — Mutual assured destruction. The doctrine of preventing nuclear war by creating a situation in which any use of nuclear weapons would result in the certain destruction of both the attacker and the defender.

- ABM — Anti-Ballistic Missile. Missiles designed to intercept and destroy ballistic missiles. Can also refer to the ABM treaty, signed by Richard Nixon and Leonid Brezhnev, which halted the development and use of such systems due to fears that such systems could counter the MAD scenario and, thereby, increase the likelihood that an ABM protected country would use their nuclear weapons aggressively.
- SDI — Strategic Defence Initiative, more commonly known as Star Wars. A system proposed by Ronald Reagan to use space-based systems to detect, intercept and destroy ICBMs and MIRVs. Criticized for its costs, doubts that it would be effective, and concerns that it would violate the ABM treaty and offset MAD, it was not supported by the US Congress at that time.

Types of Nuclear Warfare

Nuclear warfare, or atomic warfare, is a military conflict or political strategy in which nuclear weapons are used. Compared to conventional warfare, nuclear warfare is vastly more destructive in range and extent of damage. A major nuclear exchange could have severe long-term effects, primarily from radiation release but also from possible atmospheric pollution leading to nuclear winter, that could last for decades, centuries, or even millennia after the initial attack. Nuclear war is considered to bear existential risk for civilization on Earth.

The first, and to date only, nuclear war was World War II: near the end of the war, the United States dropped atomic bombs on Hiroshima and Nagasaki, Japan. At the time of those bombings, the United States was the only country to possess atomic weapons. After World War II, nuclear weapons were also developed by the United Kingdom, France, the Soviet Union, and the People's Republic of China, which contributed to the state of conflict and tension that became known as the Cold War. In the 1970s, India and 1990s, Pakistan, countries openly hostile to each other, developed nuclear weapons. After the collapse of the Soviet Union in 1991 and the resultant end of the Cold War, the threat of a major nuclear war between the superpowers was generally thought to have receded. Since then, concern over nuclear weapons has shifted to the prevention of localized nuclear conflicts resulting from nuclear proliferation, and the threat of nuclear terrorism.

Types of Nuclear Warfare

The possibility of using nuclear weapons in war is usually divided into two subgroups, each with different effects and potentially fought with different types of nuclear armaments.

The first, a *limited nuclear war* (sometimes *attack* or *exchange*), refers to a small scale use of nuclear weapons by one or more parties. A "limited nuclear war" would consist of a limited exchange between two nuclear powers targeting each others military facilities, either as an attempt to pre-emptively cripple the enemy's ability to attack as a defensive measure or as a prelude to an invasion by conventional forces as an offensive measure. This term would apply to any limited use of nuclear weapons, which may involve either military or civilian targets.

The second, a *full-scale nuclear war*, consists of large numbers of weapons used in an attack aimed at an entire country, including military, economic and civilian targets. Such an attack would seek to destroy the entire economic, social, and military infrastructure of a nation by means of an overwhelming nuclear attack.

Some Cold War strategists argued that a limited nuclear war could be possible between two heavily armed superpowers (such as the United States and the Soviet Union) and if so several predicted that a limited war could "escalate" into an all-out war. Others have called limited nuclear war "global nuclear holocaust in slow motion" arguing that once such a war took place others would be sure to follow over a period of decades, effectively rendering the planet uninhabitable in the same way that a "full-scale nuclear war" between superpowers would, only taking a much longer and more agonizing path to achieve the same result.

Even the most optimistic predictions of the effects of a major nuclear exchange foresee the death of a hundred million people within a very short amount of time; more pessimistic predictions argue that a full-scale nuclear war could bring about the extinction of the human race or its near extinction with a handful of survivors (mainly in remote areas) reduced quality of life and life expectancy for centuries after and cause permanent damage to most complex life on the planet, Earth's ecosystems, and the global climate, particularly if predictions of nuclear winter are accurate. It is in this latter mode that nuclear warfare is usually alluded to as a doomsday scenario. Such hypothesized civilization-ending nuclear wars have been a staple of the science fiction literature and film genre for decades.

Either a limited or full-scale nuclear exchange could be an *accidental nuclear war,* in which a nuclear war is triggered unintentionally. Possible triggers for this scenario have included malfunctioning early warning devices and targeting computers, deliberate malfeasance by rogue military commanders, accidental straying of planes into enemy airspace, reactions to unannounced missile tests during tense diplomatic periods, reactions to military exercises, mistranslated or miscommunicated messages, and so forth. A number of these scenarios did actually occur during the Cold War, though none resulted in a nuclear exchange. Many such scenarios have been depicted in popular culture, such as in the 1962 novel *Fail-Safe* (released as a film in 1964) and the film *Dr. Strangelove or: How I Learned to Stop Worrying and Love the Bomb,* also released in 1964.

History

Hiroshima to Semipalatinsk

The United States is the only nation to have ever used nuclear weapons during war, using two atomic bombs on the Japanese cities of Hiroshima and Nagasaki in 1945. Immediately after the bombings of Japan, the status of atomic weapons in international and military relations was unclear. Presumably, the United States hoped atomic weapons could offset the Soviet Union's superior conventional ground forces in Eastern Europe, and possibly be used to pressure Soviet leader Joseph Stalin into concessions. Despite Stalin's palpable fear of the bomb, he was pursuing his own atomic capabilities through scientific research and espionage against the American program. The Soviets believed that the Americans were unlikely to begin another world war with their limited nuclear arsenal and the Americans were not confident they could prevent a Soviet takeover of Europe, despite their atomic advantage. Within the United States the authority to produce and develop nuclear weapons was removed from military control and put instead under the civilian control of the United States Atomic Energy Commission. This decision reflected an understanding that nuclear weapons had unique risks and benefits separate from other military technology.

For several years after World War II, the US developed and maintained a strategic force based on the Convair B-36 bomber that would be able to attack any potential enemy from bomber bases in the US. It deployed atomic bombs around the world for potential use in conflicts. Over a period of a few years, many in the US defence community became increasingly convinced of the invincibility of the United States to a nuclear attack. Indeed, it became generally believed that the threat of nuclear war would deter any strike against the United States.

Many proposals were suggested to put all US nuclear weapons under international control—for example, by the newly formed United Nations—as an effort to deter both their usage and an arms race. However no terms could be arrived at that made either the United States or the USSR feel secure—the US was not willing to give up its atomic monopoly, and the USSR did not trust UN inspections on its soil.

On August 29, 1949 the USSR tested its first nuclear weapon at Semipalatinsk in Kazakhstan. Scientists in the United States from the Manhattan Project had warned that, in time, the Soviet Union would certainly develop nuclear capabilities of its own. Nevertheless, the effect upon military thinking and planning in the US was dramatic, primarily because American military strategists had not anticipated the Soviets would "catch up" so soon. However, at this time, they had not discovered that the Russians had conducted significant espionage of the project from spies at Los Alamos, the most significant of which was done by the theoretical physicist Klaus Fuchs. The first Soviet bomb was more or less a deliberate copy of the Fat Man device.

With the monopoly over nuclear technology broken, worldwide nuclear proliferation accelerated. The United Kingdom tested its first independent atomic bomb in 1952, followed by France in 1960 and then the People's Republic of China in 1964.

While much smaller than the arsenals of the USA and the USSR, Western Europe's nuclear reserves were nevertheless a significant factor in strategic planning during the Cold War. A top-secret white paper produced for the British Government in 1959, compiled by the Royal Air Force, estimated that British atomic bombers were capable of destroying key cities and military targets in the Soviet Union, with an estimated 16 million deaths in the USSR (half of whom were estimated to be killed on impact and the rest fatally injured) *before* bomber aircraft from the United States' Strategic Air Command reached their targets.

1950s

Though the USSR had nuclear weapon capabilities in the beginning of the Cold War, the US still had an advantage in terms of bombers and weapons. In any exchange of hostilities, the US would have been capable of bombing the USSR, while the USSR would have more difficulties arranging the reverse.

The widespread introduction of jet-powered interceptor aircraft upset this balance somewhat by reducing the effectiveness of the US bomber fleet. In 1949 Curtis LeMay was placed in command of the Strategic Air Command and instituted a program to update the bomber fleet to one that was all-jet. During the early 1950s the B-47 and B-52 were introduced, providing the ability to bomb the USSR more easily.

Before the development of a capable strategic missile force in the Soviet Union, much of the war-fighting doctrine held by western nations revolved around using a large number of smaller nuclear weapons used in a tactical role. It is debatable whether such use could be considered "limited" however, because it was believed that the US would use their own strategic weapons (mainly bombers at the time) should the USSR deploy any kind of nuclear weapon against civilian targets. Douglas MacArthur, an American general, was fired by President Harry Truman, partially because he persistently requested permission to use his own discretion in deciding whether to use atomic weapons on the People's Republic of China in 1951 (as the Korean War was raging).

Several scares about the increasing ability of the USSR's strategic bomber forces surfaced during the 1950s. The defensive response by the US was to deploy a fairly strong layered defence consisting of interceptor aircraft and anti-aircraft missiles, like the Nike, and guns, like the Skysweeper, near larger cities. However this was a small response compared to the construction of a huge fleet of nuclear bombers. The principal nuclear strategy was to massively penetrate the USSR. Because such a large area could not be defended against this overwhelming attack in any credible way, the USSR would lose any exchange.

This logic became ingrained in US nuclear doctrine and persisted for the duration of the Cold War. As long as the strategic US nuclear forces could overwhelm their USSR counterparts, a Soviet preemptive strike could be averted. Moreover, the USSR could not afford to build any reasonable counterforce as the economic output of the United States was far larger than that of the Soviets, and they would be unable to achieve nuclear parity.

Soviet nuclear doctrine, however, did not match US nuclear doctrine. Soviet planning expected a large-scale nuclear exchange followed by a conventional war which itself would involve heavy use of tactical nuclear weapons. Unfortunately, US doctrine rather assumed that Soviet doctrine was similar—the *mutual* in Mutually Assured Destruction necessarily requiring that the other side see things in much the same way, rather than believing, as the Soviets did, that they could fight a large-scale, combined nuclear and conventional war.

A revolution in nuclear strategic thought occurred with the introduction of the intercontinental ballistic missile (ICBM), which the USSR first successfully tested in August 1957. In order to deliver a warhead to a target, a missile was more cost-effective than a bomber, and enjoyed a higher survivability due to the enormous difficulty of interception of the ICBMs due to their high altitude and speed. The USSR could now afford to achieve nuclear parity with the US in terms of raw numbers, although for a time they appeared to have chosen not to.

Photos of Soviet missile sites set off a wave of panic in the US military, something the launch of Sputnik would do for the public a few months later. Politicians, notably then-US Senator John Kennedy suggested a "missile gap" between the Soviets and the US. The US military gave missile development programs the highest national priority, and several spy aircraft and reconnaissance satellites were designed and deployed to observe Soviet progress.

1960s

Issues came to a head during the Cuban Missile Crisis in 1962. The Soviet Union placed medium range missiles 90 miles (140 km) from the US-a move considered by many as a direct response to American Jupiter missiles placed in Turkey; however, these Jupiter missiles were already somewhat obsolete. After intense negotiation, the Soviets ended up removing the missiles from Cuba and decided to institute a massive building program of their own. In exchange, the US dismantled its launch sites in Turkey, although this was done secretly and was not publicly revealed for over two decades. Khrushchev did not even reveal this part of the agreement when he came under fire by political opponents for mishandling the crisis.

By the late 1960s, the number of ICBMs and warheads was so high on both sides that either the USA or USSR was capable of completely destroying the other country's infrastructure. Thus a balance of power system known as mutually assured destruction (*MAD*) came into being. It was thought that any full-scale exchange between the powers could not produce a victorious side and thus neither would risk initiating one.

One drawback of this doctrine was the possibility of a nuclear war occurring without either side intentionally striking first. Early warning systems were notoriously error-prone. On 78 occasions in 1979, for example, a "missile display conference" was called to evaluate detections potentially threatening to the North American continent. Some of these were trivial errors, spotted quickly. But several went to more serious levels. On September 26, 1983, Stanislav Petrov received convincing indications of a US first strike launch against the USSR but positively identified the warning as a false alarm. Though it is unclear what role Petrov's actions played in preventing a nuclear war, he has been honoured by the United Nations for his actions.

Similar incidents happened many times in the US, due to failed computer chips, flights of geese, test programs, and bureaucratic failures to notify early warning military personnel of legitimate launches of test or weather missiles. For many years, US strategic bombers were kept airborne on a rotating basis round the clock, until the number and severity of accidents persuaded policymakers it was not worthwhile.

1970s

By the late 1970s, citizens in the US and USSR (and indeed the entire world) had been living with MAD for about a decade. It became deeply ingrained into the popular culture. Such an exchange would have killed many millions of individuals directly and possibly induced a nuclear winter which could have led to the death of a large portion of humanity and, potentially, the collapse of global civilization. In May 18, 1974, India conducted its first nuclear test in the Pokhran test range. The name of the operation was Smiling Buddha and India termed the test as a "peaceful nuclear explosion".

According to the 1980 United Nations report *General and Complete Disarmament: Comprehensive Study on Nuclear Weapons: Report of the Secretary-General*, it was estimated that in total there were approximately 40,000 nuclear warheads in existence at that time with a total yield of approximately 13,000 megatons of TNT. By comparison, when the volcano Mount Tambora erupted in 1815 (turning 1816 into the Year Without A Summer due to the levels of ash expelled), it exploded with a force of roughly 1,000 megatons of TNT. Many people believed that a full-scale nuclear war could result in the extinction of the human species, though not all analysts agreed on the assumptions required for these models.

The idea that any nuclear conflict would eventually escalate was a challenge for military strategists. This challenge was particularly severe for the United States and its NATO allies because it was believed until the 1970s that a Soviet tank invasion of Western Europe would quickly overwhelm NATO conventional forces, leading to the necessity of escalating to tactical nuclear weapons.

A number of interesting concepts were developed. Early ICBMs were inaccurate, which led to the concept of countervalue strikes—attacks directly on the enemy population leading to a collapse of the enemy's will to fight. However, it appears that this was the American interpretation of the Soviet stance while the Soviet strategy was never clearly anti-population. During the Cold War the USSR invested in extensive protected civilian infrastructure such as large nuclear-proof bunkers and non-perishable food stores. In the US, by comparison, smaller scale civil defence programs were instituted starting in the 1950s where schools and other public buildings had basements stocked with non-perishable food supplies, canned water, first aid, dosimeter and Geiger counter radiation measuring devices. Many of the locations were given "Fallout Shelter" designation signs. Also, CONELRAD Radio information systems were adopted, whereby the commercial radio sector would broadcast on two AM frequencies in the event of a CD emergency. These two frequencies can be seen on 50's vintage radios on online auction sites and museums, with many of these radios still in use on tabletops across America. Also, the occasional backyard fallout shelter was built by private individuals.

This strategy had one major and possibly critical flaw, soon realised by military analysts but highly underplayed by the US military: Conventional NATO forces in the European theatre of war were outnumbered by similar Soviet and Warsaw Pact forces, and while the western countries invested heavily in high-tech conventional weapons to counter this imbalance, it was assumed that in case of a major Soviet attack (commonly perceived as the "red tanks rolling towards the North Sea" scenario) that NATO, in the face of conventional defeat, would soon have no other choice but to resort to tactical nuclear strikes. Most analysts agreed that once the first nuclear exchange had occurred, escalation to global nuclear war would become almost inevitable.

As missile technology improved, the emphasis moved to counter-force strikes: ones that directly attacked the enemy's means of waging war. This was the predominant doctrine from the late 1960s onwards. Additionally the development of warheads (at least in the US) moved towards delivering a small explosive force more accurately and with a "cleaner" blast (with fewer long-lasting radioactive isotopes). In any conflict therefore, damage would have been initially limited to military targets, there may well have been "withholds" for targets near civilian areas. The argument was that the destruction of a city would be a military advantage to the *attacked*. The enemy had used up weapons and a threat in the destruction while the attacked was relieved of the need to defend the city and still had their entire military potential untouched.

Only if a nuclear conflict were extended into a number of "spasm" strikes would direct strikes against civilians occur, as the more accurate weapons would be expended early; if one side were "losing", the potential for using less accurate submarine-launched missiles would occur.

The 1980s

In the late seventies and early eighties the balance, in terms of nuclear weapons, shifted towards the Soviets. However, with the ascension to the presidency by Ronald Reagan, the US renewed its commitment to a powerful military, which required large spending on military programs. These programs included spending on conventional and nuclear weapons systems, as well as defensive systems like Strategic Defence Initiative.

Another major shift in nuclear doctrine was the development of the submarine-launched ballistic (nuclear) missile, the SLBM. It was hailed by some military theorists as a weapon that would make nuclear war less likely. SLBMs, which can move with stealth virtually anywhere in the world, give a nation a "second strike" capability. Before the advent of SLBMs, thinkers feared that a nation might be tempted to initiate a first strike if it felt confident that such a strike would incapacitate the nuclear arsenal of its enemy, making retaliation impossible. With the advent of SLBMs, no nation could be certain that a first strike would incapacitate its enemy's entire nuclear arsenal. To the contrary, it would have to fear a retaliatory second strike from SLBMs. Thus a first strike was much less of a feasible option, and nuclear war was held to be less likely.

However, it was soon realized that submarines could "sneak up" close to enemy coastlines and decrease the warning time—the time between detection of the launch and impact of the missile—from as much as half an hour to under three minutes. This effect was especially significant to the United States, Britain, and China, with their capitals all within 100 miles (160 km) of their coasts.

Moscow was more secure from this type of threat. This greatly increased the credibility of a "surprise first strike" by one of the factions and theoretically made it possible to knock out or disrupt the chain of command before a counterstrike could be ordered. It strengthened the notion that a nuclear war could be "won", resulting not only in greatly increased tension, and increasing calls for fail-deadly control systems, but also in a dramatic increase in military spending. The submarines and their missile systems were very expensive (one fully equipped nuclear powered nuclear missile submarine could easily cost more than the entire GNP of a third world nation), but the greatest cost came in the development of both sea-and land-based anti-submarine defenses and in improving and strengthening the chain of command. As a result, military spending skyrocketed.

South Africa developed a nuclear weapon capability during the 1970s and early 1980s. It was operational for a brief period before being dismantled in the early 1990s. On Sept. 1, 1983, Korean Air Lines Flight 007 was shot down by Soviet Jet Fighters. On the 26th, a Soviet early warning station under the command of Stanislav Petrov falsely detected 5 inbound intercontinental ballistic missiles from US. Petrov correctly assessed the situation as a false alarm, and hence did not report his finding to his superiors. This highly likely prevented World War III, as the Soviet policy at that time was immediate nuclear response upon discovering inbound ballistic missiles.

The world came unusually close to nuclear war (although perhaps not as close as during the Cuban Missile Crisis) when the Soviet Union thought the NATO military exercise Able Archer 83 was a cover up to begin a nuclear strike. The Soviets responded by readying their nuclear arsenal. Soviet fears of an attack went away once the exercise concluded without incident.

Post–Cold War

Although the dissolution of the Soviet Union ended the Cold War and greatly reduced tensions between the United States and Russia (the Soviet Union's formal successor state), both nations remained in a "nuclear stand-off" due to the continuing presence of a significant number of warheads in both nations. Additionally, the end of the Cold War led the United States to become increasingly concerned with the development of nuclear technology by other nations outside of the former Soviet Union. In 1995, a branch of the US Strategic Command produced an outline of forward-thinking strategies in the document "Essentials of Post-Cold War Deterrence".

The former chair of the United Nations disarmament committee states there are more than 16,000 strategic and tactical nuclear weapons ready for deployment and another 14,000 in storage. The U.S. has nearly 7,000 ready for action and 3,000 in storage and Russia has about 8,500 on hand and 11,000 in storage, he said. China has 400 nuclear weapons, Britain 200, France 350, India 160, and Pakistan 60. North Korea is confirmed as having nuclear weapons, though it is not known how many (a common estimate is between 1 and 10). Israel is also widely believed to have nuclear weapons. NATO has stationed 480 US nuclear weapons in Belgium, the Netherlands, Italy, Germany, and Turkey, with several other countries in pursuit of an arsenal of their own.

A key development in nuclear warfare in the 2000s has been the proliferation of nuclear weapons to the developing world, with India and Pakistan both publicly testing nuclear devices and North Korea conducting an underground nuclear test on October 9, 2006. The US Geological Survey measured a 4.2 magnitude earthquake in the area where the test occurred. A further test was announced by the North Korean government on May 25, 2009. Iran, meanwhile, has embarked on a nuclear program which, while officially for civilian purposes, has come under scrutiny by the United Nations and individual states.

Recent studies undertaken by the CIA cite the enduring India-Pakistan conflict as the most likely to escalate into nuclear war. During the Kargil War in 1999, Pakistan came close to using their nuclear weapons in case of further deterioration. In fact, Pakistan's foreign minister had even warned that they would "use any weapon in our arsenal", hinting at a nuclear strike against India; the statement was condemned by the international community with Pakistan denying it later on. It remains the only war between two declared nuclear powers. The 2001-2002 India-Pakistan standoff again stoked fears of nuclear war between the two countries. Despite these very serious threats, relations between India and

Pakistan have been improving somewhat over the last few years. A bus line directly linking Indian and Pakistani-administered Kashmir has recently been established. However, with the November 26, 2008 Mumbai terror attacks, India does not rule out war with Pakistan.

Another flashpoint which has analysts worried is a possible conflict between the United States and the People's Republic of China over Taiwan. Although economic forces have decreased the possibility of military conflict, there remains the worry that increasing military buildup (China is rapidly increasing their naval capacity) and a move toward Taiwan independence could spin out of control.

Israel is another possibility as it is thought to possess between one hundred and four hundred nuclear warheads. It has been asserted that the submarines which Israel received from Germany have been adapted to carry missiles with nuclear warheads, so as to give Israel a second strike capacity. Israel has been involved in wars with its neighbours on numerous occasions, and its small geographic size would mean that in the event of future wars the Israeli military might have very little time to react to a future invasion or other major threat; the situation could escalate to nuclear warfare very quickly in some scenarios.

In the Persian Gulf, Iran appears to many observers to be in the process of developing a nuclear weapon, which has heightened fears of a nuclear conflict in the Middle East, either with Israel or with Iran's Sunni neighbours.

Potential Consequences of a Regional Nuclear War

A study presented at the annual meeting of the American Geophysical Union in December 2006 asserted that even a small-scale, regional nuclear war could produce as many direct fatalities as all of World War I and disrupt the global climate for a decade or more. In a regional nuclear conflict scenario in which two opposing nations in the subtropics each used 50 Hiroshima-sized nuclear weapons (ca. 15 kiloton each) on major populated centres, the researchers estimated fatalities from 2.6 million to 16.7 million per country. Also, as much as five million tons of soot would be released, which would produce a cooling of several degrees over large areas of North America and Eurasia, including most of the grain-growing regions. The cooling would last for years and could be "catastrophic" according to the researchers.

Sub-strategic Use

The above examples envisage nuclear warfare at a strategic level, i.e. total war. However, many nuclear powers are believed to have the ability to launch more limited engagements. The United Kingdom has reserved the possibility of launching a sub-strategic nuclear strike against an enemy, described by its Parliamentary Defence Select Committee as "the launch of one or a limited number of missiles against an adversary as a means of conveying a political message, warning or demonstration of resolve". This would see the deployment of strategic nuclear weapons in a very limited role rather than the battlefield exchanges of tactical nuclear weapons. Such a strategy is based on the assumption that an enemy country such as the Russian Federation or the People's Republic of China with a larger stockpile of nuclear weapons would not retaliate with far greater force than had been used by Britain.

British Trident-armed *Vanguard* class nuclear submarines are believed to carry some missiles for this purpose, potentially allowing a strike as low as one kiloton against a single target. Former Defence Secretary Malcolm Rifkind argued that this capacity offset the reduced credibility of fullscale strategic nuclear attack following the end of the Cold War. Commodore Tim Hare, former Director of Nuclear Policy at the British Ministry of Defence, has described it as offering the Government "an extra option in the escalatory process before it goes for an all-out strategic strike which would deliver unacceptable damage". However, this sub-strategic capacity has been criticized as potentially increasing the acceptability of using nuclear weapons. The related consideration of new generations of limited-yield nuclear weapons by the United States has also alarmed anti-nuclear groups, who believe it will make the use of nuclear weapons more acceptable.

Nuclear Terrorism

Nuclear terrorism by non-state organizations is an unknown factor in nuclear deterrence thinking, as states possessing nuclear weapons are susceptible to retaliation in kind, but sub-or trans-state actors are not. The collapse of the Soviet Union led to the possibility that former Soviet nuclear weapons might become available on the black market (so-called 'loose nukes'), while no warheads are known to have been mislaid, it has been alleged that suitcase-size bombs might be unaccounted for. A similar threat may exist via dirty bombs.

An Overview of the History of Nuclear Warfare

The discovery that it is possible to release the energy within the atomic structure of certain elements has led to the manufacture of weapons of unprecedented destructiveness. Such weapons present a great danger as they are capable of causing damage on an immense scale and possibly killing hundreds of millions of people while destroying the basis of civilized life over wide areas. In the 19th century, the rapid advance of modern technology and industrial organization greatly increased both the destructive power of armed forces and the capacity of societies both to resist and to recover from an attack. In the present century, these advances have already resulted in two massively destructive world wars. These experiences led many to question whether modern war on a large scale remained a practical—let alone a morally justifiable—way to achieve political purposes. Nuclear weapons carry the possibilities of destruction to a new level for Nuclear weapons are able to inflict far greater damage within a few hours than previously resulted from years of warfare! This not only makes the consequences of war worse but also raises new concerns about controlling such a destructive process. Fearing the consequences of losing control, the nations possessing nuclear weapons, have, therefore, become extremely cautious in managing these dangers and in their dealing with each other. A more in depth view of the history of nuclear warfare is on the nuclear past page.

Countermeasures

Nuclear Deterrence

Over the past few decades, ways of living with nuclear weapons have evolved, creating political systems that everyone hopes will prevent such weapons from ever being used. The main feature of these systems is known as nuclear deterrence. Quite soon after the destructive power of nuclear weapons was realized, people understood that an active defence, such as shooting down bombers, was impossible. But a passive defence (building air raid shelters, evacuating people, etc.) would not do much good either. Safety could only come from persuading potential attackers not to attack at all. This could best be done by convincing them that they would suffer an equally bad attack in return. This threat of retaliation, therefore, would perhaps serve to deter the possible aggressor. While deterrence is not a new idea, what is new about nuclear deterrence is, first, that it may be the only defence possible and, secondly, that a well-designed nuclear force could create retaliatory threats so great that no leader would ever act to bring about such destruction deliberately. Consequently, whatever its other military policies, each of the nuclear powers has tried to develop a nuclear retaliatory force that could—even if its enemies struck first—deliver in a second strike a blow that would result in unacceptable damage to the aggressor. That is the principle behind nuclear deterrence. It can be argued that nuclear deterrence is effective because no nuclear weapons have been used in warfare ever since 1945, but a world of nuclear deterrence has several obvious drawbacks:

- Because nuclear weapons continue to exist, there is the permanent danger of catastrophe, and the system might produce catastrophe rather than stalemate.
- The system requires that nuclear powers regard each other as possible enemies, keeping calculating military balances against each other, and watching nervously for signs that others have found ways to break the stalemate in their favour and engage in nuclear blackmail, or even an attack.
- While, theorectically, deterrence could be maintained by only a few nuclear weapons, the kind of suspicion and uncertainty that exists tends to drive nuclear powers to heavy expenditures in order to increase or improve their arsenals. This, in turn, reinforces mutual suspicion.
- As such suspicions illustrate, simple nuclear deterrence is based on the assumption that there is no adequate defence yet. In recent years, however, this assumption has been undermined in two ways:

— First, ways of intercepting bombers and missiles have been much improved. Although any adequate defence against a large-scale nuclear attack in the near future seems unlikely, would-be deterers have to worry about possible defence against their retaliation. This, however, can increase suspicion and competition.

— Secondly, missiles have become more accurate. While early intercontinental missiles typically missed targets by a mile or two, they can now achieve accuracies of a few hundred feet and will soon be able to arrive within a few yards. Therefore, it might be possible to seek defence by destroying an enemy's retaliatory force before it could be used. The possibility of such a counterforce strike against enemy forces rather than against cities or industry could be combined with active defenses against the weakened surviving retaliatory force.

For all these reasons, deterrence cannot be assured simply by possessing a few nuclear weapons. The weapons also have to be effective against an agressor's range of countermeasures. Such a situation creates an arms competition that would be expensive at best and, at the worst, might produce tensions and uncertainties that could lead a nuclear power to believe that attacking was the only way to avert or minimize an attack on itself.

Ways to Control Nuclear Forces

The destructiveness of nuclear weapons, and the danger of escalation to higher levels of warfare if even one or two were used, makes governments possessing nuclear weapons anxious to guarantee their use only when absolutely necessary. Consequently, great care has been taken to perfect the systems that control nuclear weapons, and systems for Command, Control, and Communication, or C^3.

Closely connected to this system for controlling forces are the systems used to determine the size and capabilities of potentially hostile forces and to provide warning of an impending attack. Most of these activities are now performed by the many kinds of sensors carried by space satellites and by ground-based radars such as the three U.S. Ballistic Missile Early Warning Systems (BMEWS) that are located in Alaska, Greenland, and England. The systems for preventing unintended use of nuclear weapons can be divided into three categories:

- o safety devices to prevent accidental explosions or launching of weapons
- o laws and military discipline for making sure that people obey orders
- o devices to prevent people from acting without authority

While military discipline is nothing new, the special dangers of nuclear weapons have inspired ingenious physical controls. Weapons are being guarded with electronic locks that require the insertion of a code number before operators can act. These are often supplemented by devices that will make the weapon unusable if anyone tries to bypass the locks.

Surveillance Satellites

Satellites provide their owners with much information about the activities of other countries and also provide useful reassurance that nothing too dangerous is happening or that an atttack is not imminent. If nuclear war were tragically to occur, satellites could help to control it by providing reliable information about what was actually happening and therefore, could reduce the typical confusion that is often referred to as the "fog of war."

Antimissile Weapons

It takes only a very few of the larger nuclear weapons to create great destruction. Power nuclear warheads are now only a few feet in length so they can be delivered by ballistic missiles, which cannot be stopped by traditional air defenses. For many years, it was thought that no defence was possible against ballistic missiles, but now the situation has changed. This is an important development because the revolution created by nuclear weapons would be significantly reversed if effective defenses against missiles were to be developed.

In the past, developments in rocketry and in electronic guidance made it possible for one rocket to intercept another and destroy it. But while it was possible to intercept single test rockets, catching all of a numerous incoming attack still seemed impossible. As it only took a few penetrations to cause a disaster, U.S. experts did not think building a defensive network was worth the great expense. A further reason to be doubtful about ballistic missile defenses then was the probable ease with which an attacker could make the defender's job more difficult. Although the most expensive, the simplest way would be to buy more offensive missiles to "saturate" the defence. Cheaper ways would be to equip reentry vehicles with devices such as chaff and decoys—lightweight imitations that acted like the real thing while outside the atmosphere—to confuse the defensive radar.

There are also broader arguments against ballistic missile defenses, and one is that such defenses could accelerate an arms race such as the Cold War mentioned in the nuclear past section. Many people believe that if all parties in a nuclear balance of power know they have no defence, they will be cautious and content with fairly small attacking forces. But if an attacker faced with defenses, tries to get through by increasing the size of its attack, the result might be more rather than less destruction if the defenses failed. On the other hand, if one side were confident in its defence, it might be more tempted to use its own offensive forces. It was this kind of thinking that led to the U.S. and the Soviet Union signing the Anti-Ballistic Missile (ABM) Treaty of 1972. That treaty limited each side to one defended area. The Soviet Union has one around Moscow, but the United States has yet to build the system permitted by the treaty.

Star Wars

Although the challenge of intercepting a reentry vehicle was technologically mastered in the 1960s, it still seemed impossible to offer a really worthwhile defence to a full-scale sttack. By the 1980s, however, a variety of technological advances had made such a defence seem possible. Because space operations played such an important role in these efforts, the U.S. program, officially called the Strategic Defence Initiative (SDI), became known as Star Wars.

Many different technologies contributed to this new optimism. Radars had become more efficient, and computers were much more capable of rapidly processing the information they received.

Interceptor rockets could more quickly meet attacking warheads and, where earlier systems had to rely on nuclear explosions to destroy hostile reentry vehicles, more accurate interception made it possible to employ non-nuclear kill methods such as conventional explosions and shrapnel-like clusters of solid projectiles, or kinetic kill. the most Star Wars-like idea was to use laser beams from the ground or from satellites to damage offensive vehicles. As rockets rose slowly and vulnerably from the ground with all their later-to-be-dispersed multiple warheads aboard, they might be destroyed by kinetic or laser deviecs in satellites over enemy launch-sites. These ideas offered the possibility of a layered defence, whereby the offensive force would be attacked during all three stages of its flight: the boost phase, the mid-course phase, and the reentry, or terminal, phase. Thus, the defence would have several chances to attack and could enjoy a good overall performance, even if each phase had been only partially successful.

There are still many difficulties with a layered defence, however, and many of the necessary devices are still in the experimental stage. It is particularly difficult to get the necessary energy for lasers into space because the atmosphere has the effect of shielding the ground. Moreover, the attacker can use countermeasures such as decoys and can "harden," or strengthen, its weapons against lasers. It can also increase the acceleration of its boosters to permit the separation of the warheads while they are still within the atmosphere, which will give them some shielding from lasers. They enemy can, of course, also nicrease the attack by aircraft or cruise missiles, which means the defender must also have a good antiaircraft system. Once an option becomes technologically possible, its usefulness always depends on the cost. for instance, can an attacker afford to maintain the effectiveness of its attack? Most experts believe it will be a long time, if ever, before a "leak-proof umbrella of defence" can be built. But before then, defenses may become efficient enough to reduce an attacker's confidence in success and thus promote deterrence.

Nuclear Terrorism—something Bad to Consider

So far in this nuclear age, nuclear weapons have been in the possession of only very few nations. While the danger of an increasing number of countries gaining possession of these powerful new weapons has long been recognized, much less attention has been given to the possibility that private groups might gain access to a nuclear weapon. In an age of widespread terrorism, it is not difficult to imagine the attraction that such a terrifying instrument might have for those seeking power for coercion or blackmail. In theory, terrorists might either seize an existing weapon or set up a secret organization to make one.

On the whole, obtaining nuclear weapons by unauthorized individuals or groups seems unlikely because nuclear materials are difficult to acquire and to handle. Military weapons and nuclear power stations and manufacturing facilities are closely guarded, often by special police forces or by technological devices. Also, nuclear weapons often contain mechanism that not only prevent accidental explosions but also disable the weapon if an unauthorized person tampers with it.

Radioactive material is so dangerous, however, that it might not be necessary for terrorists to obtain a weapon. Instead, they could create immense fear and panic if they were only suspected of possessing a nuclear bomb and threatened to release radioactive material. As the amount of radioactive waste in the world increases, this might offer one of the easier methods for terrorists.

Aftermath of Nuclear War

The detonation of nuclear weapons has a number of very powerful effects. Chief among them are the immediate release of X-ray energy followed by thermal radiation, atmospheric blast and the subsequent movement of longer-term radiation, which is carried in dust from the bomb and residue from any crater. These longer term aftereffects depend on the design of the weapon and how it was used—whether on the earth's surface or below the ground or in or above the atmosphere. The weather is also a factor. Wind can cause long-distance travel of particles, and fog can shield against thermal radiation.

The explosive nuclear components of a typical weapon instantly rise to temperatures of several million degrees and create a massive fireball of heat and radiation, usually culminating in fallout. An explosion in the atmosphere also causes a shock wave of compressed air that travels at about one-half mile in two seconds.

This causes over-pressure. Here the first wave meets a reactive reflection. Thermal radiation also occurs, and animals up to some 12 miles from where the bomb detonated can be burned. Buildings will suffer damage chiefly from explosion and fire. Buildings are also destroyed by fires caused by the thermal radiation. Although people are usually injured by the collapse of buildings rather than by the over-pressure, the various forms of radiation also kill people, either quickly or slowly.

2

Nuclear Weapons

There are two basic types of nuclear weapon. The first type produces its explosive energy through nuclear fission reactions alone. Such fission weapons are commonly referred to as atomic bombs or atom bombs (abbreviated as A-bombs), though their energy comes specifically from the nucleus of the atom. In fission weapons, a mass of fissile material (enriched uranium or plutonium) is assembled into a supercritical mass—the amount of material needed to start an exponentially growing nuclear chain reaction—either by shooting one piece of sub-critical material into another (the "gun" method), or by compressing a sub-critical sphere of material using chemical explosives to many times its original density (the "implosion" method). The latter approach is considered more sophisticated than the former, and only the latter approach can be used if plutonium is the fissile material.

A major challenge in all nuclear weapon designs is to ensure that a significant fraction of the fuel is consumed before the weapon destroys itself. The amount of energy released by fission bombs can range between the equivalent of less than a ton of TNT upwards to around 500,000 tons (500 kilotons) of TNT.

The second basic type of nuclear weapon produces a large amount of its energy through nuclear fusion reactions. Such fusion weapons are generally referred to as thermonuclear weapons or more colloquially as hydrogen bombs (abbreviated as H-bombs), as they rely on fusion reactions between isotopes of hydrogen (deuterium and tritium). However, all such weapons derive a significant portion – and sometimes a majority – of their energy from fission (including fission induced by neutrons from fusion reactions). Unlike fission weapons, there are no inherent limits on the energy released by thermonuclear weapons. Only six countries—United States, Russia, United Kingdom, People's Republic of China, France and India—have conducted thermonuclear weapon tests. (Whether India has detonated a "true," multi-staged thermonuclear weapon is controversial.)

Thermonuclear bombs work by using the energy of a fission bomb in order to compress and heat fusion fuel. In the Teller-Ulam design, which accounts for all multi-megaton yield hydrogen bombs, this is accomplished by placing a fission bomb and fusion fuel (tritium, deuterium, or lithium deuteride) in proximity within a special, radiation-reflecting container. When the fission bomb is detonated, gamma and X-rays emitted first compress the fusion fuel, then heat it to thermonuclear temperatures. The ensuing fusion reaction creates enormous numbers of high-speed neutrons, which then can induce fission in materials which normally are not prone to it, such as depleted uranium. Each of these components is known as a "stage," with the fission bomb as the "primary" and the fusion capsule as the "secondary." In large hydrogen bombs, about half of the yield, and much of the resulting nuclear fallout, comes from the final fissioning of depleted uranium.

By chaining together numerous stages with increasing amounts of fusion fuel, thermonuclear weapons can be made to an almost arbitrary yield; the largest ever detonated (the Tsar Bomba of the USSR) released an energy equivalent to over 50 million tons (50 megatons) of TNT. Most thermonuclear weapons are considerably smaller than this, due for instance to practical constraints in fitting them into the space and weight requirements of missile warheads. There are other types of nuclear weapons as well. For example, a boosted fission weapon is a fission bomb which increases its explosive yield through a small amount of fusion reactions, but it is not a fusion bomb. In the boosted bomb, the neutrons produced by the fusion reactions serve primarily to increase the efficiency of the fission bomb. Some weapons are designed for special purposes; a neutron bomb is a thermonuclear weapon that yields a relatively small explosion but a relatively large amount of neutron radiation; such a device could theoretically be used to cause massive casualties while leaving infrastructure mostly intact and creating a minimal amount of fallout.

The detonation of a nuclear weapon is accompanied by a blast of neutron radiation. Surrounding a nuclear weapon with suitable materials (such as cobalt or gold) creates a weapon known as a salted bomb. This device can produce exceptionally large quantities of radioactive contamination. Most variety in nuclear weapon design is in different yields of nuclear weapons for different types of purposes, and in manipulating design elements to attempt to make weapons extremely small.

Nuclear Strategy

Nuclear warfare strategy is a way for either fighting or avoiding a nuclear war. The policy of trying to ward off a potential attack by a nuclear weapon from another country by threatening nuclear retaliation is known as the strategy of nuclear deterrence. The goal in deterrence is to always maintain a second strike status (the ability of a country to respond to a nuclear attack with one of its own) and potentially to strive for first strike status (the ability to completely destroy an enemy's nuclear forces before they could retaliate). During the Cold War, policy and military theorists in nuclear-enabled countries worked out models of what sorts of policies could prevent one from ever being attacked by a nuclear weapon.

Different forms of nuclear weapons delivery allow for different types of nuclear strategy, primarily by making it difficult to defend against them and difficult to launch a pre-emptive strike against them. Sometimes this has meant keeping the weapon locations hidden, such as putting it on submarines or train cars whose locations are very hard for an enemy to track, and other times this means burying them in hardened bunkers. Other responses have included attempts to make it seem likely that the country could survive a nuclear attack, by using missile defence (to destroy the missiles before they land) or by means of civil defence (using early warning systems to evacuate citizens to a safe area before an attack). Note that weapons which are designed to threaten large populations or to generally deter attacks are known as strategic weapons. Weapons which are designed to actually be used on a battlefield in military situations are known as tactical weapons. There are critics of the very idea of nuclear strategy for waging nuclear war who have suggested that a nuclear war between two nuclear powers would result in mutual annihilation. From this point of view, the significance of nuclear weapons is purely to deter war because any nuclear war would immediately escalate out of mutual distrust and fear, resulting in mutually assured destruction. This threat of national, if not global, destruction has been a strong motivation for anti-nuclear weapons activism.

Critics from the peace movement and within the military establishment have questioned the usefulness of such weapons in the current military climate. The use of (or threat of use of) such weapons would generally be contrary to the rules of international law applicable in armed conflict, according to an advisory opinion issued by the International Court of Justice in 1996.

Perhaps the most controversial idea in nuclear strategy is that nuclear proliferation would be desirable. This view argues that, unlike conventional weapons, nuclear weapons successfully deter all-out war between states, and they are said to have done this during the Cold War between the U.S. and the Soviet Union. Political scientist Kenneth Waltz is the most prominent advocate of this argument.

It has been claimed that the threat of potentially suicidal terrorists possessing nuclear weapons (a form of nuclear terrorism) complicates the decision process. Mutually assured destruction may not be effective against an enemy who expects to die in a confrontation, as they may feel they will be rewarded in a religious afterlife as martyrs and would not therefore be deterred by a sense of self-preservation. Further, if the initial act is from rogue groups of individuals instead of a nation, there is no fixed nation or fixed military targets to retaliate against. It has been argued, especially after the September 11, 2001 attacks, that this complication is the sign of the next age of nuclear strategy, distinct from the relative stability of the Cold War.

Weapons Delivery

Nuclear weapons delivery—the technology and systems used to bring a nuclear weapon to its target—is an important aspect of nuclear weapons relating both to nuclear weapon design and nuclear strategy. Additionally, developing and maintaining delivery options is among the most resource-intensive aspects of nuclear weapons: according to one estimate, deployment of nuclear weapons accounted for 57% of the total financial resources spent by the United States in relation to nuclear weapons since 1940.

Historically the first method of delivery, and the method used in the two nuclear weapons actually used in warfare, is as a gravity bomb, dropped from bomber aircraft. This method is usually the first developed by countries as it does not place many restrictions on the size of the weapon, and *weapon miniaturization* is something which requires considerable weapons design knowledge. It does, however, limit the range of attack, the response time to an impending attack, and the number of weapons which can be fielded at any given time.

Additionally, specialized delivery systems are usually not necessary; especially with the advent of miniaturization, nuclear bombs can be delivered by both strategic bombers and tactical fighter-bombers, allowing an air force to use its current fleet with little or no modification. This method may still be considered the primary means of nuclear weapons delivery; the majority of U.S. nuclear warheads, for example, are represented in free-fall gravity bombs, namely the B61.

More preferable from a strategic point of view are nuclear weapons mounted onto a missile, which can use a ballistic trajectory to deliver a warhead over the horizon. While even short range missiles allow for a faster and less vulnerable attack, the development of intercontinental ballistic missiles (ICBMs) and submarine-launched ballistic missiles (SLBMs) has allowed some nations to plausibly deliver missiles anywhere on the globe with a high likelihood of success. More advanced systems, such as multiple independently targetable reentry vehicles (MIRVs) allow multiple warheads to be launched at several targets from any one missile, reducing the chance of any successful missile defence. Today, missiles are most common among systems designed for delivery of nuclear weapons. Making a warhead small enough to fit onto a missile, though, can be a difficult task.

Tactical weapons have involved the most variety of delivery types, including not only gravity bombs and missiles but also artillery shells, land mines, and nuclear depth charges and torpedoes for anti-submarine warfare. An atomic mortar was also tested at one time by the United States. Small, two-man portable tactical weapons (somewhat misleadingly referred to as suitcase bombs), such as the Special Atomic Demolition Munition, have been developed, although the difficulty to combine sufficient yield with portability limits their military utility.

Governance, Control, and Law

Because of the immense military power they can confer, the political control of nuclear weapons has been a key issue for as long as they have existed; in most countries the use of nuclear force can only be authorized by the head of government or head of state. In the late 1940s, lack of mutual trust was preventing the United States and the Soviet Union from making ground towards international arms control agreements, but by the 1960s steps were being taken to limit both the proliferation of nuclear weapons to other countries and the environmental effects of nuclear testing. The Partial Test Ban Treaty (1963) restricted all nuclear testing to underground nuclear testing, to prevent contamination from nuclear fallout, while the Nuclear Non-Proliferation Treaty (1968) attempted to place restrictions on the types of activities which signatories could participate in, with the goal of allowing the transference of non-military nuclear technology to member countries without fear of proliferation.

In 1957, the International Atomic Energy Agency (IAEA) was established under the mandate of the United Nations in order to encourage the development of the peaceful applications of nuclear technology, provide international safeguards against its misuse, and facilitate the application of safety measures in its use. In 1996, many nations signed and ratified the Comprehensive Test Ban Treaty which prohibits all testing of nuclear weapons, which would impose a significant hindrance to their development by any complying country.

Additional treaties have governed nuclear weapons stockpiles between individual countries, such as the SALT I and START I treaties, which limited the numbers and types of nuclear weapons between the United States and the Soviet Union.

Nuclear weapons have also been opposed by agreements between countries. Many nations have been declared Nuclear-

Weapon-Free Zones, areas where nuclear weapons production and deployment are prohibited, through the use of treaties. The Treaty of Tlatelolco (1967) prohibited any production or deployment of nuclear weapons in Latin America and the Caribbean, and the Treaty of Pelindaba (1964) prohibits nuclear weapons in many African countries. As recently as 2006 a Central Asian Nuclear Weapon Free Zone was established amongst the former Soviet republics of Central Asia prohibiting nuclear weapons.

In the middle of 1996, the International Court of Justice, the highest court of the United Nations, issued an Advisory Opinion concerned with the "Legality of the Threat or Use of Nuclear Weapons". The court ruled that the use or threat of use of nuclear weapons would violate various articles of international law, including the Geneva Conventions, the Hague Conventions, the UN Charter, and the Universal Declaration of Human Rights.

Additionally, there have been other, specific actions meant to discourage countries from developing nuclear arms. In the wake of the tests by India and Pakistan in 1998, economic sanctions were (temporarily) levied against both countries, though neither were signatories with the Nuclear Non-Proliferation Treaty. One of the stated *casus belli* for the initiation of the 2003 Iraq War was an accusation by the United States that Iraq was actively pursuing nuclear arms (though this was soon discovered not to be the case as the program had been discontinued). In 1981, Israel had bombed a nuclear reactor in Osirak, Iraq, in what it called an attempt to halt Iraq's previous nuclear arms ambitions.

Disarmament

Beginning with the 1963 Partial Test Ban Treaty and continuing through the 1996 Comprehensive Test Ban Treaty, there have been many treaties to limit or reduce nuclear weapons testing and stockpiles. The 1968 Nuclear Non-Proliferation Treaty has as one of its explicit conditions that all signatories must "pursue negotiations in good faith" towards the long-term goal of "complete disarmament". However, no nuclear state has treated that aspect of the agreement as having binding force. Only one country—South Africa—has ever fully renounced nuclear weapons they had independently developed. A number of former Soviet republics—

Belarus, Kazakhstan, and Ukraine—returned Soviet nuclear arms stationed in their countries to Russia after the collapse of the USSR.

Uses

Apart from their use as weapons, nuclear explosives have been tested and used for various non-military uses, and proposed, but not used for large-scale earth moving. When long term health and clean-up costs were included, there was no economic advantage over conventional explosives. Synthetic elements, such as einsteinium and fermium, created by neutron bombardment of uranium and plutonium during thermonuclear explosions, were discovered in the aftermath of the first thermonuclear bomb test. In 2008 the worldwide presence of new isotopes from atmospheric testing beginning in the 1950s was developed into a reliable way of detecting art forgeries, as all paintings created after that period may contain traces of cesium-137 and strontium-90, isotopes that did not exist in nature before 1945.

Nuclear explosives have also been seriously studied as potential propulsion mechanisms for space travel.

History of Nuclear Weapons

The history of nuclear weapons chronicles the development of nuclear weapons. Nuclear weapons are devices that possess enormous destructive potential derived from nuclear fission or nuclear fusion reactions. Starting with the scientific breakthroughs of the 1930s which made their development possible, and continuing through the nuclear arms race and nuclear testing of the Cold War, the issues of proliferation and possible use for terrorism still remain in the early 21st century. The first fission weapons, also known as "atomic bombs," were developed jointly by the United States, Britain and Canada during World War II in what was called the Manhattan Project to counter the assumed Nazi German atomic bomb project. In August 1945 two were dropped on Japan ending the Pacific War. An international team was dispatched to help work on the project. The Soviet Union started development shortly thereafter with their own atomic bomb project, and not long after that both countries developed even more powerful fusion weapons called "hydrogen bombs."

During the Cold War, the Soviet Union and United States each acquired nuclear weapons arsenals numbering in the thousands, placing many of them onto rockets which could hit targets anywhere in the world. Currently there are at least nine countries with functional nuclear weapons. A considerable amount of international negotiating has focused on the threat of nuclear warfare and the proliferation of nuclear weapons to new nations or groups. There have been (at least) four major false alarms, the most recent in 1995, that resulted in the activation of either the US's or Russia's nuclear attack early warning protocols.

Physics and Politics in the 1930s

In the first decades of the twentieth century, physics was revolutionized with developments in the understanding of the nature of atoms. In 1898, French physicist Pierre Curie and his Polish wife Maria Sklodowska-Curie had discovered that present in pitchblende, an ore of uranium, was a substance which emitted large amounts of radioactivity, which they named radium. This raised the hopes of both scientists and lay people that the elements around us could contain tremendous amounts of unseen energy, waiting to be tapped. Experiments by Ernest Rutherford in 1911 indicated that the vast majority of an atom's mass was contained in a very small nucleus at its core, made up of protons, surrounded by a web of whirring electrons. In 1932, James Chadwick discovered that the nucleus contained another fundamental particle, the neutron, and in the same year John Cockcroft and Ernest Walton "split the atom" for the first time, the first occasion on which an atomic nucleus of one element had been successfully changed to a different nucleus by artificial means.

In 1934 the idea of chain reaction via neutron was proposed by Leó Szilárd, who patented the idea of the atomic bomb. The patent was transferred in secret to Britain's Royal Navy in 1936. In a very real sense, Szilárd was the father of the atomic bomb academically. In 1934, French physicists Irène and Frédéric Joliot-Curie discovered that artificial radioactivity could be induced in stable elements by bombarding them with alpha particles, and in the same year Italian physicist Enrico Fermi reported similar results when bombarding uranium with neutrons. In December 1938, the German chemists Otto Hahn and Fritz Strassmann sent a manuscript to *Naturwissenschaften* reporting they had detected the element barium after bombarding uranium with neutrons; simultaneously, they communicated these results to Lise Meitner. Meitner, and her nephew Otto Robert Frisch, correctly interpreted these results as being nuclear fission. Frisch confirmed this experimentally on 13 January 1939. Even before it was published, Meitner's and Frisch's interpretation of the work of Hahn and Strassmann crossed the Atlantic Ocean with Niels Bohr, who was to lecture at Princeton University. Isidor Isaac Rabi and Willis Lamb, two Columbia University physicists working at Princeton, heard the news and carried it back to Columbia. Rabi said he told Fermi; Fermi gave credit to Lamb. Bohr soon thereafter went from Princeton to Columbia to see Fermi. Not finding Fermi in his office, Bohr went down to the cyclotron area and found Herbert Anderson. Bohr grabbed him by the shoulder and said: "Young man, let me explain to you about something new and exciting in physics."

It was clear to a number of scientists at Columbia that they should try to detect the energy released in the nuclear fission of uranium from neutron bombardment. On 25 January 1939, an experimental team at Columbia University conducted the first nuclear fission experiment in the United States, which was done in the basement of Pupin Hall; the members of the team were Herbert L. Anderson, Eugene T. Booth, John R. Dunning, Enrico Fermi, G. Norris Glasoe, and Francis G. Slack. As the Nazi army marched into first Czechoslovakia in 1938, and then Poland in 1939, beginning World War II, many of Europe's top physicists had already begun to flee from the imminent conflict. Scientists on both sides of the conflict were well aware of the possibility of utilizing nuclear fission as a weapon, but at the time no one was quite sure how it could be done. In the early years of the Second World War, physicists abruptly stopped publishing on the topic of fission, an act of self-censorship to keep the opposing side from gaining any advantages.

From Los Alamos to Hiroshima

By the beginning of World War II, there was concern among scientists in the Allied nations that Nazi Germany might have its own project to develop fission-based weapons. Organized research first began in Britain as part of the "Tube Alloys" project, and in the United States a small amount of funding was given for research into uranium weapons starting in 1939 with the Uranium Committee under Lyman James Briggs. At the urging of British scientists, though, who had made crucial calculations indicating that a fission weapon could be completed within only a few years, by 1941 the project had been wrested into better bureaucratic hands, and in 1942 came under the auspices of a Military Policy Committee led by General Leslie Groves as the Manhattan Project.

Scientifically led by the American physicist Robert Oppenheimer, the project brought together the top scientific minds of the day (many exiles from Europe) with the production power of American industry for the goal of producing fission-based explosive devices before Germany could. Britain and the U.S. agreed to pool their resources and information for the project, but the other Allied power—the Soviet Union under Joseph Stalin—was not informed. A massive industrial and scientific undertaking, the Manhattan Project involved many of the world's great physicists in the scientific and development aspects. The United States made an unprecedented investment into wartime research for the project, which was spread across more than 30 sites in the U.S. and Canada. Scientific knowledge was centralized at a secret laboratory known as Los Alamos, previously a small ranch school near Santa Fe, New Mexico.

Uranium appears in nature primarily in two isotopes: uranium-238 and uranium-235. When the nucleus of uranium-235 absorbs a neutron, it undergoes nuclear fission, splitting into two "fission products" and releasing energy and 2.5 neutrons on average. Uranium-238, on the other hand, absorbs neutrons but does not split, effectively putting a stop to any ongoing fission reaction. It was discovered that an atomic bomb based on uranium would need to be made of almost completely pure uranium-235 (at least 80% pure), or else the presence of uranium-238 would quickly curtail the nuclear chain reaction. The team of scientists working on the Manhattan Project immediately realized that one of the largest problems they would have to solve was how to remove uranium-235 from natural uranium, which was composed of 99.3% uranium-238. Two methods were developed during the wartime project, both of which took advantage of the fact that uranium-

238 has a slightly greater atomic mass than uranium-235: electromagnetic separation and gaseous diffusion—methods which separated isotopes based on their differing weights. Another secret site was erected at rural Oak Ridge, Tennessee, for the large-scale production and purification of the rare isotope. It was a massive investment: at the time, one of the Oak Ridge facilities (K-25) was the largest factory under one roof. The Oak Ridge site employed tens of thousands of employees at its peak, most of whom had no idea what they were working on.

Though uranium-238 cannot be used for the initial stage of an atomic bomb, when U-238 absorbs a neutron, it transforms first into an unstable element, uranium-239, and then decays into neptunium-239, and finally the relatively stable plutonium-239, an element which does not exist in nature. Plutonium is also fissile and can be used to create a fission reaction, and after Enrico Fermi achieved the world's first sustained and controlled nuclear chain reaction in the creation of the first "atomic pile"—a primitive nuclear reactor—in a basement at the University of Chicago, massive reactors were secretly created at what is now known as Hanford Site in the state of Washington, using the Columbia River as cooling water, to transform uranium-238 into plutonium for a bomb.

For a fission weapon to operate, there must be a critical mass—the amount needed for a self-sustaining nuclear chain reaction—of fissile material bombarded with neutrons at any one time. The simplest form of nuclear weapon is a gun-type fission weapon, where a sub-critical mass of fissile material (such as uranium-235) would be shot at another sub-critical mass of fissile material. The result would be a super-critical mass which, when bombarded with neutrons, would undergo fission at a rapid rate and create the desired explosion. The weapons envisaged in 1942 were the two gun-type weapons, Little Boy (uranium) and Thin Man (plutonium), and the Fat Man plutonium implosion bomb. In early 1943 Oppenheimer determined that two projects should proceed forwards: the "Thin Man" project (plutonium gun) and the "Fat Man" project (plutonium implosion). The plutonium gun was to receive the bulk of the research effort, as it was the project with the most uncertainty involved. It was assumed that the uranium gun-type bomb could then be adapted from it.

But in April 1944 it was found by Emilio Segrè that plutonium produced by the Hanford reactors had too high a level of background neutron radiation, and underwent spontaneous fission to a very small extent, due to the presence of impurities of the Pu-240 isotope. If such plutonium were used in a "gun assembly," the chain reaction would start in the split seconds before the critical mass was assembled, blowing the weapon apart before it would have any great effect (this is known as a fizzle). So development of Fat Man, the implosion bomb, was given high priority. Chemical explosives were used to implode a sub-critical sphere of plutonium, thus increasing its density and making it into a critical mass. The difficulties with implosion were in the problem of making the chemical explosives deliver a perfectly uniform shock wave upon the plutonium sphere— if it were even slightly asymmetric, the weapon would fizzle (which would be expensive, messy, and not a very effective military device). This problem was circumvented by the use of hydrodynamic "lenses"—explosive materials of differing densities—which would focus the blast waves inside the imploding sphere, akin to the way in which an optical lens focuses light rays.

After D-Day, General Groves had ordered a team of scientists—Project Alsos—to follow eastward-moving victorious Allied troops into Europe in order to assess the status of the German nuclear program (and to prevent the westward-moving Russians from gaining any materials or scientific manpower). It was concluded that while Nazi Germany had also had an atomic bomb program, headed by Werner Heisenberg, the government had not made a significant investment in the project, and had been nowhere near success. Historians claim to have found a rough schematic showing a Nazi nuclear bomb. Research was conducted in the German nuclear energy project. In March 1945, a Nazi scientific team was directed by the physicist Kurt Diebner to develop a primitive nuclear device in Ohrdruf, Thuringia.

By the unconditional surrender of Germany on May 8, 1945, the Manhattan Project was still months away from a working weapon. That April, after the death of American President Franklin D. Roosevelt, former Vice-President Harry S. Truman was told about the secret wartime project for the first time. Because of the difficulties in making a working plutonium bomb, it was decided that there should be a test of the weapon, and Truman wanted to know for sure if it would work before his meeting with Joseph Stalin at an upcoming conference on the future of postwar Europe. On July 16, 1945, in the desert north of Alamogordo, New Mexico, the first nuclear test took place, code-named "Trinity," using a device nicknamed "the Gadget." The test, a plutonium implosion type device, released the equivalent of 19 kilotons of TNT, far mightier than any weapon ever used before. The news of the test's success was rushed to Truman, who used it as leverage at the upcoming Potsdam Conference, held near Berlin.

After hearing arguments from scientists and military officers over the possible uses of the weapons against Japan (though some recommended using them as "demonstrations" in unpopulated areas, most recommended using them against "built up" targets, a euphemistic term for populated cities), Truman ordered the use of the weapons on Japanese cities, hoping it would send a strong message which would end in the capitulation of the Japanese leadership and avoid a lengthy invasion of the island. There were suggestions to drop the atomic bomb on Tokyo, the capital of Japan, but concerns about Tokyo's cultural heritage changed the plan. On May 10–11, 1945 The Target Committee at Los Alamos, led by J. Robert Oppenheimer, recommended Kyoto, Hiroshima, Yokohama, and the arsenal at Kokura as possible targets. On August 6, 1945, a uranium-based weapon, "Little Boy", was let loose on the Japanese city of Hiroshima. Three days later, a plutonium-based weapon, "Fat Man", was dropped onto the city of Nagasaki. The atomic bombs killed at least one hundred thousand Japanese outright, most of them civilians, with the heat, radiation, and blast effects.

Many tens of thousands would die later of radiation sickness and related cancers. Truman promised a "rain of ruin" if Japan did not surrender immediately, threatening to eliminate Japanese cities, one by one; Japan surrendered on August 15. Truman's threat was in fact a bluff, since the US had but one remaining uranium-gun type bomb completed.

Soviet Atomic Bomb Project

The Soviet Union was not invited to share in the new weapons developed by the United States and the other Allies. During the war, information had been pouring in from a number of volunteer spies involved with the Manhattan Project (known in Soviet cables under the code-name of *Enormoz*), and the Soviet nuclear physicist Igor Kurchatov was carefully watching the Allied weapons development. It came as no surprise to Stalin when Truman had informed him at the Potsdam conference that he had a "powerful new weapon." Truman was shocked at Stalin's lack of interest. The Soviet spies in the U.S. project were all volunteers and none were Russians. One of the most valuable, Klaus Fuchs, was a German émigré theoretical physicist who had been a part in the early British nuclear efforts and had been part of the UK mission to Los Alamos during the war. Fuchs had been intimately involved in the development of the implosion weapon, and passed on detailed cross-sections of the "Trinity" device to his Soviet contacts. Other Los Alamos spies—none of whom knew each other—included Theodore Hall and David Greenglass. The information was kept but not acted upon, as Russia was still too busy fighting the war in Europe to devote resources to this new project.

In the years immediately after World War II, the issue of who should control atomic weapons became a major international point of contention. Many of the Los Alamos scientists who had built the bomb began to call for "international control of atomic energy," often calling for either control by transnational organizations or the purposeful distribution of weapons information to all superpowers, but due to a deep distrust of the intentions of the Soviet Union, both in postwar Europe and in general, the policy-makers of the United States worked to attempt to secure an American nuclear monopoly. A half-hearted plan for international control was proposed at the newly formed United Nations by Bernard Baruch ("The Baruch Plan"), but it was clear both to American commentators—and to the Soviets—that it was an attempt primarily to stymie Russian nuclear efforts. The Soviets vetoed the plan, effectively ending any immediate postwar negotiations on atomic energy, and made overtures towards banning the use of atomic weapons in general.

All the while, the Soviets had put their full industrial and manpower might into the development of their own atomic weapons. The initial problem for the Soviets was primarily one of resources—they had not scouted out uranium resources in the

Soviet Union and the U.S. had made deals to monopolise the largest known (and high purity) reserves in the Belgian Congo. The USSR used penal labour to mine the old deposits in Czechoslovakia—now an area under their control—and searched for other domestic deposits (which were eventually found). Two days after the bombing of Nagasaki, the U.S. government released an official technical history of the Manhattan Project, authored by Princeton physicist Henry DeWolf Smyth, known colloquially as the Smyth Report. The sanitized summary of the wartime effort focused primarily on the production facilities and scale of investment, written in part to justify the wartime expenditure to the American public.

The Soviet program, under the suspicious watch of former NKVD chief Lavrenty Beria (a participant and victor in Stalin's Great Purge of the 1930s), would use the Report as a blueprint, seeking to duplicate as much as possible the American effort. The "secret cities" used for the Soviet equivalents of Hanford and Oak Ridge literally vanished from the maps for decades to come. At the Soviet equivalent of Los Alamos, Arzamas-16, physicist Yuli Khariton led the scientific effort to develop the weapon. Beria distrusted his scientists, however, and he distrusted the carefully collected espionage information. As such, Beria assigned multiple teams of scientists to the same task without informing each team of the other's existence. If they arrived at different conclusions, Beria would bring them together for the first time and have them debate with their newfound counterparts. Beria used the espionage information as a way to double-check the progress of his scientists, and in his effort for duplication of the American project even rejected more efficient bomb designs in favour of ones which more closely mimicked the tried-and-true "Fat Man" bomb used by the U.S. against Nagasaki.

Working under a stubborn and scientifically ignorant administrator, the Soviet scientists struggled on. On August 29, 1949, the effort brought its results, when the USSR tested its first fission bomb, dubbed "Joe-1" by the U.S., years ahead of American predictions. The news of the first Soviet bomb was announced to the world first by the United States, which had detected the nuclear fallout it generated from its test site in Kazakhstan. The loss of the American monopoly on nuclear weapons marked the first tit-for-tat of the nuclear arms race. The response in the U.S. was one of apprehension, fear, and scapegoating, which would lead eventually into the Red-baiting tactics of McCarthyism. Yet recent information from unclassified Venona intercepts and the opening of the KGB archives after the fall of the Soviet Union show that the USSR had useful spies that helped their program, although none were identified by the McCarthy. Before this, though, President Truman would announce his decision to begin a crash program to develop a far more powerful weapon than those which were used against Japan: the hydrogen bomb.

The First Thermonuclear Weapons

The notion of using a fission weapon to ignite a process of nuclear fusion can be dated back to 1942. At the first major theoretical conference on the development of an atomic bomb hosted by J. Robert Oppenheimer at the University of California, Berkeley, participant Edward Teller directed the majority of the discussion towards Enrico Fermi's idea of a "Super" bomb which would utilize the same reactions which powered the Sun itself. It was thought at the time that a fission weapon would be quite simple to develop and that perhaps work on a hydrogen bomb would be possible to complete before the end of the Second World War. However, in reality the problem of a "regular" atomic bomb was large enough to preoccupy the scientists for the next few years, much less the more speculative "Super." Only Teller continued working on the project—against the will of project leaders Oppenheimer and Hans Bethe.

After the atomic bombings of Japan, many scientists at Los Alamos rebelled against the notion of creating a weapon thousands of times more powerful than the first atomic bombs. For the scientists the question was in part technical—the weapon design was still quite uncertain and unworkable—and in part moral: such a weapon, they argued, could only be used against large civilian populations, and could thus only be used as a weapon of genocide. Many scientists, such as Bethe, urged that the United States should not develop such weapons and set an example towards the Soviet Union. Promoters of the weapon, including Teller, Ernest Lawrence, and Luis Alvarez, argued that such a development was inevitable, and to deny such protection to the people of the United States—

especially when the Soviet Union was likely to create such a weapon themselves—was itself an immoral and unwise act.

Oppenheimer, who was now head of the General Advisory Committee of the successor to the Manhattan Project, the Atomic Energy Commission, presided over a recommendation against the development of the weapon. The reasons were in part because the success of the technology seemed limited at the time (and not worth the investment of resources to confirm whether this was so), and because Oppenheimer believed that the atomic forces of the United States would be more effective if they consisted of many large fission weapons (of which multiple bombs could be dropped on the same targets) rather than the large and unwieldy predictions of massive super bombs, for which there were a relatively limited amounts of targets of the size to warrant such a development. Furthermore, were such weapons developed by both the U.S. and the USSR, they would be more effectively used against the U.S. than by it, as the U.S. had far more regions of dense industrial and civilian activity which would serve as ideal targets for the large weapons than the Soviet Union did.

In the end, President Truman made the final decision, looking for a proper response to the first Soviet atomic bomb test in 1949. On January 31, 1950, Truman announced a crash program to develop the hydrogen (fusion) bomb. At this point, however, the exact mechanism was still not known: the "classical" hydrogen bomb, whereby the *heat* of the fission bomb would be used to ignite the fusion material, seemed highly unworkable. However, an insight by Los Alamos mathematician Stanislaw Ulam showed that the fission bomb and the fusion fuel could be in separate parts of the bomb, and that *radiation* of the fission bomb could first work in a way to *compress* the fusion material before igniting it.

Teller pushed the notion further, and used the results of the boosted-fission "George" test (a boosted-fission device using a small amount of fusion fuel to boost the yield of a fission bomb) to confirm the fusion of heavy hydrogen elements before preparing for their first true multi-stage, Teller-Ulam hydrogen bomb test. Many scientists initially against the weapon, such as Oppenheimer and Bethe, changed their previous opinions, seeing the development as being unstoppable. The first fusion bomb was tested by the United States in *Operation Ivy* on November 1, 1952, on Elugelab Island in the Enewetak (or Eniwetok) Atoll of the Marshall Islands, code-named "Mike". "Mike" used liquid deuterium as its fusion fuel and a large fission weapon as its trigger. The device was a prototype design and not a deliverable weapon: standing over 20 ft (6 m) high and weighing at least 140,000 lb (64 t) (its refrigeration equipment added an additional 24,000 lb as well), it could not have been dropped from even the largest planes.

Its explosion yielded 10.4 megatons of energy—over 450 times the power of the bomb dropped onto Nagasaki— and obliterated Elugelab, leaving an underwater crater 6240 ft (1.9 km) wide and 164 ft (50 m) deep where the island had once been. Truman had initially tried to create a media blackout about the test—hoping it would not become an issue in the upcoming presidential election—but on January 7, 1953, Truman announced the development of the hydrogen bomb to the world as hints and speculations of it were already beginning to emerge in the press. Not to be outdone, the Soviet Union exploded its first thermonuclear device, designed by the physicist Andrei Sakharov, on August 12, 1953, labeled "Joe-4" by the West. This created concern within the U.S. government and military, because, unlike "Mike," the Soviet device was a deliverable weapon, which the U.S. did not yet have. This first device though was arguably not a "true" hydrogen bomb, and could only reach explosive yields in the hundreds of kilotons (never reaching the megaton range of a "staged" weapon). Still, it was a powerful propaganda tool for the Soviet Union, and the technical differences were fairly oblique to the American public and politicians.

Following the "Mike" blast by less than a year, "Joe-4" seemed to validate claims that the bombs were inevitable and vindicate those who had supported the development of the fusion program. Coming during the height of McCarthyism, the effect was most pronounced by the security hearings in early 1954 which revoked former Los Alamos director Robert Oppenheimer of his security clearance, on the grounds that he was unreliable, had not supported the American hydrogen bomb program, and had made long-standing, left-wing ties in the 1930s. Edward Teller participated in the hearing as the only major scientist to testify against Oppenheimer, a role which resulted in his virtual expulsion from the physics community. On February 28, 1954, the U.S. detonated its first deliverable thermonuclear weapon (which used isotopes of lithium as its fusion fuel), known as the "Shrimp" device of the "Castle Bravo" test, at Bikini Atoll, Marshall Islands. The device yielded 15 megatons of energy, over twice its expected yield, and became the worst radiological disaster in U.S. history. The combination of the unexpectedly large blast and poor weather conditions caused a cloud of radioactive nuclear fallout to contaminate over 7,000 square miles, including Marshall Island natives and the crew of a Japanese fishing boat, as a snow-like mist. The contaminated islands were evacuated (and are still uninhabitable), but the natives received enough of a radioactive dose that they suffered far elevated levels of cancer and birth defects in the years to come.

The crew of the Japanese fishing boat, *Lucky Dragon 5*, returned to port suffering from radiation sickness and skin burns. Their cargo, many tons of contaminated fish, managed to enter into the market before the cause of their illness was determined. When a crew member died from the sickness and the full results of the contamination were made public by the U.S., Japanese concerns were reignited about the hazards of radiation and resulted in a boycott on eating fish (a main staple of the island country) for some weeks. The hydrogen bomb age had a profound effect on the thoughts of nuclear war in the popular and military mind. With only fission bombs, nuclear war could be considered something which could easily be "limited." Dropped by planes and only able to destroy the most built up areas of major cities, it was possible to consider fission bombs simply a technological extension of previous wartime bombing (such as the extensive firebombing which took place against Japan and Germany during World War II), and claims that such weapons could lead to worldwide death or harm were easily brushed aside as grave exaggeration.

Even the decades before the development of fission weapons there had been speculation about the possibility for human beings to end all life on the planet by either accident or purposeful maliciousness, but technology had never allowed for such a capacity. The far greater power of hydrogen bombs made this seem ever closer. The "Castle Bravo" incident itself raised a number of questions about the survivability of a nuclear war. Government scientists in both the U.S. and the USSR had insisted that fusion weapons, unlike fission weapons, were "cleaner" as fusion reactions did not result in the dangerously radioactive by-products as did fission reactions. While technically true, this hid a more gruesome point: the last stage of a multi-staged hydrogen bomb often used the neutrons produced by the fusion reactions to induce fissioning in a jacket of natural uranium, and provided around half of the yield of the device itself.

This fission stage made fusion weapons considerably more "dirty" than they were made out to be, a fact made evident by the towering cloud of deadly fallout which followed the "Bravo" test. When the Soviet Union tested its first megaton device in 1955, the possibility of a limited nuclear war seemed even more remote in the public and political mind: even if a city or country was not the direct target of a nuclear attack, the clouds of fallout and harmful fission products would disperse along with normal weather patterns and embed themselves in the soil and water of non-targeted areas of the planet as well. Speculation began to look towards what would happen as the fallout and dust created by a full-scale nuclear exchange would affect the world as a whole, rather than just the cities and countries which had been directly involved. In this way, the fate of the world was now tied to the fate of the bomb-wielding superpowers.

Deterrence and Brinkmanship

Throughout the 1950s and the early 1960s a number of trends were enacted between the U.S. and the USSR as they both endeavored in a tit-for-tat approach to disallow the other power from acquiring nuclear supremacy. This took form in a number of ways, both technologically and politically, and had massive political and cultural effects during the Cold War. The first atomic bombs dropped on Hiroshima and Nagasaki were large, custom-made devices, requiring highly trained personnel for their arming and deployment. They could be dropped only from the largest bomber planes—at the time the B-29 Superfortress—and each plane could only hold a single bomb in its hold.

The first hydrogen bombs were similarly massive and complicated. This ratio of one plane to one bomb was still fairly impressive in comparison with conventional, non-nuclear weapons, but against other nuclear-armed countries it was considered to be a grave danger. In the immediate postwar years, the U.S. expended much effort on making the bombs "G.I.-proof"—capable of being used and deployed by members of the U.S. Army, rather than Nobel Prize–winning scientists, and in the 1950s a program of nuclear testing was undertaken in order to improve the nuclear arsenal. Starting in 1951, the Nevada Test Site (in the Nevada desert) became the primary location for all U.S. nuclear testing (in the USSR, Semipalatinsk Test Site in Kazakhstan served a similar role). Tests were divided into two primary categories: "weapons related" (verifying that a new weapon worked or looking at exactly how it worked) and "weapons effects" (looking at how weapons behaved under various conditions or how structures behaved when subjected to weapons).

In the beginning, almost all nuclear tests were either "atmospheric" (conducted above ground, in the atmosphere) or "underwater" (such as some of the tests done in the Marshall Islands). Testing was used as a sign of both national and technological strength, but also raised questions about the safety of the tests, which released nuclear fallout into the atmosphere (most dramatically with the Castle Bravo test in 1954, but in more limited amounts with almost all atmospheric nuclear testing). Because testing was seen as a sign of technological development (the ability to design usable weapons without some form of testing was considered dubious), halts on testing were often called for as stand-ins for halts in the nuclear arms race itself, and many prominent scientists and statesmen lobbied for a ban on nuclear testing. In 1958, the U.S., USSR, and the United Kingdom (a new nuclear power) declared a temporary testing moratorium for both political and health reasons, but by 1961 the Soviet Union had broken the moratorium and both the USSR and the U.S. began testing with great frequency.

As a show of political strength, the Soviet Union tested the largest-ever nuclear weapon in October 1961, the massive Tsar Bomba, which was tested in a reduced state with a yield of around 50 megatons—in its full state it was estimated to have been around 100 Mt. The weapon was largely impractical for actual military use, but was hot enough to induce third-degree burns at a distance of 62 mi (100 km) away. In its full, "dirty" design, it would have increased the amount of worldwide fallout since 1945 by 25%. In 1963, all nuclear and many non-nuclear states signed the Limited Test Ban Treaty, pledging to refrain from testing nuclear weapons in the atmosphere, underwater, or in outer space. The treaty permitted underground tests.

Most tests were considerably more modest, and worked for direct technical purposes as well as their potential political overtones. Weapons improvements took on two primary forms. One was an increase in efficiency and power, and within only a few years fission bombs were being developed which were many times more powerful than the ones created during World War II. The other was a program of miniaturization, reducing the size of the nuclear weapons themselves. Smaller bombs meant that bombers could carry more of them, and thus become even more of a threat against even the most rigorous air defenses, and they could also be used in conjunction with the development in rocketry during the 1950s and 1960s. U.S. rocket efforts had received a large boost in the postwar years, largely from the acquiring of engineers who had worked on the Nazi rocketry program during the war, such as Wernher von Braun, who had been involved in the design and manufacture of the V-2 rockets which were launched across the English Channel. An American program, Project Paperclip, had endeavored to move scientists of this sort into American hands (and kept out of Soviet hands) and put them to work on projects for the U.S.

Weapons Improvement

The first nuclear-tipped rockets, such as the MGR-1 Honest John, first deployed by the U.S. in 1953, were surface-to-surface missiles with relatively short ranges (around 15 mi/25 km maximum) with yields around twice the size of the first fission weapons. The limited range of these weapons meant that they could only be used in certain types of potential military situations—the U.S. rocket weapons could not, for example, threaten the city of Moscow with the threat of an immediate strike, and could only be used as "tactical" weapons (that is, for small-scale military situations). For "strategic" weapons—weapons which would serve to threaten an entire country—for the time being, only long-range bombers capable of penetrating deep into enemy territory would work. In the U.S. this resulted in the creation of the Strategic Air Command in 1946, a system of bombers headed by General Curtis LeMay (who had previously presided over the firebombing of Japan during WWII), which kept a number of nuclear-armed planes in the sky at all times, ready to receive orders to attack Moscow whenever commanded.

These technological possibilities enabled nuclear strategy to develop a logic considerably different than previous military thinking had allowed. Because the threat of nuclear warfare was so awful, it was first thought that it might make any war of the future impossible. President Dwight D. Eisenhower's doctrine of "massive retaliation" in the early years of the Cold War was a message to the USSR, saying that if the Red Army attempted to invade the parts of Europe not given to the Eastern bloc during the Potsdam Conference (such as West Germany), nuclear weapons would be used against the Soviet troops and potentially the Soviet leaders. With the development of more rapid-response technologies (such as rockets and long-range bombers), this policy began to shift. If the Soviet Union also had nuclear weapons and a policy of "massive retaliation" was carried out, it was reasoned, then any Soviet forces not killed in the initial attack, or launched while the attack was ongoing, would be able to serve their own form of nuclear "retaliation" against the U.S. Recognizing this to be an undesirable outcome, military officers and game theorists at the RAND think tank developed a nuclear warfare strategy that would eventually become known as Mutually Assured Destruction (MAD).

MAD divided potential nuclear war into two stages: first strike and second strike. A first strike would be the first use of nuclear weapons by one nuclear-equipped nation against another nuclear-equipped nation. If the attacking nation did not prevent the attacked nation from a nuclear response, then a second strike could be deployed against the attacking nation. In this situation, whether the U.S. first attacked the USSR or the USSR first attacked the U.S., the end result would be that both nations would be damaged perhaps to the point of utter social collapse. According to game theory, because starting a nuclear war would be suicidal, no logical country would willfully enter into a nuclear war.

However, if a country were capable of launching a first strike which would utterly destroy the ability of the attacked country to respond in kind, then the balance of power would be disturbed and nuclear war could then be safely undertaken.

MAD played on two seemingly opposed modes of thought: cold logic and emotional fear. The phrase by which MAD was often known, "nuclear deterrence", was translated as "dissuasion" by the French and "terrorization" by the Russians. This apparent paradox of nuclear war was summed up by British Prime Minister Winston Churchill as "the worse things get, the better they are"—the greater the threat of mutual destruction, the safer the world would be. This philosophy made a number of technological and political demands on participating nations. For one thing, it said that it should always be assumed that an enemy nation may be trying to acquire "first strike capability," something which must always be avoided. In American politics this translated into demands to avoid "missile gaps" and "bomber gaps" where the Soviet Union could potentially "out shoot" American efforts (most of these supposed "gaps" proved to be political figments, but this hardly mattered at the time). It also encouraged the production of thousands of nuclear weapons by both the U.S. and the USSR, far more than would be needed to simply destroy the major civilian and military infrastructures of the opposing country.

These policies and strategies were satirized in the 1964 Stanley Kubrick film Dr. Strangelove, in which the Soviets, unable to keep up with the US's first strike capability, instead plan for MAD by building a Doomsday Machine, and thus, after a (literally) mad US General orders a nuclear attack on the USSR, the end of the world is brought about. The policy also encouraged the development of the first early warning systems. Conventional war, even at its fastest, was fought over time scales of days and weeks. With long-range bombers, the time from the start of an attack to its conclusion was reduced to mere hours. With rockets, it could be reduced to minutes. It was reasoned that conventional command and control systems could not be expected to adequately respond to a nuclear attack, and so great lengths were taken to develop the first computers which could look for enemy attacks and direct rapid responses. In the U.S., massive funding was poured into the development of SAGE, a system which would track and intercept enemy bomber aircraft using information from remote radar stations, and was the first computer system to feature real-time processing, multiplexing, and display devices—the first "general" computing machine, and a direct predecessor of modern computers.

Anti-nuclear

Bombers and short-range rockets were not reliable: planes could be shot down, and earlier nuclear missiles could cover only a limited range— for example, the first Soviet rockets' range limited them to targets in Europe. However, by the 1960s, both the United States and the Soviet Union had developed intercontinental ballistic missiles, which could be launched from extremely remote areas far away from their target; and submarine-launched ballistic missiles, which had less range but could be launched from submarines very close to the target without any radar warning. This made any national protection from nuclear missiles increasingly impractical. The military realities made for a precarious diplomatic situation. The international politics of brinkmanship led leaders to exclaim their willingness to participate in a nuclear war rather than concede any advantage to their opponents, feeding public fears that their generation may be the last. Civil defence programs undertaken by both superpowers, exemplified by the construction of fallout shelters and urging civilians about the "survivability" of nuclear war, did little to ease public concerns.

The climax of brinksmanship came in early 1962, when an American U-2 spy plane photographed a series of launch sites for medium-range ballistic missiles being constructed on the island of Cuba, just off the coast of the southern United States, beginning what became known as the Cuban Missile Crisis. The U.S. administration of John F. Kennedy concluded that the Soviet Union, then led by Nikita Khrushchev, was planning to station Russian nuclear missiles on the island, which was under the control of Communist Fidel Castro. On October 22, Kennedy announced the discoveries in a televised address, and declared that a naval quarantine would be put around Cuba to turn back any Soviet nuclear shipments, and warned that the military was prepared "for any eventualities." The missiles would have a range of 2,400 miles (4,000 km), and allow the Soviet Union to easily destroy many major American cities on the Eastern Seaboard if a nuclear war were started. The leaders of the two superpowers stood nose to nose, seemingly poised over the beginnings of a third world war. Khrushchev's ambitions for putting the weapons on the island were motivated in part by the fact that the U.S. had stationed similar weapons in Britain, Italy, and nearby Turkey, and had previously attempted to sponsor an invasion of Cuba the year before in the failed Bay of Pigs Invasion. On October 26, an offer was sent from Khrushchev to Kennedy offering to withdraw all missiles if Kennedy would commit to a policy of no future invasions of Cuba. Khrushchev worded the threat of assured destruction eloquently: "You and I should not now pull on the ends of the rope in which you have tied a knot of war, because the harder you and I pull, the tighter the knot will become. And a time may come when this knot is tied so tight that the person who tied it is no longer capable of untying it, and then the knot will have to be cut. What that would mean I need not explain to you, because you yourself understand perfectly what dreaded forces our two countries possess."

A day later, however, the Russians put forward another offer, this time demanding that the U.S. remove its missiles from Turkey before any missiles would be withdrawn from Cuba. On the same day, a U-2 plane was shot down over Cuba and another was almost intercepted over Russia, and Soviet merchant ships were nearing the quarantine zone. Kennedy responded by accepting the first deal publicly, and sending his brother Robert to the Soviet embassy to accept the second deal in private. On October 28, the Soviet ships stopped at the quarantine line and, after some hesitation, turned back towards the Soviet Union. Khrushchev announced that he had ordered the removal of all missiles in Cuba, and U.S. Secretary of State Dean Rusk was moved to comment, "We went eyeball to eyeball, and the other fellow just blinked."

The Crisis was later seen as the closest the U.S. and the USSR ever came to nuclear war and had been narrowly averted by last-minute compromise by both superpowers. Fears of communication difficulties led to the installment of the first hotline, a direct link between the superpowers which would allow them to more easily discuss future military activities and political maneuverings. It had been made clear that with their missiles, bombers, submarines, and computerized firing systems, the escalation of any situation to Armageddon could be done far more easily than anybody desired. After stepping so close to the brink, both the U.S. and the USSR worked to reduce their nuclear tensions in the years immediately following. The most immediate culmination of this work was the signing of the Partial Test Ban Treaty in 1963, in which the U.S. and USSR agreed to no longer test nuclear weapons in the atmosphere, underwater, or in outer space. Testing underground continued, allowing for further weapons development, but the worldwide fallout risks were purposefully reduced, and the era of using massive nuclear tests as a form of saber-rattling ended.

In December 1979, NATO decided to deploy cruise and Pershing II missiles in Western Europe in response to Soviet deployment of intermediate range mobile missiles, and in the early 1980s, a "dangerous Soviet-US nuclear confrontation" arose. In New York on June 12, 1982, one million people gathered to protest nuclear weapons, and to support the second UN Special Session on Disarmament. As the nuclear abolitionist movement grew, there were many protests at the Nevada Test Site. For example, on February 6, 1987, nearly 2,000 demonstrators, including six members of Congress, protested against nuclear weapons testing and more than 400 people were arrested. Four of the significant groups organizing this renewal of anti-nuclear activism were Greenpeace, The American Peace Test, The Western Shoshone, and Nevada Desert Experience.

Initial Proliferation

The United Kingdom had been an integral part of the Manhattan Project following the Quebec Agreement in 1943. The passing of the McMahon Act by the United States in 1946 unilaterally broke this partnership and prevented the passage of any further information to the United Kingdom. The British Government under Clement Attlee determined that it would be essential for there to be a British Bomb. Because of the involvement in the Manhattan Project Britain had extensive knowledge in some areas, but not in others.

An improved version of 'Fat Man' was developed, and on 26 February 1952, Prime Minister Winston Churchill announced that the United Kingdom also had an atomic bomb and a successful test took place on the 3rd October 1952. At first these were free-fall bombs and then there was a missile, Blue Steel, and a later-canceled MRBM, Blue Streak. Anglo-American cooperation on Nuclear weapons was restored by the 1958 US-UK Mutual Defence Agreement. As a result of this and the Polaris Sales Agreement, the United Kingdom has bought United States designs for submarine missiles and fitted its own warheads. It retains full independent control over the use of the missiles. It no longer possesses any free-fall bombs. France had been heavily involved in nuclear research before World War II through the work of the Joliot-Curies. This was discontinued after the war because of the instability of the Fourth Republic and the lack of finance available. However, in the 1950s a civil nuclear research program was started, a byproduct of which would be plutonium.

In 1956 a secret Committee for the Military Applications of Atomic Energy was formed and a development program for delivery vehicles started. With the return of Charles de Gaulle to the presidency of France in 1958 the final decisions to build a bomb were taken, and a successful test took place in 1960. Since then France has developed and maintained its own nuclear deterrent. In 1951 China and the Soviet Union signed an agreement whereby China would supply uranium ore in exchange for technical assistance in producing nuclear weapons. In 1953 China had established a research program under the guise of civilian nuclear energy. Throughout the 1950s the Soviet Union provided large amounts of equipment, but as the relations between the two countries worsened, the amount of assistance was reduced, and in 1959 the donation of a bomb for copying purposes was refused. Despite this, rapid progress was made with the test of an atomic bomb on the 16th October 1964 at Lop Nur, a nuclear missile on 25 October 1966, and of a hydrogen bomb on the 14th June 1967.

Nuclear warheads were produced from 1968 and thermonuclear warheads from 1974. It is also thought that Chinese warheads have been successfully miniaturised from 2200 kg to 700 kg through the use of designs obtained by espionage from the United States. The current number of weapons is unknown owing to strict secrecy, but it is thought that up to 2000 warheads may have been produced, though far fewer may be available for use.

China is the only nuclear weapons state to have guaranteed the non-first use of nuclear weapons.

Cold War

After World War II, the balance of power between the Eastern and Western blocs, resulting in the fear of global destruction, prevented the further military use of atomic bombs. This fear was even a central part of Cold War strategy, referred to as the doctrine of Mutually Assured Destruction ("MAD" for short). So important was this balance to international political stability that a treaty, the Anti-Ballistic Missile Treaty (or ABM treaty), was signed by the U.S. and the USSR in 1972 to curtail the development of defenses against nuclear weapons and the ballistic missiles which carry them. This doctrine resulted in a large increase in the number of nuclear weapons, as each side sought to ensure it possessed the firepower to destroy the opposition in all possible scenarios and against all perceived threats. Early delivery systems for nuclear devices were primarily bombers like the United States B-29 Superfortress and Convair B-36, and later the B-52 Stratofortress. Ballistic missile systems, based on Wernher von Braun's World War II designs (specifically the V2 rocket), were developed by both United States and Soviet Union teams (in the case of the U.S., effort was directed by the German scientists and engineers although the Soviet Union also made extensive use of captured German scientists, engineers, and technical data).

These systems, after testing, were used to launch satellites, such as Sputnik, and to propel the Space Race, but they were primarily developed to create the capability of Intercontinental Ballistic Missiles (ICBMs) with which nuclear powers could deliver that destructive force anywhere on the globe. These systems continued to be developed throughout the Cold War, although plans and treaties, beginning with the Strategic Arms Limitation Treaty (SALT I), restricted deployment of these systems until, after the fall of the Soviet Union, system development essentially halted, and many weapons were disabled and destroyed. There have been a number of potential nuclear disasters. Following air accidents U.S. nuclear weapons have been lost near Atlantic City, New Jersey (1957); Savannah, Georgia (1958); Goldsboro, North Carolina (1961); off the coast of Okinawa (1965); in the sea near Palomares,

Spain (1966); and near Thule, Greenland (1968). Most of the lost weapons were recovered, the Spanish device after three months' effort by the DSV Alvin and DSV Aluminaut.

The Soviet Union was less forthcoming about such incidents, but the environmental group Greenpeace believes that there are around forty non-U.S. nuclear devices that have been lost and not recovered, compared to eleven lost by America, mostly in submarine disasters. The U.S. has tried to recover Soviet devices, notably in the 1974 Operation Jennifer using the specialist salvage vessel *Hughes Glomar Explorer*. On January 27, 1967, more than 60 nations signed the Outer Space Treaty, banning nuclear weapons in space.

The end of the Cold War failed to end the threat of nuclear weapon use, although global fears of nuclear war reduced substantially. In a major move of symbolic de-escalation, Boris Yeltsin, on January 26, 1992, announced that Russia planned to stop targeting United States cities with nuclear weapons.

Second Nuclear Age

Although it had started before the end of the Cold War, the *second nuclear age*-proliferation of nuclear weapons among lesser powers and for reasons other than the American-Soviet rivalry-really began with the end of the Cold War. India's first atomic-test explosion was in 1974 with Smiling Buddha, which it described as a "peaceful nuclear explosion". India tested fission and perhaps fusion devices in 1998, and Pakistan successfully tested fission devices that same year, raising concerns that they would use nuclear weapons on each other. All of the former Soviet bloc countries with nuclear weapons returned their warheads to Russia by 1996.

In January 2004, Pakistani metallurgist and weapons scientist Abdul Qadeer Khan confessed to having been a part of an international proliferation network of materials, knowledge, and machines from Pakistan to Libya, Iran, and North Korea. South Africa also had an active program to develop uranium-based nuclear weapons, but dismantled its nuclear weapon program in the 1990s. It is not believed that it actually tested such a weapon though it later claimed to have constructed several crude devices which it eventually dismantled. In the late 1970s American spy satellites detected a "brief, intense, double flash of light near the southern tip of Africa." Known as the Vela Incident, it was speculated to have been a South African or possibly Israeli nuclear weapons test, though some feel that it may have been caused by natural events.

Israel is widely believed to possess an arsenal of potentially up to several hundred nuclear warheads, but this has never been officially confirmed or denied (though the existence of their Dimona nuclear facility were confirmed by Mordechai Vanunu in 1986). North Korea announced in 2003 that it also had several nuclear explosives though it has not been confirmed and the validity of this has been a subject of scrutiny amongst weapons experts. The first detonation of a nuclear weapon by the Democratic People's Republic of Korea was the 2006 North Korean nuclear test, conducted on October 9, 2006. On the 25th of May 2009 North Korea continued nuclear testing, violating United Nations Security Council Resolution 1718.

In Iran, Ayatollah Ali Khamenei issued a fatwa forbidding the production, stockpiling and use of nuclear weapons on August 9, 2005. The full text of the fatwa was released in an official statement at the meeting of the International Atomic Energy Agency (IAEA) in Vienna. Despite this, however, there is mounting concern in many nations about Iran's refusal to halt its nuclear power program, which many (including some members of the US Government) fear is a cover for weapons development.

Use of Nuclear Weapons

The fact that nuclear weapons are a subject of separate negotiations cannot be taken to exempt them from established international law. It is obvious that the applicability of law to a nuclear setting requires consideration of the likely physical consequences of the use of nuclear weapons. Firstly, can it ever be possible to reconcile the use of nuclear weapons with the accepted principles. In particular, is it possible to use nuclear weapons in a way which distinguishes between combatants and non-combatants, which represents proportionality of force, which can ever be selective or discriminating, and which does not violate the rights of neutral states.

The Tribunal heard much evidence to the effect that nuclear weapons are extremely destructive of both persons and property (Iwasa, Sagan, Myers, Greene, Steadman, Dawson, Haines, Saito, Thompson, Percival, Alcalay). The detonation of just one, one-megaton nuclear warhead over a major city would result in 900,000 immediate deaths primarily from blast and heat, and a further 900,000 from the effects of radiation, making a total of 1.8 million. The health and emergency services of the European countries could not cope with just one such detonation. Evidence from the British Medical Association indicated, that the medical services would be completely overwhelmed by one such bomb.

General Effects of Nuclear Weapons

Potentially lethal and destructive effects such as fire and blast may extend over ten miles in radius from the centre (ground-zero) of a nuclear explosion, while lethal levels of radioactive fallout dust would be deposited as far as 50 to 100 miles down-wind depending upon wind speed and local precipitation. The highly destructive nature of the nuclear weapons means that it is extremely difficult, and in most cases impossible to hit military targets without also devastating civilian habitations and environments nearby or down-wind. Evidence from Hiroshima and Nagasaki in Japan and from US atomic bomb tests established that long-term (20 to 30 years later) effects include eye cataracts, cancers of various types and impaired reproductive ability. Thus the detonation of just one weapon in the megaton range over or near to a civilian centre of population would be a breach of the law on the following counts, inter alia: indiscriminate, unnecessary suffering, disproportionate force and lack of protection to civilians or injured non-combatants.

The detonation of up to 200 nuclear weapons in the 10 to 100 kiloton range on purely military targets in central Europe would result in 5-14 million deaths, primarily of civilians. Civilian casualties would exceed military casualties by a factor of 16 to 1. It was noted that in areas such as the Middle East or most of Europe, the use of even relatively few nuclear weapons-less than 0.1% of the current nuclear arsenals-would result in very high casualties. This is because in such areas military and civilian targets are highly interspersed. The legal provisions to protect property, buildings and undefended cities could not be kept. The possible erection of a so-called Star Wars or SDI (Strategic Defence Initiative) shield as envisaged at present would also not achieve the aim of separating civil and military targets. In the final or 'terminal' phase of such a putative shield, nuclear weapons would have to be destroyed in the atmosphere above cities and military bases.

If these weapons were 'salvage fused', that is if they detonated with a nuclear explosion if hit, a most likely response to SDI, these low endo-atmospheric explosions would still cause severe blast and heat damage to cities.

Weapons intercepted in the mid-course or this final phase would still deposit large quantities of highly radioactive elements and isotopes upon their intended targets. Thus a 'limited' nuclear exchange would lead to a breach of the law on all the counts above, with the addition of the following: devastation of the environment and violation of neutrality (by fallout and blast). Countries such as Switzerland, Sweden and Hungary would suffer casualties to their populations, disruption of trade and imports and the poisoning of tracts of land making movement hazardous for many weeks and farming for up to a year.

Once nuclear weapons are used in larger quantities, that is up to 1-2% of the current arsenals, or even possibly at the 'tactical' level, a further effect of nuclear weapons becomes important. The heat of the nuclear fire-balls will start many fires creating huge clouds of smoke.

These smoke clouds will merge and reduce the levels of light and heat from the sun and furthermore create a 'greenhouse' effect as with normal water vapour clouds. The result will be a general reduction of local and northern hemispheric average temperatures. If sufficient weapons are detonated, the resultant smoke particles could lead to the so-called 'nuclear winter', in which light levels and land temperatures would be severely reduced for up to many months.

Causation of the nuclear winter would be an extreme violation of all the categories of the laws of war on every count. Countries very far removed from the theatres of war would suffer the most severe effects, leading to the starvation of estimated billions in the Third World as a result of crop and rains failure and world climatic catastrophe.

Medical and Environmental Effects of Nuclear War

The Tribunal heard much evidence about the medical and environmental effects of the use of nuclear weapons.

Consequences of Nuclear Attack on the UK

Bearing in mind the special situations represented in the evidence from Japan, the Tribunal was anxious to establish the impact of a major nuclear attack on a modern and highly developed society using weapons currently existing in the arsenals of the major nuclear powers. Evidence was presented by Mr. Greene and Dr. Steadman of the Open University on the results of computer simulations of large scale nuclear attacks on the UK. Their evidence gave a detailed account of calculations of short-term effects, the numbers killed and injured, the extent of physical damage caused by blast and fire, and the extent of radioactive contamination by fall-out. These calculations are based primarily on direct evidence of the effects of modern weapons which are detailed in a recent joint US Department of Energy/Department of Defence report which provides the most comprehensive technical summary of nuclear explosion effects openly available. The US report is based principally on the results of a large number of nuclear tests carried out by the United States during the 1950s and 1960s. Notably, results from British nuclear tests are still not openly available.

The Steadman and Greene evidence focused on assumed attack levels of 219 megatons and 348 megatons which are based on attacks covering (i) all major nuclear and conventional military bases including command centres, as well as power stations, oil and gas refineries, ports and a few heavy industrial plants and (ii) as in (i) but with a few general urban-industrial targets added as well. These attacks are regarded as primarily counterforce and countervalue attacks aimed at eliminating military forces and reducing industrial/economic recovery. Steadman and Greene assume that one-third to one-quarter of the nuclear warheads available to the Soviet Union in its Eurostrategic arsenal would be allocated for use against the United Kingdom on account of its key role within NATO and the high density of military targets and American nuclear bases. However only about one third of these levels are used in their attack scenarios. Steadman and Greene also pointed out that up until 1981 the British Home Office made the assumption for the purposes of civil defence planning that an attack by the Soviet Union would be of roughly 200 megatons. More recently government spokesmen have been asserting that more limited attacks (e.g. of 50 megatons) are "more probable" than an all-out attack though this remains an issue of deep contention.

The effects of the two attack patterns presented by Steadman and Greene. Both levels of attack which are not aimed principally at population centres generate substantial civilian casualty rates. The Tribunal interpret this as being indicative of the fact that it is impossible to distinguish between military and non-military targets with modern nuclear weaponry.

During his oral evidence, Dr. Steadman provided the Tribunal with estimates of the indirect effects of the attack scenarios on energy supply, agriculture, and the provision of food and water. He pointed out that the effects of blast damage, the electromagnetic pulse and radiation would seriously damage all public services and hamper if not eradicate all chance of post-attack recovery within a predictable or reasonable time-scale. Mr. Greene was cross-examined at length on differences between their calculations and similar ones carried out by the UK Home Office which generated a casualty level of only 17 million. Mr. Greene pointed out that many independent scientists have been critical of assumptions in the Home Office models relating to the extent of blast damage and the radiation protection offered by damaged buildings.

The members of the Tribunal noted with some concern that there appears to be substantial disagreement within the scientific community vis a vis the extent of blast damage from nuclear explosions, the protection factors for modern housing stock, and LDSO values for radiation injury. Nevertheless the Tribunal accepted that even allowing for the most optimistic assumptions the consequences of any nuclear attack against a nation would be extremely dire and that there could be no effective civil defence for whole populations particularly when long-term effects are taken into account.

The Tribunal noted that the UK Home Office had not been prepared to send representatives to the Tribunal to explain its own calculations and assumptions. Finally Steadman and Greene presented the Tribunal with a publication outlining a number of other attack scenarios on the UK. Two other recent publications on British assessments of the effects of nuclear attack were also made available to the Tribunal, one dealing with an attack on London, the other with the detailed consequences for the British housing stock.

Nuclear War and the Provision of Health Services

In assessing the overall effects of nuclear war the Tribunal sought to identify more clearly the scale of physical and psychological damage to civilian populations and the ability of health services to provide for victims.

The first witness to appear in this category was Dr. Dawson, Under Secretary of the British Medical Association. He presented the Tribunal with copies of the report by the BMA's Board of Science and Education on the medical effects of nuclear war as his prime proof of evidence. This report reviewed all the major studies of nuclear attacks on the UK and examined mortality rates and medical response. The BMA report establishes that in the UK there are approximately 160,000 acute beds available within the National Health Service (NHS) in peace-time. After a nuclear attack the majority of these would have been destroyed. Many victims would suffer from serious second and third degree burn injuries, orthopaedic, abdominal, spinal and thoracic injury from blast effects, as well as from the effects of high levels of radioactivity and infection. The report points out that substantial numbers of victims of nuclear attack even if they survive the first few days would require major surgery for blast trauma plus plasma and blood transfusions for burn and radiation injury. The majority of victims requiring such treatment (likely to be many millions) are certain to die. The report concludes : "The explosion of a single nuclear bomb of the size used at Hiroshima over a major city in the UK is likely to produce so many cases of trauma and burns requiring hospital treatment that the remaining medical services in the UK would be completely overwhelmed. An attack with, for example, 200 megatons represents an explosive power some 15,000 times greater than the Hiroshima bomb or the equivalent of forty (40) times all the conventional explosive used in the whole of the

Second World War. The NHS could not deal with the casualties that might be expected following the detonation of a single one megaton weapon over the UK. It follows that multiple nuclear explosions over several, possibly many, cities would force a breakdown in medical services across the country as a whole. There is no possibility of increasing the production of certain drugs in a short period of tension before a war, and if it is wished to have large quantities of blood products available for transfusion purposes or the bulk of the present generation of medical practitioners in the country trained for certain eventualities, then all of these things would have to be done now and the country must exist on a more or less permanent emergency footing."

Dr. Dawson indicated that the BMA had taken the view in its study that the calculations performed by independent scientists on the effects of attacks on the UK were more realistic than those of the British Home Office. The members of the Tribunal note that regardless of who is right or wrong on this issue, the essential conclusions of the BMA report remain indisputable. Additional evidence on the effects of nuclear war on the medical services was provided by Dr. Haines of the Department of Community Medicine at the Middlesex Hospital, London.

A third witness in this section, Dr Thompson, provided the Tribunal with useful information on the possible psychological reactions to nuclear disasters. Such evidence is based on observed reactions to past natural disasters and extrapolation to a post-nuclear society is difficult. Under examination Dr. Thompson expressed the view that approximately one half of the survivors of an attack would probably suffer from a 'disaster syndrome' in which people would feel 'dazed, stunned, bewildered, and apathetic and behave mechanically'. He estimated that a further 25% would be capable of reacting usefully but would suffer from a role conflict, i.e. family versus duty. The remaining 25% would be incapable of reacting. The Tribunal accepted that severe psychological disturbance was likely to be a major indirect effect of the use of nuclear weapons which would pose a serious threat to the continuing existence of initial survivors even at 'limited' scales of attack. The lack of a normal outside world would be a critical factor in amplifying the psychological effects.

The attention of the Tribunal was also drawn to a recent report by the International Committee of Experts in Medical Sciences and Public Health to the World Health Organization. The report concludes that: "The immediate and the delayed loss of human and animal life would be enormous, and the effect on the fabric of civilization would be either to impede its recovery or make recovery impossible. The plight of survivors would be physically and psychologically appalling. The partial or complete disruption of the health services would deprive survivors of effective help. The committee is convinced that there is a sound professional basis for its conclusions that nuclear weapons constitute the greatest immediate threat to the health and welfare of mankind."

Longer Term Effects of Low-Level Radiation

The Tribunal accepted evidence from several witnesses on the long-term effects of nuclear weapons in terms of low-level radiation and the human body. One, Dr. Glenn Alcalay, concentrated on long-term medical effects experienced by inhabitants of the Marshall Islands in the Pacific where a large number of American nuclear tests were conducted in the 1950s. This evidence was particularly revealing as it concerned the effects on populations who were not direct or intended victims of nuclear attack. In a written report, Dr. Alcalay revealed that on several occasions the Marshall Islanders were subjected to accidental radioactive contamination from fall-out. In one particular 15 megaton detonation, the BRAVO test of March 1954, a total of fourteen islands was affected. Three days after the explosion (at Bikini Atoll) the inhabitants of Kongelap Island were evacuated by the US Navy. They were returned to the island in 1957 but began to experience medical problems. On several occasions women gave birth to "creatures like monkeys, some like octupi, and some like bunches of grapes". A few years later other islanders were found to be suffering from thyroid problems and leukaemia. Dr. Alcalay's report notes that the long-term effects on the islanders eventually included late-occurring thyroid effects including tumours and thyroid dysfunction with concomitant growth abnormalities, as well as blood changes and chromosome aberrations, adverse birth outcomes and the effects of ecosystem contamination and the uptake of radionuclides in the food-chain. The Tribunal noted with concern that his report indicated that data from the Marshall Islands suggests that low levels of ionizing radiation may cause as much cancer as higher levels over a long period of time. A group exposed to a whole-body gamma dose of 14 rads (considered by many experts to be insignificant) appears to have experienced the same rate of thyroid cancer as a group exposed to 175 rads.

Long-Term Effects on the Global Ecosphere

Apart from examining the medical effects of nuclear weapons the Tribunal sought to address the recent and spectacular conclusions of a number of atmospheric and biological scientists who now believe that nuclear warfare can result in such drastic changes to the global climate that the continued existence of many life-forms would be questionable. The Tribunal recognized that the recent predictions of the so-called 'nuclear winter effect' needed special attention for three primary reasons:

i. the nuclear winter theory is based largely, but not exclusively, on mathematical model predictions

ii. a nuclear winter would be the ultimate factor determining the eventual survival of the human race whether or not extensive civil defence provisions were available in the short-term

iii. the nuclear winter theory suggests that the global biosphere is at risk as the consequences of a nuclear exchange would be carried far beyond the nations involved directly in the military conflict. This has serious implications for the validity of the nuclear weapon as an instrument of war between nations.

The Tribunal received written evidence from four experts one of whom, Professor Ian Percival FRS of Queen Mary College London appeared before the Tribunal in person for cross-examination. The Tribunal was presented with papers from Professor Carl Sagan of Cornell University reporting the original research work which predicted a nuclear winter and the biological effects; a paper from Dr. Norman Myers on the environmental consequences; and a paper from Mr. Jonathon Porritt, also on the impact on the biosphere. During the course of the oral proceedings

Professor Percival outlined the main causes of the nuclear winter and its effects. He explained that one major effect of a nuclear war would be that dust and smoke from large fires would be carried high into the atmosphere where it would be carried around the globe acting as a barrier to sunlight causing darkness and extreme cold at the Earth's surface. He explained that if the dust and smoke reached the comparatively stable stratosphere as the computer models predicted then it could remain air-borne for many months and even up to one or two years resulting in severe biological consequences.

The precise nature of these consequences was outlined in some detail in the other written evidence. Basically the occurrence of very low light levels (down to a few percent of normal) combined with protracted periods of cold would effectively obliterate agriculture as plant photosynthesis would cease. In addition damage to the Earth's ozone layer caused by massive quantities of nitrogen oxides generated as a by-product of nuclear explosions would result in an increased level of ultraviolet light reaching the Earth once the dust had cleared, posing a further threat to any life-forms which might have survived the cold and the dark. In addition the Earth's surface and atmosphere may be contaminated not only with enhanced levels of long-lived radioactivity but also with hazardous chemical pollutants resulting from the combustion of plastics and other materials prevalent in a modern highly industrialized society. If such predictions are correct then the consequences for human survivors are clear. With failing agriculture and no relief from the cold or dark the long term survival of the human race appears to be in some doubt on the basis of these startling scientific predictions.

The Tribunal attempted to ascertain what minimum level of nuclear exchange could give rise to the nuclear winter. Results from calculations by Professor Sagan and others indicate that sub-zero temperatures averaged over a hemisphere would exist for up to 3 months after only a 100 megaton city attack corresponding to a small 'theatre' exchange. The Tribunal was also interested in assessing the certainty of the nuclear winter predictions or the lack of it. Under cross-examination Professor Percival accepted that the nuclear winter theory depends very much on estimates of the extent of fires, the amount of soot and smoke generated, the height to which soot and smoke particles rise, and the rates at which they fall out. Professor Percival accepted that there were many imponderables in the models but that the best judgment could be reached by examining a variety of studies.

Tribunal Conclusions on Global Ecosphere Effects

After careful consideration of all the evidence submitted on the nuclear winter the members of the Tribunal were drawn to a number of significant conclusions:

1. There appears to be genuine controversy within the scientific community on the certainty or severity of a nuclear winter after a nuclear exchange. However, a number of major computational studies carried out independently in the USA and USSR appear to come to the same conclusion: that a nuclear winter is a likely consequence of nuclear war.
2. Experimental evidence has shown that dust emitted by volcanoes can encircle the globe within 20 days and that there is an historical correlation between frost damage to tree rings and occurrences of major dust-creating volcanic eruptions.
3. A nuclear winter arising from a theatre or strategic nuclear exchange may render human life impossible in one or both hemispheres of the Earth on a long-term basis. This effect may far outweigh the short-term effects of nuclear weapons on civilians and combatants.
4. In view of the fact that the nuclear winter theory cannot be indisputably disproved short of a test in the form of a real war and that the evidence seems to point to it as a real and likely outcome of even a theatre nuclear war (for example, limited to Europe), then it is apparent that the use of nuclear weapons within a limited scenario must be regarded as a grossly irresponsible act on a global scale having consequences far beyond any conceivable military objective within the theatre of use.

Nuclear Weapons and Strategy

Such deliberate use takes the threat of use to its next logical conclusion. Such use is itself illegal for the various reasons examined in the cases given below, but in addition and more importantly such use is illegal if it is likely to bring about limited or general nuclear exchanges leading to a gross breach of all the principles of the laws of war as above.

Detonation of Single Weapon in Water

Use of a single, one kiloton nuclear warhead accurately targeted upon a surface ship even as large as an aircraft carrier would completely destroy it, with the probably loss of all hands. This would be in breach of the laws of war to the extent that disproportionate force would have been used. The same military objective could be achieved with the use of several successful torpedo or conventional missile attacks. If the weapon was detonated at very low altitude very substantial amounts of soluble radioactive isotopes would be generated and dispersed creating a large local environmental impact to the aquatic food-chains and a radioactive fallout plume lethal several miles downwind. Injection of radioactive material into the upper atmosphere would be unlikely. These effects would bring a further charge of unlawfulness to the extent that an. area would be poisoned.

Use of Single Weapon on Land

Assuming that a small detonation was made in a remote pass before enemy troops could reach the area and that prevailing winds did not blow fallout over the territory of neighbouring countries the only breach of the law is that of poisoning of the environment. In reality it is very difficult to envisage all such eventualities being fulfilled and such use would be most likely to breach the neutrality of any neighbouring countries, to kill civilians, and to be indiscriminate use.

Use of Single Weapon as Demonstration

Such use would be a very explicit example of terroristic diplomacy and a very clear threat of further use on a possibly inhabited area or upon a military target.

Tendency of Weaponry and Strategies Towards Use

Here the Tribunal considered factors such as the disposition of various nuclear states to use nuclear weapons, cumulative tendencies to use nuclear weapons, crisis stability, specific technologies and strategies leading towards use and the likely influence of possible defensive components (for example, the SDI) in conjunction with the highly offensive nuclear weapons. A large body of evidence was presented and several specialist witnesses were cross-examined.

Strong evidence was presented to the Tribunal that nuclear strategies currently in force, particularly western strategies, had detailed contingency plans for the first-use of nuclear weapons in response to conventional attack — known as 'extended' deterrence. Nuclear weapons were not seen as purely existing to make a devastating response to any nuclear attack. Soviet declared strategy differed in that the Soviets had made a unilateral pledge not to use nuclear weapons first, against non-nuclear states or neutrals. Despite this declared strategy, evidence was presented that the Soviet Union might in certain circumstances, such as in anticipation of an imminent nuclear attack by NATO, launch nuclear weapons first. Nevertheless the strategic trends were that NATO was more ready to threaten or actually to initiate nuclear weapons use than the Soviet Union. This was a clear asymmetry between the positions of the two superpowers.

Relating to the weapons themselves, the trend in weaponry is towards larger numbers of smaller and more accurate warheads. The accuracy of present-day warheads is far above that needed to target cities, which gives rise to the fear that these weapons are targeted upon other nuclear weapons in their silos and that they might be used in a nuclear 'first strike'. Neither side has sufficient weapons of sufficient accuracy to achieve such a disarming first strike over the other, also both sides possess submarine launched weapons whose positions were not sufficiently well-known to be hit. Nevertheless this trend in weaponry and in anti-submarine warfare was to increase the numbers of weapons systems potentially vulnerable to first-strike. The US was 5 to 10 years ahead of the Soviet Union in this technology.

New conventional weapons also 'fudge' the firebreak between nuclear and non-nuclear use for two reasons: (a) new dual-capable weapons systems are planned using cruise and Pershing type missiles to strike Warsaw Pact airfields and fixed targets, these launches would be indistinguishable from nuclear launches; (b) certain weapons such as the fuel-air explosion have explosive powers larger than the smallest nuclear weapons, others are intended to be just as destructive as neutron warheads to tank concentrations (MLRS Phase 3 warhead), others such as the cluster bomb can devastate large areas with withering blasts of shrapnel and deposit plastic minelets for area denial purposes. Witnesses (Boyle, Meyrowitz) referred to the Rand Study to support a proposition that more accurate and smaller weaponry could be an attempt to legitimize nuclear weaponry by reducing collateral damage. Evidence was presented that although individual warheads are smaller, intermixing of military and civilian targets would lead to inevitable and unlawful killing of civilians. Also increased forward basing of land-based weapons in highly populated areas such as Europe could only exacerbate the problem.

Both sides have deployed weapons which could be targeted upon the other's command and control networks and reaching them in 5 to 10 minutes from launch. These deployments were judged by the Tribunal to be diminishing stability in a crisis by reason of the very short flight times and the vulnerability of command and control networks. This trend represented, in the view of the Tribunal an increase in risk taking which was deemed to be both unnecessary and reckless endangerment.

The influence of possible future defensive measures was considered. The US SDI is defensive only insofar as its intention is to destroy incoming warheads. Both the US and the USSR possess large numbers of highly offensive weapons including long-range nuclear warheads. Such offensive capability in conjunction with a new defensive ability, would enhance both the defensive and the offensive capability of any power deploying an SDI system. If one side deploys SDI the result is simply a greater degree of threat to the side not possessing it, because as far as it is successful a certain proportion of the nuclear warheads of one's opponent are made useless. SDI could be interpreted as enhancing a possible first strike option because any response after first strike could be stopped by the shield. It can also be interpreted as removing the deterrent ability of the smaller nuclear powers. In both these respects it is de-stabilizing. SDI as presently envisaged cannot defend Europe, because tactical weapons do not go up into space, or defend against low-flying weapons of longer range. Anti-tactical Ballistic Missile (ATBM) systems are being considered for the point defence of US airfields in Europe. As far as SDI is successful and the belief that any retaliatory strike may be sufficiently blunted is enhanced, the likelihood of further unlawful and unethical risk-taking is increased.

Evidence was given to the effect that the nuclear state could only exist by means of excessive state security and was thus by its nature counter-democratic leading to a gradual erosion of human rights (Kaldor).

The existence of nuclear weapons had led to a militarization of international relations since the Second World War. Successive nuclear threats were known to have been made by the US in Korea, but the effectiveness of these threats as a means of nuclear coercion or blackmail was severely questioned. It seemed that the only successful case of nuclear blackmail was by a small nuclear state (Israel) against the US.

The Tribunal found that the trends in weaponry and strategy made the unlawful use of nuclear weapons more likely, both the threat of use and the actual detonation of weapons. Many of the newer, smaller types of weapons particularly the US cruise missile, made verification of future treaties more difficult (cruise is outside existing arms control treaties such as Salt-2).

This also applied to a lesser extent to mobile weapons such as the Soviet SS-20. Modern developments made the likelihood of escalation to all-out nuclear war from serious conventional conflicts almost inevitable and constituted an unlawful and unethical degree of risk taking. The US SDI initiative was seen as a further de-stabilizing development, particularly as an existing arms control treaty, the ABM treaty, was likely to be threatened.

One positive trend which emerged from the technology was that with the extremely high sensitivity of satellite monitoring operating at many different frequencies and new technologies for higher frequency seismic analysis-the transparency revolution-the possibility of any side cheating on any arms control agreements was more remote. This could not be used as a valid reason for not ratifying the Comprehensive Test Ban Treaty (CTBT) or a implementing a freeze on deployment, testing and development.

Lawful Use of Nuclear Weapons

In evidence before the Tribunal, Professor Meyrowitz stated that, of all those scholars who have expressly considered the topic, the substantial majority have concluded that the use of nuclear weapons would contravene international law. The minority opinion, predominantly American, is that the use of nuclear weapons would be lawful so long as their use complies with the standards of discrimination and proportionality. To be meaningful, this last assertion requires an answer to the question of whether the real (and not theoretical) use of nuclear weapons could be discriminating and proportionate. The Tribunal did not consider that the likely reality supports the assertion, and reached this conclusion based upon the evidence of the capabilities of existing nuclear weapons, the unlikelihood of a limited use of nuclear weapons and the medical and environmental consequences of their actual use.

Professor Boyle stated, "one might be able to conceive some totally insignificant situation in which a bomb could be blown off and perhaps not violate international law". Professor Griffith offered a few examples such as the use of a small 'clean' tactical weapon against an enemy ship in mid-ocean or against a small force in mid-desert.

The Tribunal considered these examples to be unlikely. In reality any major nuclear exchange would be an unprecedented human and environmental catastrophe proving a serious threat to the survival of all life on the planet. Even the use of a few tactical nuclear warheads would result in substantial incidental loss of civilian life and civilians would be subjected to unnecessary suffering far outweighing any immediate political or military objectives.

There are the strongest religious and moral objections to the destruction of a society through the use of nuclear weapons. Indeed, it is difficult to identify any real value system that justifies their use. As for the rights of neutral states, missiles, which are not included within any of the treaties regulating air traffic, but which will inevitably fly over neutral territory are in breach of Article

II of the fifth Hague Convention. The use of nuclear weapons would inflict considerable damage on neutral nations, most obviously upon Austria and Switzerland. It is the most extraordinary proposition that two warring states, engaged in a private conflict, may legitimately destroy their neutral neighbours.

Upon the evidence, the use of nuclear weapons cannot distinguish between combatants and non-combatants, that it could not represent a proportionate use of force, that it cannot be selective or discriminating, and that it violates the rights of neutral nations. In short, the use of nuclear weapons is unlawful. It is clear therefore that the use of nuclear weapons involves, inter alia, infringements the Charter of the United Nations, the Hague Conventions of 1899 and 1907 on the Law of War, the Geneva Conventions of 1949 and the Geneva Protocols of 1977. It is also clear that mere *possession* (certainly in terms of testing nuclear weapons) has already involved quite unlawful actions against civilian populations and exposed certain populations to unacceptable risks and actual damage.

3

Aerial Warfare

Aerial warfare is the use of military aircraft and other flying machines in warfare, including military airlift of cargo to further the national interests as was demonstrated in the Berlin Airlift. Developing from unpowered observation hot air balloons in the 18th century and even older kite, aerial warfare has become a high-technology affair that has led to many advances in technology and techniques such as propulsion, radar, and use of composites and engineered materials such as carbon fibers.

Kite Warfare

The earliest documented aerial warfare took place in ancient China, when a manned Kite was set off to spy for military intelligence and communication. Ancient Chinese soldiers also mounted massive aerial fire arrow attacks from war kites, where they would send a volley of flaming arrows from the war kite onto the ground target, carrying out the world's first-ever air attacks.

Balloon Warfare— Balloon warfare in Ancient China

In or around the 2nd or 3rd century, a prototype Hot air balloon, the Kongming lantern was invented in China serving as military communication.

Balloon Warfare in Europe

Some minor warfare use was made of balloons in the infancy of aeronautics. The first instance was by the French Aerostatic Corps at the Battle of Fleurus in 1794, who used a tethered balloon, *L'entreprenant,* to gain a vantage point. Balloons had disadvantages. They could not fly in bad weather, fog, or high winds. They were at the mercy of the winds and were also very large targets.

American Civil War—Union Army Balloon Corps

The American Civil War was the first war to witness significant use of aeronautics in support of battle.. Thaddeus Lowe made noteworthy contributions to the Union war effort using a fleet of balloons he created In June 1861 Professor Thaddeus S. C. Lowe left his work in the private sector as a scientist/balloonist and offered his services as an aeronaut to President Lincoln, who took some interest in the idea of an air war. Lowe's demonstration of flying his balloon *Enterprise* over Washington, DC, and transmitting a telegraph message to the ground was enough to have him introduced to the commanders of the Topographical Engineers; initially it was thought balloons could be used for preparing better maps.

Lowe's first action was at the First Battle of Bull Run in July 1861 with General Irvin McDowell and the Grand Army of the Potomac. *Enterprise* did a free flight observation of the Confederate positions.

In another demonstration, Lowe was called to Fort Corcoran by artillery General W. F. Smith. Lowe ascended to a given altitude in order to spot rebel encampments at Falls Church, Virginia. With flag signals he directed artillery fire onto the sleeping encampment. As the General put it, *"The signals from the balloon have enabled my gunners to hit with a fine degree of accuracy an unseen and dispersed target area."*

By October, Lowe had orders in hand to build four balloons with portable hydrogen gas generators for use in aerial reconnaissance. Working with several other prominent American balloonists he formed the Union Army Balloon Corps who never received commissions, working as civilian contractors, This was of great concern should the aeronauts be shot down over enemy lines, as civilian spying is summarily punishable by death. Therefore Lowe insisted on the strict use of tethered (as opposed to free) flight. By attaining altitudes from 1,000 feet (300 m) to as much as 3-1/2 miles, an expansive view of the battle field and beyond could be had.

Lowe built seven balloons: *Eagle*, his first; *Constitution*, one of the smaller balloons; its sister, *Washington*; *Intrepid*, a larger balloon and his favorite; a sister, *Union*; *Excelsior*; and *United States*, which never came out of storage. As the Confederates retreated toward Richmond, the War turned into the Peninsular Campaign. Due to the heavy forests on the peninsula, the balloons were unable to follow on land. Lowe was introduced to *George Washington Parke Custis*, a coal barge converted to operate balloons. The balloons and their gas generators were loaded aboard and taken down the Potomac, where reconnaissance of the peninsula could continue. *Custis* was taken up the Pawmunkey River, where Lowe was reunited with McClellan's army.

Lowe's most dramatic action came in the Battle of Fair Oaks, where he was able to view the advancing of Lee's army onto the isolated detachment of General Heintzelman. Working from two balloon camps, one at Mechanicsville and one at Gaine's Farm, Lowe galloped six miles (10 km) twice daily to keep up with the reconnaissance reports. McClellan was sure the rebels were feigning an attack, but Lowe could see differently. Heintzelman was left stranded on the other side of the Chickahominy River with the bridges having been taken out overnight by the swollen waters. Lowe sent a dispatch of utmost urgency to have the bridge repaired immediately and reserves sent to Heintzelman's aid. He then sent dispatch from Mechanicsville to Gaine's Farm calling for the immediate inflation of the large balloon *Enterprise*, which would aid him in overlooking the imminent battle.

When Lowe arrived at Gaine's Farm, *Intrepid* will still far from being inflated. In a quick work of inventive ingenuity, Lowe had the bottom of a camp kettle cut out and joined the valve ends of the *Intrepid* and the partially inflated *Constitution* hooked together, thereby transferring the gas from the latter into the former. Within 15 minutes he was in the air to oversee the battle.

Lowe fell prey to malaria during Fair Oaks and was out of commission for more than a month. On his return he found the Balloon Corps had been stripped of horses and wagons and left out of service for Antietam. Lowe was called back into service at Sharpsburg and later responded to Gen. Burnside's army at Vicksburg. The ensuing defeat of the Union Army in what was referred to as the "Mud March" led to Gen. Joseph Hooker relieving Burnside. By this time, the Balloon Corps had been assigned to the Engineers Corps, and a newly promoted Captain Comstock cut Lowe's pay dramatically. Lowe tendered his resignation and was released from military duty in May 1863. The Balloon Corps continued to operate with Lowe's handlers, but Union generals' continuing ignoring and mistrust of ballooning resulted in balloon-intelligence not being utilized. By August, the Union Army Balloon Corps was disbanded.

Silk Dress Balloons

Due to the effectiveness of the Union Army Balloon Corps, the Confederates felt compelled to incorporate balloons as well. As coke gas was not always available in Richmond, the first balloons were made of the Montgolfier rigid style, cotton stretched over wood framing and filled with hot smoke from fires made of oil-soaked pinecones. They were piloted by Captain John R. Bryant for use at Yorktown. Though Bryant's performance was not all that bad, his handlers were poorly experienced and his balloon was left in the air spinning like a top. Another incident had one of the handlers becoming entangled in the ascending tether rope which had to be chopped loose, leaving the Captain free-flying over his own Confederate positions whose troops threatened to shoot him down.

Attempts at making gas-filled silk balloons were hampered by the South's inability to obtain any imports at all. They did fashion a balloon from dress silk (purportedly silk for making dresses, not from silk dresses themselves). The inflated spheres appeared as multi-colored orbs over Richmond and were piloted by Captain Landon Cheeves. Before the first balloon could be used it was captured during transportation on the James River by the crew of the Monitor. A second balloon did see action until summer 1863, when it was blown from its mooring and taken by Union forces only to be divided up as souvenirs for members of the Federal Congress. As the Union Army reduced its use of balloons, so did the Confederates—much to their relief.

Zeppelins, Airships and Blimps

As powered aircraft with wings dominated military aviation during World War I, rigid dirigibles and zeppelins were used by the Germans to attack cities. After World War I, the United States Navy researched the use of airships, including their use as a base for fighter aircraft, but efforts were cancelled after losses in storms. In World War II, barrage balloons were used as obstacles against aircraft, and blimps were used as observation and radar platforms.

Before World War I

The armies of many countries evaluated the use of aircraft for observation purposes. Naval aviation was pursued as well; several tests were made in which floatplanes were launched by catapult from ships at sea, and recovered later by crane.

The U.S. Navy had been interested in naval aviation since the turn of the 20th century. In August 1910 Jacob Earl Fickel did the first experimenting with Glenn Curtiss shooting a gun from an airplane. In 1910–1911, the Navy conducted experiments which proved the practicality of carrier-based aviation. On November 14, 1910, near Hampton Roads, Virginia, civilian pilot Eugene Ely took off from a wooden platform installed on the scout cruiser *USS Birmingham* (CL-2). He landed safely on shore a few minutes later. Ely proved several months later that it was also possible to land on a ship. On January 18, 1911, he landed on a platform attached to the American cruiser *USS Pennsylvania* (ACR-4) in San Francisco harbor.

The first use of airplanes in an actual war occurred in the 1911 Italo-Turkish War with the Italian Army Air Corps bombing a Turkish camp at Ain Zara, Libya, and in the 1912 First Balkan War with the Bulgarian Air Force bombing Turkish positions at Adrianople. Airplanes were also used by the U.S. against Pancho Villa. Air reconnaissance was carried out in both wars too. The air-dropped bomb was extensively used during the First Balkan War (including in the first ever night bombing on 7 November 1912), and subsequently shared with the Imperial German Air Service during World War I.

World War I

Initially during that war both sides made use of tethered balloons and airplanes for observation purposes, both for information gathering and directing of artillery fire. A desire to prevent enemy observation led to airplane pilots attacking other airplanes and balloons, initially with small arms carried in the cockpit, but due to the technology of the time pilots couldn't have forward facing machine guns. Although the addition of deflector plates to the back of propellers by French pilot Roland Garros and designer Raymond Saulnier in the Morane-Saulnier monoplane was the first example of an aircraft able to fire through its propeller, it wasn't until the Dutch aircraft designer Anthony Fokker developed the gun synchronizer in 1915 that it became possible to aim the gun and the airplane at the same time, resulting in German *Leutnant* Kurt Wintgens scoring the first known victory for a synchronized gun-equipped fighter aircraft, on July 1, 1915.

The Allies were able to capture a Fokker *Eindecker* with a Fokker-designed *Stangensteuerung* synchronizer mechanism intact and reverse engineer it, leading to the birth of *aerial combat,* more commonly known as the dogfight. Tactics for dogfighting evolved by trial and error. The German ace Oswald Boelcke created eight essential rules of dogfighting, the *Dicta Boelcke.*

Both sides also made use of aircraft for bombing, strafing, sea reconnaissance, antisubmarine warfare, and dropping of propaganda. The German military made use of Zeppelins and, later on, bombers such as the Gotha, to drop bombs on Britain. By the end of the war airplanes had become specialized into bombers, fighters, and observation (reconnaissance) aircraft.

Between the Wars

Between 1918 and 1939 aircraft technology developed very rapidly. In 1918 most aircraft were biplanes with wooden frames, canvas skins, wire rigging and air-cooled engines. Biplanes continued to be the mainstay of air forces around the world and were used extensively in conflicts such as the Spanish Civil War. Most industrial countries also created air forces separate from the army and navy. However, by 1939 military biplanes were in the process of being replaced with metal framed monoplanes, often with stressed skins and liquid cooled engines. Top speeds had tripled; altitudes doubled; ranges and payloads of bombers increased enormously.

Some theorists, especially in Britain, considered that aircraft would become the dominant military arm in the future. They imagined that a future war would be won entirely by the destruction of the enemy's military and industrial capability from the air. The

Italian general Giulio Douhet, author of *The Command of the Air*, was a seminal theorist of this school, which has been associated with Stanley Baldwin's statement that "the bomber will always get through"; that is, regardless of air defenses, sufficient raiders will survive to rain destruction on the enemy's cities. This led to what would later be called a strategy of deterrence and a "bomber gap", as nations measured air force power by number of bombers.

Others, such as General Billy Mitchell in the United States, saw the potential of air power to augment the striking power of naval surface fleets. German and British pilots had experimented with aerial bombing of ships and air-dropped torpedoes during World War I with mixed results. The vulnerability of capital ships to aircraft was demonstrated on 21 July 1921 when a squadron of bombers commanded by General Mitchell sank the ex-German battleship SMS *Ostfriesland* with aerial bombs; although the *Ostfriesland* was stationary and defenseless during the exercise, its destruction demonstrated the potency of airplanes against ships.

It was during the Banana Wars, while fighting bandits, freedom fighters and insurgents in places like Haiti, the Dominican Republic and Nicaragua, that United States Marine Corps aviators would begin to experiment with air-ground tactics making the support of their fellow Marines on the ground their primary mission. It was in Haiti that Marines began to develop the tactic of dive bombing and in Nicaraugua where they began to perfect it. While other nations and services had tried variations of this technique, Marine aviators were the first to embrace it and make it part of their tactical doctrine Germany was banned from possessing an air force by the terms of the World War I armistice. The German military continued to train its soldiers as pilots clandestinely until Hitler was ready to openly defy the ban. This was done by forming the *Deutscher Luftsportverband*, a flying enthusiast's club, and training pilots as civilians, and some German pilots were even sent to the Soviet Union for secret training; a trained air force was thus ready as soon as the word was given. This was the beginning of the *Luftwaffe*.

World War II

Military aviation came into its own during the Second World War. The increased performance, range, and payload of contemporary aircraft meant that air power could move beyond the novelty applications of World War I, becoming a central striking force for all the combatant nations.

Over the course of the war, several distinct roles emerged for the application of air power.

Strategic Bombing

Strategic bombing of civilian targets from the air was first proposed by the Italian theorist General Giulio Douhet. In his book *The Command of the Air* (1921), Douhet argued future military leaders could avoid falling into bloody World War I–style trench stalemates by using aviation to strike past the enemy's forces directly at their vulnerable civilian populations. Douhet believed such strikes would cause these populations to force their governments to surrender.

Douhet's ideas were paralleled by other military theorists who emerged from World War I, including Sir Hugh Trenchard in Britain. In the interwar period, Britain and the United States became the most enthusiastic supporters of the strategic bombing theory, with each nation building specialized heavy bombers specifically for this task.

Imperial Japanese Air Service

Shôwa strategic bombing was independently conducted during the Second Sino-Japanese war and World War II by the Imperial Japanese Navy Air Service and the Imperial Japanese Army Air Service.

Bombing efforts mostly targeted large Chinese cities such as Shanghai, Wuhan and Chonging. The bombing of Nanjing and Canton, which began on 22 and 23 September 1937, called forth widespread protests culminating in a resolution by the Far Eastern Advisory Committee of the League of Nations.

There were also air raids on Philippines and northern Australia (Bombing of Darwin, 19 February 1942). The Imperial Japanese Navy Air Service used tactical bombing against enemy airfields and military positions, as at Pearl Harbor. The Imperial Japanese Army Air Service also attacked enemy ships and military installations.

Luftwaffe

In the early days of World War II, the Luftwaffe launched devastating air attacks against the besieged cities of Warsaw and Rotterdam. In the case of Warsaw, the bombings had little effect, but in the case of Rotterdam, the psychological effect of the bombings did have the intended effect—a relatively rapid ending of Dutch resistance (Buckley 129).

During the Battle of Britain, the *Luftwaffe*, frustrated in its attempts to gain air superiority in preparation for the planned invasion, turned to bombing of London and other large English cities. However, the *Luftwaffe* found these raids did not have the effect predicted by prewar airpower theorists.

Royal Air Force

The British, started in kind-using a strategic bombing campaign in 1940 that was to last for the rest of the war. Early British bombers were all twin-engined designs and were lacking in defensive armament. Therefore, RAF Bomber Command quickly turned to a policy of night bombing, for which the crews were untrained; their inaccuracy meant they were forced to adopt area bombing and were unable to hit specific targets such as factories or power plants until later in the war when pathfinder tactics, radio location plus ground mapping radar (OBOE and H2S) and very low-level bombing such as that used by the Dambusters in Operation Chastise were developed.

Soviet Red Air Force

Although the rapid industrialization the Soviet Union experienced in the 1930s had the *potential* to enable the Voyenno-vozdushnyye sily (VVS) to be effective against the Luftwaffe, Stalin's purges left the organization intellectually and morally weakened. However, when Germany invaded in June 1941 (Operation Barbarossa), the massive size of the VVS, in both planes and people, allowed it to absorb "horrendous" casualties and still maintain capability.

Like Japan was to do in December of that year, Nazi Germany had awoken a sleeping giant which was too large to destroy despite the Wehrmacht's superior experience and the Luftwaffe's superior training. Despite the near collapse of both the Red Army and Red Air Force, Germany's 1941 assault failed to destroy either one, and as the massive resources of the Soviet Union were reorganized toward war, Germany's impending destruction become ever more apparent.

As during the *Battle of Britain,* fundamental flaws in the Luftwaffe were exposed during Germany's war with the Soviet Union. Although strategic bombing requires that the enemy's industrial war capacity be neutralized, some Soviet war factories were moved as much as 1,000 miles (1,600 km) east—far out of reach of the Luftwaffe's bombers. And even factories and VVS facilities that were in reach of the Luftwaffe had to be ignored much of the time because the Luftwaffe's resources were needed for more critical duty in supporting the German army. The Luftwaffe became overstretched, and even victorious battles damaged the overall capability of Germany's air force due to attrition.

By 1943, the Soviets had fully rebounded from the defeats of 1941, and they were able to produce considerably more airplanes than their German rivals; for example, at Kursk, the VVS had twice the number of airplanes that the Luftwaffe had. The VVS's fighter-capability rested on the Yakovlev Yak-9 and Lavochkin La-5, and its primary bombers were the Ilyushin 2 Shturmovik and Petlyakov Pe-2. Utilizing overwhelming numerical superiority, Soviet forces were able to drive the Germans out of Soviet territory and take the war to Germany.

U.S. Army Air Force

When the U.S. Eighth Air Force arrived in England in 1942, the Americans were convinced they could carry out successful daylight raids. The Eighth was equipped with B-17 Flying Fortresses and B-24 Liberators, both high-altitude four-engined designs. The new bombers also featured the strongest defensive armament yet seen-up to 13.50 caliber machine guns, depending on the version, most of them in power-operated turrets. Flying in daylight in large, close formations, U.S. doctrine held tactical formations of heavy bombers would be sufficient to gain air superiority in the absence of escort fighters. The intended raids would hit hard on chokepoints in the German war economy such as oil refineries or ball bearing factories. The U.S.A.A.F. was compelled to change its doctrine since bombers alone, no matter how heavily armed, could not achieve air superiority against single-engined fighters. Loss rates rose from five to twenty *per* cent in a series of missions between August 17 and October 14, 1943, when raids against Regensburg and Schweinfurt, penetrating beyond the range of fighter cover, resulted in the loss of 60 bombers on one mission.

Air Superiority

During the Battle of Britain, many of the best *Luftwaffe* pilots had been forced to bail out over British soil, where they were captured. As the quality of the *Luftwaffe* fighter arm decreased, the Americans introduced the long-range P-38 Lightning and P-51 Mustang escort fighters, carrying drop tanks. Newer, inexperienced German pilots—flying potentially superior aircraft, such as the Focke-Wulf Fw 190, Heinkel He 162, and the Messerschmitt Me 262—gradually became less and less effective at thinning the late-war bomber streams. Adding fighters to the daylight raids gave the bombers much-needed protection and greatly improved the impact of the strategic bombing effort.

Over time, from 1942 to 1944, the Allies' air forces became stronger and stronger while the Luftwaffe became weaker and weaker. During 1944, the Luftwaffe experienced a 78 percent reduction in its strength, and Germany's air force lost control over Germany's skies. As a result *nothing* in Germany could be securely protected—not stationary army units, nor moving army units, nor war factories, nor their workers, nor civilians in cities such as Hamburg and Dresden, nor the nation's capital—Berlin. Germans had to watch as their soldiers and civilians began to be slaughtered in the thousands by aerial bombardment—much as the Germans had done to Poland, Rotterdam, Britain, and the Soviet Union.

Effectiveness

Strategic bombing by non-atomic means did not win the war for the Allies, nor did it succeed in breaking the will to resist of the German (and Japanese) people. But in the words of the German armaments minister Albert Speer, it created "a second front in the air." Speer succeeded in increasing the output of armaments right up to mid-1944 in spite of the bombing. Still, the war against the

British and American bombers demanded enormous amounts of resources: antiaircraft guns, day and night fighters, radars, searchlights, manpower, ammunition, and fuel.

On the Allied side, strategic bombing diverted material resources, equipment (such as radar) aircraft, and manpower away from the Battle of the Atlantic (where even a couple of squadrons of B-24s could be priceless) and Allied armies. As a result, German army groups in Russia, Italy, and France rarely saw friendly aircraft and constantly ran short of tanks, trucks, and anti-tank weapons. The only option left was to create World War I–style slit trench defenses quite unlike the *blitzkriegs* of 1939–1941.

U.S. Bombing of Japan

The long-range Boeing B-29 was used to bomb Japan. On 15 June 1944, 47 B-29s launched from Chengdu, China, bombed the Imperial Iron and Steel Works at Yawata Japan. This was the first attack on Japanese islands since the Doolittle Raid in April 1942. The entire B-29 effort was gradually shifted to the new bases in the Marianas Islands in the Central Pacific.

The first mission against Japan from bases in the Marianas was flown on 24 November 1944, with 111 B-29s sent to attack Tokyo. From that point, increasingly intense raids were launched regularly until the end of the war. Tactics evolved from high-altitude to lower altitude attacks, largely removing most defensive guns and switching to incendiary bombs. These attacks succeeded in devastating almost all large Japanese cities.

The most famous B-29 was the *Enola Gay*, which dropped the atomic bomb 'Little Boy' on Hiroshima on 6 August 1945. *Bockscar*, another B-29, dropped 'Fat Man' on Nagasaki three days later. Although the ethics of nuclear warfare remain controversial, these two actions, along with the Soviet invasion of Manchuria on 9 August 1945, brought about the Japanese surrender, and the official end of World War II.

Tactical Air Support

By contrast with the British strategists, the primary purpose of the *Luftwaffe* was to support the Army. This accounted for the presence of large numbers of dive bombers on strength and the scarcity of long-range heavy bombers. This 'flying artillery' greatly assisted in the successes of the German Army in the Battle of France (1940). Hitler determined air superiority was essential for the invasion of Britain. When this was not achieved in the Battle of Britain, the invasion was canceled, making this the first major battle whose outcome was determined primarily in the air.

The war in Russia forced the Luftwaffe to devote the majority of its resources to providing tactical air support for the beleaguered German army. In that role, the Luftwaffe used the Junkers Ju 87, Henschel Hs 123 and modified fighters—Bf 109 and FW 190.

The Red Air Force was also primarily used in the tactical support role, and towards the end of the war was very effective in the support of the Red Army in its advance across Eastern Europe. An aircraft of importance to the Soviets was the *Ilyushin Il-2 Sturmovik*—appropriately called "flying artilery"; the Il-2 was able to make life very difficult for panzer crews, and the Il-2 was an important part of the Soviet victory at Kursk—one of the biggest tank battles in history.

Military Transport Aviation and Use of Airborne Troops

Military transport aviation was invaluable to all sides in maintaining supply and communications of ground troops, and was used on many notable occasions such as resupply of German troops in and around Stalingrad after Operation Uranus, and employment of airborne troops. After the first trials in use of airborne troops by the Red Army displayed in the early 1930s many European nations and Japan also formed the airborne troops, and these saw extensive service on in all Theatres of the Second World War.

However their effectiveness as shock troops employed to surprise enemy static troops proved to be of limited success. Most airborne troops served as light infantry by the end of the war despite attempts at massed use in the Western Theatre by US and Britain during the Operation Market Garden.

Naval Aviation

Aircraft and the aircraft carrier first became important in naval battles in World War II. Carrier based aircraft are specialized as dive bombers, torpedo bombers, and fighters, evolving from biplanes such as the Swordfish and fighters such as the F4F Wildcat which were based on biplanes to the F4U Corsair which outperformed many land based types, and the TBF Avenger which had an enclosed gun turret.

Surface based aircraft such as the PBY Catalina help find submarines and surface fleets. The aircraft carrier replaces the battleship as the most powerful naval offensive weapons system as battles between fleets are fought entirely out of gun range by aircraft. The Yamato, the most powerful battleship ever built is first turned back by light escort carrier aircraft, and later sunk lacking its own air cover.

In the Doolittle Raid, the US launches normally land-based B-25 Mitchell bombers from carriers in a raid against Tokyo and other Japanese mainland targets. Small escort carriers and light carriers are built in large numbers to escort slow cargo convoys or supplement fast carriers. Aircraft for observation or light raids are also carried by battleships and cruisers, while blimps are used to search for attack submarines.

- Battle of the Atlantic, aircraft carried by low-cost escort carriers are used for antisubmarine patrol, defence, and attack
- Battle of Taranto
- Attack of Pearl Harbor First attack on US territory is carried out entirely by carrier based aircraft, destroying or sinking most US battleships, but not finding any US carriers in port.
- Sinking of *Prince of Wales* and *Repulse,* the first time a battleship underway was sunk solely by aircraft
- Battle of the Coral Sea, the first where neither fleet was in visual contact with the other and all fighting was carried out by aircraft
- Battle of Midway
- Battle of the Bismarck Sea
- Battle of the Philippine Sea
- Battle of Leyte Gulf, with the first appearance of kamikazes, perhaps the largest naval battle in history. Japan's last

carriers and pilots are deliberately sacrificed as a decoy, the super battleship *Musashi* is sunk by aircraft. The Japanese Navy ceases to be an effective fighting force.

- Battle off Samar A powerful fleet led by the Japanese battleship Yamato catches the light escort carrier "Taffy" task forces within gun range. Although largely unprepared to attack armored ships, aircraft and screening "tin-can" destroyers caused enough damage, sinking or forcing the scuttling of 3 cruisers and 1 destroyer, to turn the Japanese force back.
- Operation Ten-Go The sinking of a fleet with the Yamato and nine other warships with no air cover demonstrated U.S. air supremacy in the Pacific theatre by this stage in the war and the vulnerability of surface ships without air cover to aerial attack.

Cold War

Military aviation in the post-war years was dominated by the needs of the Cold War. The post-war years saw the almost total conversion of combat aircraft to jet power, which resulted in enormous increases in speeds and altitudes of aircraft. Until the advent of the Intercontinental Ballistic Missile major powers relied on high-altitude bombers to deliver their newly-developed nuclear deterrent; each country strove to develop the technology of bombers and the high-altitude fighters that could intercept them. The concept of air superiority began to play a heavy role in aircraft designs for both the United States and the Soviet Union.

The Americans developed and made extensive use of the high-altitude observation aircraft for intelligence-gathering. The U-2, and later the SR-71 Blackbird were developed in great secrecy. The U-2 at its time was supposed to be invulnerable to defensive measures, due to its extreme altitude. It therefore came as a great shock when the Soviets downed one piloted by Gary Powers with a surface-to-air missile.

Air combat was also transformed through increased use of air-to-air guided missiles with increased sophistication in guidance and increased range. In the 70s and 80s it became clear that speed and altitude was not enough to protect a bomber against air defences. The emphasis shifted therefore to maneuverable attack aircraft that could fly 'under the radar', at altitudes of a few hundred feet.

Korean War

The Korean War was best remembered for jet combat, but was one of the last major wars where propeller-powered fighters such as the P-51 Mustang, F4U Corsair and aircraft carrier-based Hawker Sea Fury and Supermarine Seafire were used. Turbojet fighter aircraft such as F-80s, F-84 Thunderjets and F9F Panthers came to dominate the skies, overwhelming North Korea's propeller-driven Yakovlev Yak-9s and Lavochkin La-9s.

From 1950, North Koreans flew the Soviet-made MiG-15 jet fighters which introduced the near-sonic speeds of swept wings to air combat. Though an open secret during the war, the most formidable pilots today now admit that they were experienced Soviet Air Force pilots, a *casus belli* deliberately overlooked by the UN allied forces who suspected the use of Russians but were reluctant to engage in open war with the Soviet Union and the People's Republic of China.

At first, UN jet fighters, which also included Royal Australian Air Force Gloster Meteors, had some success, but straight winged jets were soon outclassed in daylight by the superior speed of the MiGs. At night, however, radar-equipped Marine Corps F3D Skynight night fighters claimed five MiG kills with no losses of their own, and no B-29s under their escort were lost to enemy fighters.

In December 1950, the U.S. Air Force rushed in their own swept-wing fighter, the F-86 Sabre. The MiG could fly higher, 50,000 vs. 42,000 feet (12,800 m), offering a distinct advantage at the start of combat. In level flight, their maximum speeds were comparable — about 660 mph (1,060 km/h). The MiG could climb better, while the Sabre could turn and dive better with an all-flying tailplane. For weapons, the MiG carried two 23 mm and one 37 mm cannon, compared to the Sabre's six.50 (12.7 mm) caliber machine guns. The American.50 caliber machine guns, while not packing the same punch, carried many more rounds and were aimed with a more accurate radar-ranging gunsight. The U.S. pilots also had the advantage of G-suits, which were used for the first time in this war.

Even after the Air Force introduced the advanced F-86, its pilots often struggled against the jets piloted by Soviet pilots, dubbed "honchos". The UN gradually gained air superiority over most of Korea that lasted until the end of the war — a decisive factor in helping the UN first advance into the north, and then resist the Chinese invasion of South Korea.

After the war, the USAF claimed 792 MiG-15s and 108 additional aircraft shot down by Sabres for the loss of 78 Sabres, a ratio in excess of 10:1, though some other studies show a gap of close to 2:1 against the best Russian pilots. Some post-war research has been able to confirm only 379 victories, although the USAF continues to maintain its official credits and the debate is possibly irreconcilable.

The Soviets claimed about 1,100 air-to-air victories and 335 combat MiG losses at that time. China's official losses were 231 planes shot down in air-to-air combat (mostly MiG-15) and 168 other losses. The number of losses of the North Korean Air Force was not revealed. It is estimated that it lost about 200 aircraft in the first stage of the war, and another 70 aircraft after Chinese intervention.

Soviet claims of 650 victories over the Sabres, and China's claims of another 211 F-86s, are considered to be exaggerated by the USAF. According to a recent U.S. publication, the number of F-86s ever present in the Korean peninsula during the war totaled only 674 and the total F-86 losses from all causes were about 230.

The Korean war was the first time the helicopter was used extensively in a conflict. While helicopters such as the YR-4 were used in World War II, their use was rare, and Jeeps like the Willys MB were the main method of removing an injured soldier. In the Korean war helicopters like the H-19 partially took over in the non combat Medevac area.

India-Pakistan War of 1965

The war saw the Indian Air Force and the Pakistani Air Force being involved in full scale combat for the first time since independence. Though the two forces had previously faced off in the First Kashmir War during the late 1940s, it was limited in scale compared to the '65 conflict.

Both countries hold highly contradictory claims on combat losses during the war and hardly any neutral sources have thoroughly verified the claims of both countries' claim. PAF claimed it had shot down 104 IAF planes losing only 19 in the process. India meanwhile claimed that 35 IAF planes were lost while shooting down 73 PAF aircraft.

Pakistan's main strike force comprised the U.S. made F-86 Sabre jets, which claimed a fair share of Indian planes, though remaining vulnerable to the dimunitive Folland Gnat, nicknamed "Sabre Slayer". The PAF's F-104 Starfighter was by far the fastest fighter on the subcontinent at that time. On the other hand, the Indian Air Force relied largely on the Hawker Hunter for attacks. Unlike the PAF, whose strength largely comprised American craft, IAF flew an assortment of planes from de Havilland Vampires to Dassault Mysteres, many of which were outdated in comparison to PAF planes, with even Gnats and Hunters being outmatched by Sabres and Starfighters.

Some of the fiercest dogfights occurred over Sargodha, which was PAF's main base housing the bulk of its planes; IAF planes attacked the base but PAF was able to repulse the attacks. PAF responded by attacking Indian bases with some success, especially in air to ground attacks but were soon forced to back off, in order to provide cover for its ground troops elsewhere. In one incident, the Gujarat Chief Minister, Balawant Rai Mehta's civilian craft was shot down by PAF Sabres inside Indian territory, killing him and the crew. By the end of the war, neither the numerically larger IAF, nor the PAF which possessed a qualitative advantage, achieved air superiority.

Vietnam War

The South Vietnamese Air Force (VNAF) was originally equipped with helicopters such as the CH-21 and propeller powered aircraft such as the T-28 Trojan when jet aircraft were disallowed by treaty. As US involvement increased, most airpower was directly flown by US forces. Large scale use of helicopters by the US Army in Vietnam led to a new class of airmobile troops, and the introduction of "Air Cavalry" in the U.S, culminating in extensive use of the UH-1 Huey helicopter which would become a symbol of that war, while the CH-54 Tarhe "Skycrane" and CH-47 Chinook lifted heavier loads such as vehicles or artillery. Troops were able to land unexpectedly, strike, and leave again, and evacuate wounded. The specialized AH-1 Cobra was developed from the Huey for escort and ground support duties, The later Soviet campaign in Afghanistan would also see widespread use of helicopters as part of the Air Assault brigades and regiments.

US forces provided close support of ground force over South Vietnam, and strategic bombing of targets over North Vietnam. Many types flying close support or COIN (Counter Insurgency Warfare) missions were propeller powered types such as the O-1 and OV-10 Bronco FAC spotters, A-1 Skyraider, B-26 Invader, and AC-47 "Spooky" gunship. C-123 Provider and C-130 Hercules transports flew supplies into battlefields such as Khe Sanh.

"Fast movers" included the supersonic F-100 Super Sabre, while the giant B-52 Stratofortress would be modified to unload a massive high explosive payload on enemy troop concentrations. The AC-130 would become the ultimate gunship, while the AX specification to replace the Skyraider would evolve into the A-10 Thunderbolt II.

The USAF F-105 Thunderchiefs flew the bulk of strike missions against North Vietnam in Operation Rolling Thunder, while carrier-based A-4 Skyhawks were flown by the Navy. That first campaign was marred by carefully measured regulations that prohibited attacks against SAM missile sites and fighter bases, and frequent bombing halts, and produced little in political results. Rolling Thunder saw the first combat use of electronic computers aboard PIRAZ ships to display comprehensive real-time aircraft position information for force commanders.

Lessons learned were applied to the later Operation Linebacker which employed Phantoms, B-52s, swing-wing F-111s, A-7 Corsairs and all-weather A-6 Intruders was more successful in bringing North Vietnam to the negotiating table after a massive ground invasion. North Vietnam effectively combined Soviet and Chinese anti-aircraft artillery, SA-2 guided missiles, and MiG fighters to create the most heavily defended airspace up to that time.

US air strikes would combine the use of airbone radar platforms such as the EC-121 Warning Star, KC-135 Stratotankers for air refueling, radar jamming aircraft and specialized "Wild Weasel" units to attack SAM missile sites. Jolly Green Giant helicopter crews escorted by A-1 "Sandy"s would retrieve downed pilots over hostile territory.With the use of "smart" guided bombs late in the war, this would set the model for future US air operations.

Experts were surprised when advanced F-105s were shot down in its first encounter against the elderly but nimble MiG-17. Dogfights were thought to be obsolete in the age of missiles, but pilots now needed maneuverability. The F-4 Phantom was quickly tasked with protecting against MiGs, but sorely lacked a built-in gun when missiles were often unreliable. Air combat training schools such as TOPGUN would improve kill ratios, but combat experience started programs that would produce agile air superiority fighters with guns such as the F-15 Eagle by the 1970s.

South Vietnam fell without US air support when faced with a massive assault in 1975. The VNAF South Vietnamese Air Force was never supplied with powerful fighters and bombers such as the Phantom and B-52 which could strike at North Vietnam.

Middle East

In the Six-Day War of 1967, the Israeli Air Force launched pre-emptive strikes which destroyed opposing Arab air forces on the ground. The Yom Kippur War of 1973 saw the Arab deployment of mobile SA-6 missiles which proved effective against low-flying Israeli aircraft until they were neutralized by ground forces.

Post Cold War

The collapse of the Soviet Union in 1991 forced Western air forces to undergo a shift from the massive numbers felt to be necessary during the Cold War to smaller numbers of multi-role aircraft. The closure of several military bases overseas and the U.S. Base Realignment and Closure program have served to highlight the effectiveness of aircraft carriers in the absence of dedicated military or air forces bases, as the Falklands war and U.S. operations in the Persian Gulf have highlighted. The advent of precision-guided munitions have allowed for strikes at arbitrary surface targets once proper reconnaissance is performed (network-centric warfare). In some cases such as the NATO Operation Allied Force effort against Serbian operations in Kosovo, air power was the deciding factor with ground forces mostly securing the area afterwards. However in most cases the standard military doctrine still applies: wars against third-world regional entities still cannot be won through air power alone.

Operation: Desert Storm

The role of air power in modern warfare was dramatically demonstrated during the Gulf War in 1991. Behind-the-lines air attacks were made on Iraqi command and control centres, communications facilities, supply depots, and reinforcement forces. Air superiority over Iraq was gained before major ground combat began.

The initial strikes were composed of Tomahawk cruise missiles launched from battleships situated in the Persian Gulf, F-117A Nighthawk stealth bombers with an armament of laser-guided smart bombs, and F-4G Wild Weasel aircraft armed with HARM anti-radar missiles. These first attacks allowed F-14, F-15, F-16, and F/A-18 fighter bombers to gain air superiority over the country and then continue to drop TV and laser-guided bombs.

Armed with a gatling gun and heat-seeking or optically guided Maverick missiles, A-10 Thunderbolts bombed and destroyed Iraqi armored forces, supporting the advance of US ground troops. The AH-64 Apache and AH-1 Cobra attack helicopters, fired laser guided Hellfire missiles and TOW missiles which were guided to tanks by ground observers or scout helicopters. The allied air fleet also made use of the E-3A Airborne Warning and Control Systems (AWACS) and a fleet of B-52 bombers. The aerial strike force was made up of over 2,250 combat aircraft, which included 1,800 US aircraft, which fought against an Iraqi force of about 500 Soviet-built MiG-29 and French-made Mirage F-1 fighters. More than 88,000 combat missions had been flown by allied forces with over 88,000 tons of bombs dropped by the end of the fifth week.

Operation: Iraqi Freedom

During the 2003 invasion of Iraq led by US and British forces putatively to defeat the regime of Saddam Hussein, aerial warfare continued to be decisive. The US-British alliance began its air campaign on March 19 with limited nighttime bombing on the Iraqi capital of Baghdad. Several days later, intensive bombardment began. About 14,000 sorties were flown, and at a cost of $1 million dollars each, 800 Tomahawk cruise missiles were fired at numerous targets in Iraq from March 19 until mid-April 2003. By this time Iraqi resistance had largely ended.

Iraqi anti-aircraft weapons were unable to open fire on high-altitude US bombers such as the B-52 or stealth aircraft such as the B-2 bomber and the F-117A. US and British aircraft used radar-detecting devices and aerial reconnaissance to locate Iraqi anti-aircraft weapons. Bunker buster bombs, designed to penetrate and destroy underground bunkers, were dropped on Iraqi command and control centres. Iraqi ground forces could not seriously challenge the American ground forces because of their air supremacy. By mid-April 2003, US-British forces controlled all of Iraq's major cities and oil fields.

2006 Lebanon War

In the beginning of the 2006 Lebanon War Israel utilized an intensive aerial campaign aimed to eliminate Hezbollah and destroy its military as stated by Israeli prime minister Ehud Olmert. It also aimed to return the kidnapped soldiers. The campaign started by destroying Lebanese infrastructure and Hezbollah targets. This continued during the 33 days of the war.

The importance of this war to the history of aerial campaigns lies in the fact that its the first war in the modern history that didn't reach its goals through the use of air force. Taking into consideration the results of 1990 and 2003 wars on Iraq and 1998 war on former Yugoslavia; the Israeli air force, one of the strongest in the world, were unable to accomplish their objectives. This lies on the military doctrine that Hezbollah used in the war which proved effective in facing such kinds of wars. There have also been reports during the conflict that a Hezbollah-manned flying drone penetrated Israeli airspace, and returned to Lebanese territory.

Other conflicts

A few other spans of conflicts opened up the use of aerial warfare in recent times. In 1999, India and Pakistan were involved in a brief conflict over Kashmir. The Indian Air Force used Mirage

2000 fighter jet effectively to carry out ground assault sorties against Pakistani positions. The air operations were notable given the high altitude terrain of Kashmir.

The Political Dimensions of Aerial Warfare

Any attempt to study the nature of aerial warfare immediately encounters the pervasive and controlling oversight political considerations place on the conduct of aerial war. To discuss aerial warfare without addressing the extent to which political considerations affect the application of airpower in combat is to fail to understand the nature of aerial war. Airmen often lament, with equal measures of pride and shortsightedness, how decisive airpower could be in combat if they were given free rein to prosecute an aerial attack with the full measure of destructive power theoretically at their disposal. However, the utilitarian focus of their enthusiasm entirely misses the point of the larger context against which their actions play out. Simply put, airpower is potentially so destructive and dominant that its effects must be limited.

Aerial warfare often becomes a political weapon, rather than a military one, when applied outside the lateral limits of the immediate ground battle. When aerial warfare is used to attack targets of an exclusively military character (like tanks or armored personnel carriers already engaged in combat against friendly ground forces), it obeys and is constrained by the same laws that govern every other purely military instrument of war on the battlefield. However, as aerial warfare is applied further and further from the immediate vicinity of the ground battle, the military effect of its influence decreases, while at the same time, the political effect of its employment becomes potentially more significant.

When opposing forces meet on the battlefield to engage in a violent confrontation for domination and survival, the logic and precedent for action at that moment is martial rather than political.* Kill or be killed. While the decision to employ the military instrument in pursuit of national objectives is a political one, once military forces become engaged in actual combat, the distant political motive for their employment becomes subordinated to the immediate violence, danger, and destruction that make up the character of war. This applies primarily to traditional examples of warfare like Gettysburg, Guadalcanal, or the tank battle at Kursk. Nonetheless, aerial warfare does not fit as neatly into this category of warfare (i.e. traditional warfare directed against strictly military targets) in the same way that it overflows the constricted geography of the traditional battlefield.

Aerial warfare generally ranges far beyond the limits of the immediate ground battle. While airpower is less constrained by the physical dimensions of the battlefield, it is fully and completely constrained by the political dimensions of the objectives underlying the conflict. Airpower advocates have long asserted that airpower's ability to range outside the limits of the traditional battlefield enables it to bring war directly to the heart of the enemy. Many airpower adherents believe that by bombing enemy cities and infrastructure and by disrupting communication with the military forces in the field, airpower provides the capability to extend the limits of the battlefield to bring force to bear on all segments of a society, not just its fielded military forces. In one sense, this assertion is true. The physical capacity of airpower to bring force on the enemy's civil population, infrastructure, and leadership targets is not the question. The questions are (1) do the stakes involved in the conflict warrant this extension of violence outside the traditional arena of the battlefield? and (2) to what extent do attacks on these kinds of targets, outside the traditional battle area, actually affect the outcome of war?

As to the question of whether the stakes involved in the conflict warrant extending violence beyond the limits of the traditional battlefield, the answer, simply put, is that sometimes the situation warrants this kind of attack and sometimes it does not. But, and this is the significant point, the decision to extend the application of violence beyond the zone of the ground battle is a political one. Consequently, Airmen should hardly be surprised if the political constraints applied in such situations fit more tightly than their destructive inclinations might prefer.

Thus, comprehending the effect of politics on the conduct and execution of aerial warfare requires an understanding of the following: The political effects of strategic attack may—and frequently do—outweigh the military effects of the attack.

The decision to extend the application of violence beyond the immediate limit of the traditional battlefield will be a political one.

The political constraints placed on the application of airpower in such situations will be more restrictive than those placed on the application of airpower in more traditional warfighting situations.

How Political Effects in Aerial Warfare Outweigh Military Effects

Part of the folklore of the American military experience in the Vietnam War is that President Lyndon Johnson and Secretary of Defence Robert McNamara selected bombing targets each week at their regular Tuesday luncheons in the west wing of the White House. Airmen often cite this example of political micromanagement of a military operation as axiomatic of the dangers inherent in politicians attempting to perform the work of generals. Yet, there is another lesson in this historical minuet that Airmen overlook. The fact that the president and the secretary of defence took the trouble to select targets in North Vietnam stemmed less from their interest in "playing general" than it did from their recognition of the political ramifications of applying force in the interior of North Vietnam. This is not to imply that we should adopt the example and methods of Johnson and McNamara as model behavior for the application of political oversight to military operations. Rather, Airmen should take this example as emblematic of the political gravity their actions potentially play in the prosecution of war.

For example, how could the actions of a single Airman possibly warrant the time and attention of the president of the United States? Soldiers and sailors rarely receive such unwanted oversight of their actions as they plan for combat. Essentially, three factors differentiate the application of aerial warfare and drive this increased political oversight. They relate to (1) the increase in relative target value, (2) the potential dual use of targets for both civilian and military purposes, and (3) the increased likelihood of civilian casualties from aerial attacks during offbattlefield strikes.

As aerial attacks range further and further from the lateral limits of the ground battlefield, the first political concern that arises relates to the potential variability of target value. On a traditional battlefield, the available targets are primarily, if not exclusively, military. If we destroy a tank, a truck, or an artillery piece on the battlefield, the effect on the enemy is strictly military. The result is that the enemy possesses one less piece of hardware with which to wage war and to threaten friendly forces. The political effect of such an attack is normally minimal, except to the extent to which such losses contribute to the overall outcome of the battle. But if we leave the immediate confines of the traditional battlefield, other targets (of potentially greater value) present themselves: palaces, factories, communication centres, supply depots, bridges, dams, radio towers, oil refineries, and cultural landmarks.* By definition, increased target value carries with it the possibility of increased political effect.

Along with the recognition that such targets contain greater political value comes the additional recognition that the political value of offbattlefield targets can be either positively or negatively charged. For example, while the political effect of striking an enemy's ministry of defence might be positive (from our perspective), the political effect of striking an enemy school or place of worship would be just the opposite. In either case, offbattlefield targets generally contain more political value (visàvis the achievement of wartime objectives) than they do military value.

There may be military targets outside the limits of the battlefield that, if struck, have a potentially similar effect on the outcome of the battle (an air defence sector operations center situated in an underground bunker miles from the battlefield would be one example). But, in general, targets outside the immediate area of the battlefield are of less military value, unless they directly contribute to the ongoing conduct of the battle. Of course, that is not to say that targets outside the immediate area of the battlefield do not potentially contain military value, but whatever military value they contain is outweighed—in most cases—by their potential political value.

The second reason the destruction of offbattlefield targets contains a potentially greater political (rather than military) effect stems from the increased likelihood that a target will have dual uses for both civilian and military needs. Examples of dualuse targets include a power plant, telephone exchange, or railway station. While the destruction of such targets might affect the enemy military's ability to fight, their destruction also affects the enemy's civil population. Whether or not such an effect is considered acceptable, or even desirable, depends on the situation. The potential dual use of offbattlefield targets increases the inherent political sensitivity attendant to their destruction.

The third and perhaps most important reason offbattlefield targets receive such a high degree of political oversight involves the increased probability of civilians in and around target areas as we progress further from the lateral limits of the traditional battlefield. This consideration remains, of course, a function of both culture and situation. While political and military leaders of the United States agonized over the prospect of shooting into crowds of civilians in Somalia in 1993, they showed less concern for greater numbers of civilians killed in the firebombing of Dresden during World War II. Generally, the greater the stakes involved in war, the less effect civilian casualties (or collateral damage) will have on the subsequent criteria for determining how, when, and what measure of force will be applied. Conversely, when the stakes involved in war are less compelling, the aims are more circumspect, and when the degree of oversight and transparency available to independent news media is more pervasive, then the degree to which civilian casualties undermine the achievement of war aims will be significant.

When these three factors occur in combination—hightarget value, dual civil and military use of the target, and the potential for high numbers of civilian casualties—the resulting convergence of political concerns may preclude the application of destructive force against the target in all but the most extreme cases. A fully operating nuclear power plant would be a good example of such a target.

Although the political value of a target may exceed its military value, this does not mean its destruction necessarily contributes any more or less to the achievement of the overall aims of war, since war is a political act conducted with military means. Instead, military planners assume that destroying such targets will have a more pronounced effect on the political end of the spectrum of war aims than it will on the military end of the spectrum. In either case, if the political and military goals appropriately complement one another, the effects should not contravene the overall aims of war. The problem is that political effects are subjective and more difficult to predict than military effects. Hence, there is an inevitable increase in the stake the politician bears in the process when the destructive effects of aerial warfare are applied beyond the lateral limits of the traditional battlefield.

Political Targets Versus Military Targets

If the destruction of a target can have a political effect on the outcome of a battle, we can logically conclude that in addition to traditionally defined military targets, there are also targets of a purely (or primarily) political character. The ability to range throughout the geographic limits of an adversary's homeland presents practitioners of aerial warfare (and political leaders) with the enticing conundrum of having to decide whether to focus the destructive effects of aerial attacks against traditional military targets or broaden their destructive intent to include nonmilitary targets.

The course most frequently chosen is to seek a compromise between political ramifications and military value when considering targets outside the zone of the immediate ground battle. In these cases, the litmus test used to determine target legitimacy usually includes consideration of whether a target in some way contributes to the enemy's warmaking capability. Under this guise, the selection of a power plant that supplies electricity to both military and civilian users could, for example, rise to the necessary threshold of military utility for consideration as a legitimate target. At the limit of this logical thread, the firebombing of Tokyo in World War II (and its many dispersed cottage industries supporting the Japanese war effort) also could conceivably fall under the umbrella of such justification.

Yet, sometimes targets are attacked in war despite a complete lack of military utility or contribution to the war effort. To some extent, the bombing of the town of Guernica during the Spanish Civil War fits this mold. Another example would be the blitz against London.* Still another (although the point is probably arguable) would be the atomic attacks against Hiroshima and

Nagasaki. The effects of these attacks were considerable, but not necessarily in the ways the attackers intended. In the case of Guernica, the effect was gradually to swell worldwide indignation, although not in sufficient amounts to appreciably sway the outcome of that war. The London blitz had an effect opposite to the one intended, by steeling the resolve of the British populace. In the case of Hiroshima and Nagasaki, the atomic attacks served as a final and fatal series of blows to Japanese resistance. Or, as Robert Pape argues, the attacks proved to be just one action in a series of decisive events (along with, most notably, Russia's invasion of Manchuria) that ultimately convinced Japan to surrender.

The terrorist attacks on the World Trade Center do not fit this mold. While the World Trade Center was not a military target, its destruction most certainly contributed to the war aims of the attackers. This presents an interesting conundrum. If an attacker decides to wage a cultural war of annihilation and does not mind dying in the process, then certain fundamental assumptions about negotiation and force will need to be reevaluated in the specific cultural context in which they occur. The United States faced a similar challenge at the end of World War II—with the prospect of an invasion of the Japanese mainland. Such challenges are not insurmountable. Yet, they significantly alter the threshold and the acceptability of violence. Atrocities against civilians tend to steal the resolve of the nation victimized and, rightly or wrongly, tend to be used to justify even greater applications of violence in response. Examples include the atomic attacks on Hiroshima and Nagasaki, Israeli responses to Palestinian suicide bombings, and the immediate American response both to Al Queda following 9/11 and Iraq in 2003.

Therefore, political effects are difficult to predict, even when the degree of force applied might be otherwise decisive in purely military terms. In addition, the variable political character of targets means there are sometimes targets selected for destruction that are entirely political in their character—that is to say, targets with no intrinsic military value on the outcome or the conduct of the battle.

While the number of *purely* political targets may be limited, they bear some examination. The World Trade Center is the most obvious example of a purely political target. There are others, however. A curious example from the first Persian Gulf War was the statue of the crossed swords in Baghdad, moulded in the likeness of the arms of Saddam Hussein himself. Allied war planners put the statue on their early target lists, but US political leaders removed it from consideration during the course of their review of the targets. The point is not whether that particular target was, or was not, destroyed but rather that it merited consideration as a target at all. The effect of its destruction, had it occurred, would have been purely political. That is not to say that political effects do not contribute to the achievement of a war's overall aims. The effects of a political attack can prove decisive in ways that military effects might not. Many have argued this is what happened during Operation Allied Force in Kosovo. However, this also highlights, as we discussed a moment ago, the great unpredictability of attempted political effects. That unpredictability does not restrain politicians (nor should it) from controlling the application of airpower to achieve specific political effects by deciding what should—and should not—be attacked in war. This paper examines that issue shortly and later considers the problems associated with determining the political effects of an attack against a specific target.

Problems in Attacking a Political Target

With the knowledge that targets may contain political as well as military value comes the recognition of the difficulty inherent in determining whether an attack against this type of target actually achieves the intended political effect. Measuring the success of an attack on a political target can prove dubiously inexact owing to the difficulty of establishing a direct and recognizable link between the action taken and the result, if any, observed. To illustrate the problem of ascribing political effects of an action, consider results on a battlefield. Bomb damage assessment, even in an era of sophisticated imagery, remains an inexact science. In the early airpower years, aircrews frequently overestimated the accuracy and effect of their bombs. With the development of reconnaissance platforms in more recent years, overhead imaging systems have been relied on more than the reports of aircrews.

Unfortunately, determining the success of even a straightforward military attack with poststrike imagery is sometimes difficult. Consider the following example: a bomb strikes a bunker or cave complex and burrows deep underground before detonating (as it is designed to do), but postattack imagery shows just a small hole in the roof of the complex. Has the complex been destroyed? How extensively has it been damaged? Should additional sorties be dispatched to further ensure its destruction?

The ongoing need to determine attack effects against traditional military targets is difficult enough. Attempting to determine attack effects against nonmilitary targets is just as difficult in the physical sense, but even more difficult in the psychological, social, and political sense. If we destroy an enemy bridge or power plant, determining the extent of physical damage is the first step. Assuming the attack has been physically successful, we must then determine what effect it has actually had on the enemy. Still, how do we measure the extent of our success in achieving our overall war aims? Can we establish a direct linkage between an attack taken against a largely political target and the subsequent behavior of the enemy? Do we simply assume some linkage exists, in some indirect and indeterminate way?

The truth is that the result of an attack against an enemy yields effects that are both physical and psychological. On a traditional battlefield, if you destroy a tank, there is a negative physical effect (the attrition of the tank), which is easy to measure. But there is also a psychological effect (on the other tank crews) that is more difficult to measure. The psychological effect may be negative if it triggers fear or confusion on the part of the other tank crews. Nevertheless, what if the psychological effect is to provoke anger, outrage, or blood lust? Because of the complexity of the human mind, psychological effects are not predictable. In the above example, one adjacent tank crew member might react with fear, another with outrage. On different days, their individual reactions may be reversed. Even if one assumes psychological reactions to an attack are universal, these reactions are actually unique to each situation and to each individual. Exact psychological effects cannot be predicted with certainty.

Now, expand the preceding battlefield example to one that addresses a primarily political target and predicting the psychological effects becomes less certain. An attack against the enemy's capital, for example, may have less immediate physical effect on the outcome of an ongoing ground battle, but a potentially enormous psychological effect on the enemy civil populace and the enemy leadership. However, if individual psychological effects are difficult to predict, predicting the reaction of the populace of the enemy state is more problematic.

Will the reaction be outrage or despair? Determination or panic? Perhaps all of the above. The reactions of the enemy leader may be equally problematic. Just as the individual reactions of the tank crew may vary, the reactions of an individual leader may vary from situation to situation. The psychological effects may well be profound—as they were on the Japanese after Gen James Harold "Jimmy" Doolittle's raid—but predicting with certainty exactly what those effects will be is another matter entirely.

Because political effects are difficult to measure, and even more difficult to predict, achieving a political objective may require a different approach than a military objective. Military objectives are generally measurable, political objectives much less so, at least from the standpoint of determining how a specific military action produces a recognizable political effect. Until someone develops the means to measure the degree an attack against a political target influences an enemy's behavior, the extent of airpower's contribution to the achievement of war aims will remain inconclusive. While the result of attacks on political targets may be difficult to measure, the extent to which political forces shape and determine the ways in which airpower's destructive effects are applied is profound.

Reasons Political Leaders Modulate Airpower

The nature of aerial warfare provides specific opportunities to modulate and control the intensity of aerial attack throughout the range of combat operations. This characteristic differentiates aerial warfare from many other forms of warfare. This is because more of the variables that control the intensity and duration of an aerial attack remain under the direct control of external leadership than they do in land or naval warfare. When we send an army or a navy into battle, at the outset, we can control some of the variables of time, size, intensity, and duration of the application of force.

We can increase the size of the combat forces. We may be able to accelerate the speed with which they reach the battlefield. We can specify which weapons can be used and in what context. However, once the battle starts, external (meaning political) adjustments to these objective aspects of the force engaged become significantly more difficult to apply. When an army or navy goes into battle, it does so as a single coordinated action using all available forces with a specific opportunity to fight and win. Once the battle ends, there is an opportunity to externally control how quickly, and, in what strength, they are sent into battle again. But, owing to both the cost and inertia of marshalling surface forces for battle, in most cases, these changes occur much more slowly than they do with aerial forces.

In aerial warfare, additional variables remain under external control throughout the span of combat operations. As in the previous example, at the outset, we can control both the size and the alacrity with which an aerial force is directed into battle. We can specify the weapons to be used and the context for their employment. But, even after the battle begins, additional variables often remain within the grasp of external control. We can, up to a certain physical limit, control the number of sorties produced per attack wave (notwithstanding other external influences, like weather and the actions of the enemy, for example). We can control the spacing between the attack waves, and we can control the overall duration of the attack. This is not to say that armies and navies do not control these elements in battle as well, but in the heat and furor of actual conflict, they are necessarily controlled by the engaged forces themselves and to a far less significant extent by the political leadership overseeing the conflict. To illustrate this point, a political leader is unlikely to direct a radio message to a foot soldier telling him where to aim his rifle. Yet, politicians frequently redirect or cancel an aircraft strike—even after they become airborne and are en route to the target area.

There are few military commanders who would choose to go into battle using a small portion of their available forces. When these forces sit directly in harm's way (as surface forces normally do when they are engaged in combat), political leaders normally have enough appreciation of the collective risk borne by the combatants not to suggest that their generals or admirals try to attack with anything less than the full complement of approved combat power available to them. The logic of force survival is a powerful motivator. Two thousand years of land and naval warfare experience provide numerous examples of the perils of failing to bring all available combat power to bear on the enemy at the decisive time and place. This is why, in a surface battle, we do not send out tanks or ships a few at a time to engage the enemy. To do so allows the enemy to focus his land forces against the contingent described.

But sometimes aerial commanders can find themselves (especially in limited wars) directed to strike the enemy with a fraction of their available assets. This is because, unlike army or navy forces, air bases usually sit beyond the ranges of immediate ground threats. The distance an aircraft can travel before it strikes obviates the need to maneuver the bulk of its support structure directly into harm's way to engage the enemy. If this geographic buffer were to evaporate (by the base being attacked or overrun, for example), any external mandate to restrain the use of available force would likely disappear as well. Nevertheless, it is the ability of aerial forces to conduct attacks at long range, with little commensurate threat to friendly forces back at their recovery base, which makes it possible to conduct an attack with less than maximum available aerial power.

The protection of distance and the survival of the home airfield are not the only considerations. Survival is also important when an aircraft flies into enemy territory or within the range of enemy defenses. In such situations, aircraft commanders often seek safety in numbers, since a large attack force can sometimes overwhelm an air defence system that might otherwise make mincemeat out of a smaller force. This provides a powerful argument favoring the traditional military view of attacking with overwhelming force whenever possible. We use this logic in our attack planning for surface engagements. A single tank charging into battle faces threats not only from other tanks, but also from infantry, helicopters, artillery, special operations units, and sometimes even angry mobs (as occurred in Chechnya). The threats to an aircraft are generally more specialized and less widely deployed. Consequently, another reason political leaders sometimes direct a fraction of the available aerial forces to strike the enemy is that, depending on the situation, there may be no greater risk to a small force overflying an enemy than a large force.

It may be possible sometimes to scale back the size of the attacking force without increasing the risk of the mission simply because the threat to any number of friendly aircraft, large or small, is essentially negligible. For example, in a country without a viable air defence, a lonewolf attack by a single aircraft might be an entirely appropriate attack option. Given a more robust air defence, however, the same lonewolf tactic might prove suicidal by allowing the enemy to focus its air defence on a single target.

The third and perhaps most powerful reason political leaders sometimes choose to use lessthanmaximum available aerial force is that the political ends of the situation may not justify the use of overwhelming means. For this reason, airpower is often the force application tool of choice in limited wars. Airpower is a flexible military instrument that can be used once, twice, or as many times as necessary to meet limited political ends. It can be terminated at any time, resumed at any time, or continued without letup. Violence and danger are inherent elements in war, and the military instrument of national power is nothing if not a blunt instrument. Yet, the ability to limit and continually modify aerial warfare to meet political ends makes it, in the eyes of many political leaders, the "least blunt" military instrument among those available.

The final reason political leaders are sometimes tempted, especially in limited wars, to direct the use of lessthanmaximum available aerial force in battle is simply because they can. The nature of aerial warfare itself makes this possible. When land and naval forces engage in battle, they generally sustain the application of force until the battle is either won or lost. Once combat begins, there is no natural and predictable pause during a land or naval battle (as there is when an aircraft returns to base to rearm and refuel) at which time political leaders can consciously and deliberately alter the subsequent applications of force. However, aerial warfare provides this opportunity, and political leaders sometimes avail themselves of these occasions (even in limited wars with circumscribed objectives) to adjust subsequent intensity and degree of force brought to bear on the enemy.

Appeal of the Incremental Approach

Defeating an enemy by gradually increasing the amount of force applied seems a counterintuitive approach to success in war. Logically, if military planners intend to defeat an enemy, it makes sense that we stand the greatest chance of success if we bring the greatest available military force to bear on the problem. If we bring all available force to bear at the outset, logically, it should maximize our chances for success and minimize our chances of becoming engaged in a protracted conflict. The Vietnam War is an American example of a war waged by incremental increases in the degree of force applied. Another example was Operation Allied Force in Kosovo.* And yet, owing to compelling political reasons, often states do not choose to wage war with maximum military force at the outset, but rather through the gradual application of increased levels of force.

Many political and military leaders understand the hazards associated with this incremental approach to warfare. Yet, it is still practiced. Why? If a portion of our force is used initially to engage the enemy, then the enemy stands a greater chance of surviving the attack. When this approach does not achieve quick victory, it requires an upward revision of forces to achieve the original objective and a downward revision in our expectations for a rapid resolution. Increased commitment of forces requires increased commitment of political will. With the upward migration of force levels, both political and military leaders can find themselves drawn into a greater commitment, and perhaps an entirely different mission than originally planned. These are some of the hazards associated with the incremental approach to warfare. Airpower has its own unique set of incremental pitfalls, which are discussed later. This advice against using the incremental approach applies specifically to war fighting, not deterrence. In deterrence, it is wise to proceed slowly. Consider what might have occurred during the Cuban missile crisis, for example, if either side had immediately pursued an aggressive military solution. The result might have provoked a world war. In deterrence, the incremental approach is frequently the correct approach.

Given the arguments against the use of an incremental approach in war, why does the practice persist, especially with regard to the application of airpower? The previous section highlighted the reasons political leaders have seen fit, in certain situations, to modulate the application of airpower. Again, the main reasons include (1) the exposure of fewer personnel to immediate risk, (2) the lack of a requirement—in some cases—to saturate the enemy air defenses with large numbers of aircraft, (3) the limits placed on the application of force in wars with limited political aims, and (4) the opportunity to control the application of airpower during the natural pause afforded when aircraft return to base to rearm and refuel. When politicians commit lessthanmaximum levels of destructive aerial power, unless the operation is 100 percent successful, they risk the necessity of gradually increasing force to achieve the original objectives. Enthusiasm for the measured application of force— which airpower affords—should not obscure its risk. There is a delicate balance between the military hazards associated with the incremental approach and the political imperatives to modulate the application of airpower.

There is a popular rationale favoring the incremental application of force that appeals to civilian democratic leaders involved in limited wars. The rationale presumes it is possible (particularly with airpower) to gradually increase the amount of force until an enemy finally submits. In a modern democracy, there are several attractions to this dialupthepain approach. First, it requires minimum investment of political capital. Where support for overwhelming military action does not exist, this technique allows a political leader to begin an action after which, based on the domestic and enemy reactions, a leader either can increase the level of force—assuming the prospects for military success appear favorable—or can discontinue action without having committed significant resources. Should political resolve weaken at any point during an escalating application of airpower, further applications of force can be terminated. This allows political leaders maximum control with minimal risk.

Thus, one of the reasons the incremental application of airpower appeals to political leaders is that its application of minimum levels of force precludes the political risk of overreaching the limits of the original objective. In an era when political leaders show sensitivity to the potential loss of popular domestic support, coalition consensus, and military lives, this rationale is simple enough to understand. But, the presumed effect and the actual effect of the dialupthepain approach to aerial war are very different. In contrast to the optimistic predictions of Giulio Douhet, when we use aerial warfare to strike offbattlefield targets in an enemy country, the most frequent effect on the morale of both the enemy leadership and populace is to stiffen, rather than weaken, their resolve.

When US forces make their initial strike with minimum possible combat power, they compound this effect. First, this gives the enemy the best opportunity to favorably weather the attack. Second, it builds up the resistance of enemy leaders and populace to subsequent attacks, effectively providing them with a battlefield inoculation. Thus, when a second strike occurs, the enemy is better prepared, physically and psychologically, to survive the attack. The unintended effect of increasing the pressure can prolong the time, effort, danger, and uncertainty of the campaign. Operation Allied Force and the Rolling Thunder campaign in the Vietnam War demonstrate the effects of this phenomenon.

Airpower leaders must recognize the political motives that favour an incremental approach and ensure political leaders understand the shortterm political savings of striking an enemy with minimum aerial firepower may be offset by the longterm cost of protracted aerial campaigns.

The tension in this balance results from the perceived political need, especially in limited wars, to determine exactly how much force is enough. Too little and we risk the incremental approach, with all the inherent hazards just mentioned. Too much and we risk using more than the minimum necessary force to win. On the horns of this dilemma, politicians are tempted to select the former option. The correct choice, however, is often the latter. War is not an exact science, and the use of force is not a recipe that produces a predictable and consistent effect. War is a violent and unpredictable clash of wills that should only be used to resolve the political disagreements of states when other less extreme methods have proven ineffective. The unfashionable reality of the military instrument of national power is that, even in an era of "wiz bang" technology and precisionguided munitions, it remains a blunt and bloody instrument of force.

Aerial Warfare and Civil War

In the years between the world wars, governments and military leaders theorized about the future of aerial warfare. But during this almost two-decade period, there was only one major military conflict—the Spanish Civil War. Although only a few countries officially participated, they found it invaluable preparation for World War II. The Spanish Civil War had its beginnings in Spain's elections of February 1936. The Republicans, consisting of the Communists, Socialists, and Basque and Catalonian separatists, won by a narrow margin. Under the leadership of Jose Calvo Sotelo, the right wing (monarchists, the military, and the Fascist Party) continued to oppose the elected government. In July, the Republicans arrested, then assassinated Sotelo, ostensibly in retaliation for the killing of a policeman by the Fascists. The right wing, now united as Nationalists, used this as their justification for launching a revolution. On July 17, 1936, General Francisco Franco and soldiers loyal to him seized a Spanish Army outpost in Morocco. In Spain, other Nationalist troops quickly seized other garrisons. A junta of generals, led by Franco, declared themselves the legal government, and the war officially began.

The world was forced to take sides. Many countries, including the United States and Great Britain, chose to stay neutral, believing that involvement would lead to war. However, individuals from neutral countries did volunteer with the Republican's International Brigade, feeling the cause was worth fighting for. A group of three Americans pilots formed the Patrolla Americana, which eventually grew into a unit of 20 pilots. The Soviet Union, recognizing a potential Communist nation threatened by fascism, was quick to offer aid, including equipment, soldiers, and senior advisors. Many of their planes, including the Polikarpov I-15 and I-16, formed the backbone of the Republican Air Force. And as a gesture to protect itself from being surrounded on three sides by Fascist nations, France provided some aircraft and artillery. Because a non-intervention agreement in 1936 forbade sympathetic nations to provide airplanes to the competing sides, it was difficult for the Republican government to develop a solid aviation program. It bought small amounts of aircraft where it could, which meant that its air force was composed of small numbers of a lot of different airplanes, from different companies and countries. The Republican government also accepted civilian aircraft, such as the Lockheed Orion, which it could then adapt to military use. There was also a Boeing P-26 that had been brought over as a demonstration model for the Spanish Air Force before the war and was "inherited" by the Republicans.

The Fascist nations found ways to avoid the rules of the non-intervention agreement. Benito Mussolini in Italy was quick to support Franco and sent Spain more than 700 airplanes and troops during the conflict. But it was Germany that was most instrumental in the war. Only days after the war erupted, Franco had sent a request for help to Adolph Hitler. For Germany, the Spanish Civil War came at an opportune time. The nation was initiating a rearmament program, in violation of the World War I peace treaty. A war in Spain would distract the world's governments from this transgression. Plus, Spain had raw materials that Germany could use. Hitler also liked the idea of threatening France with a Fascist government to its south. But most importantly, Spain would provide an opportunity to test equipment and train troops. Although Hitler was careful not to send enough troops to make the world perceive them as a combatant nation, 19,000 German "volunteers" gained valuable combat experience in Spain. Because the Nationalists already had strong army support, Germany sent over mostly aviators from the Luftwaffe.

The Germans were organized into the Condor Legion that was equipped with the most modern airplanes and a specially trained staff. Many of the newest airplanes were tested in real combat situations, among them the Heinkel He.111, and the Messerschmitt Bf.109. The Legion was divided into bomber, fighter, reconnaissance, seaplane, communication, medical, and anti-aircraft battalions, and also included an experimental flight group. The chief of staff was Colonel Wolfram von Richthofen, a cousin of "The Red Baron." The first challenge the German Condor Legion faced was the 20,000 Nationalist troops stranded at the outpost in Morocco, prevented by a Spanish Navy blockade that was loyal to the Republicans from joining the remainder of the Nationalist Army in Seville. The Condor Legion succeeded in evacuating the troops by air—something that had never been done before. On August 6, twenty Junkers Ju-52 transports arrived in Morocco.

Over the next two months, the Condor Legion transported all the Nationalist troops to Seville, with the loss of only one airplane. U.S. General Hap Arnold later described the airlift as the most important air power development of the interwar period.

After the evacuation, the Condor Legion settled into other jobs. It flew harassment raids against Republican forces and supported ground forces. And it initiated both strategic and tactical bombings. While military thinkers of the time were debating the validity of aerial bombing, the German troops in Spain were obtaining practical experience. The Condor Legion used tactical bombing after Soviet airplanes began arriving in October 1936 to strengthen the Republican side. Bombings would weaken the troops for the ground attack. In Bilbao, in the north of Spain, saturation bombing was used to shatter the Republican "Iron Belt"—a 35-kilometer (22-mile)-long line, leaving holes open for advancements; it also prevented Republican reinforcements from reaching the gaps.

But it was the strategic bombing attacks that attracted the most attention. In the beginning, methods were crude; Republican bombers were given tourist maps to help find their targets. But soon, the attacks became routine. Yet there were no riots or uprisings as theorists had anticipated. Instead, civilian resistance and resolve on both sides were strengthened. One British observer noted that the Spanish would "blacken every balcony so as to get a good view of bursting shrapnel."

Of all the bombing raids, it was the attack on Guernica, a city in the north of Spain, which came to symbolize the horrors of aerial bombing. Guernica was the center of Basque identity and culture, boasting the parliament building and an oak tree under which Basque leaders annually swore to uphold the liberties of the people. For three hours on the afternoon of April 26, 1937, planes from the Condor Legion dropped 100,000 pounds (almost 91 million kilograms) of bombs on the city and strafed citizens in the street by machine guns. Republican sources reported 1,500 dead. The only military target in town, a bridge, remained untouched. Instead, it appeared to many, including a London Times correspondent, that "the object of the bombardment was seemingly the demoralization of the civilian population and the destruction of the cradle of the Basque race." Everyone was shocked by the attack, which raised ethical questions all over the world. For many years, the Nationalists denied involvement and claimed that the Basques had bombed themselves for propaganda. They did not admit their involvement until they released reports in the 1970s, after Franco's death. The Republicans used the tragedy to gain support, displaying Pablo Picasso's painting Guernicain the Spanish Pavilion at the 1938 Paris World's Fair. But in the end, the greatest effect of the bombing was to make some European nations fear they might be the next Guernica and thus, they capitulated to Hitler's demands at Munich in September 1938.

At the Nuremberg trials following World War II, Luftwaffe commandant Hermann Goering said, "Spain gave me an opportunity to try out my young air force." The experience gained in Spain helped Germany in the early months of the war far more than the desktop theories and controlled tests of other nations. Having noted poor results from strategic bombing, Germany focused its funds elsewhere. Many planes were tested in real combat situations. And Germany also learned that even with air superiority, a bomber force still required a fighter escort.

But most instrumental were the 19,000 Luftwaffe personnel who rotated through the Condor Legion until the Republicans surrendered in January 1939, leaving the Fascists and Franco in power. Several months later, these veterans of the Spanish Civil War would be flying over Poland, Czechoslovakia, France, and the rest of Europe—an experienced, well-trained air force fighting for Hitler.

4

Effects of Nuclear Explosions on Human Health

Introduction

The energy released from a nuclear weapon detonated in the troposphere can be divided into four basic categories:

- Blast—40-50% of total energy
- Thermal radiation—30-50% of total energy
- Ionizing radiation—5% of total energy
- Residual radiation—5-10% of total energy.

However, depending on the design of the weapon and the environment in which it is detonated the energy distributed to these categories can be increased or decreased. The blast effect is created by the coupling of immense amounts of energy, spanning the electromagnetic spectrum, with the surroundings. Locations such as submarine, surface, airburst, or exo-atmospheric determine how much energy is produced as blast and how much as radiation. In general, denser mediums around the bomb, like water, absorb more energy, and create more powerful shockwaves while at the same time limiting the area of its effect.

The dominant effects of a nuclear weapon where people are likely to be affected (blast and thermal radiation) are identical physical damage mechanisms to conventional explosives. However the energy produced by a nuclear explosive is millions of times more powerful per gram and the temperatures reached are briefly in the tens of millions of degrees. Energy from a nuclear explosive is initially released in several forms of penetrating radiation. When there is a surrounding material such as air, rock, or water, this radiation interacts with and rapidly heats it to an equilibrium temperature (i.e. so that the matter is at the same temperature as the atomic bomb's matter). This causes vaporization of surrounding material resulting in its rapid expansion. Kinetic energy created by this expansion contributes to the formation of a shockwave. When a nuclear detonation occurs in air near sea level, much of the released energy interacts with the atmosphere and creates a shockwave which expands spherically from the hypocenter. Intense thermal radiation at the hypocenter forms a fireball and if the burst is low enough, its often associated mushroom cloud. In a burst at high altitudes, where the air density is low, more energy is released as ionizing gamma radiation and x-rays than an atmosphere displacing shockwave.

In 1942 there was some initial speculation among the scientists developing the first nuclear weapons that there might be a possibility of igniting the Earth's atmosphere with a large enough nuclear explosion. This would concern a nuclear reaction of two nitrogen atoms forming a carbon and an oxygen atom, with release of energy. This energy would heat up the remaining nitrogen enough to keep the reaction going until all nitrogen atoms were consumed. This was, however, quickly shown to be impossible, due to inverse Compton effect cooling of the fireball. Nevertheless, the notion has persisted as a rumour for many years.

Direct Effects

Blast Damage

The high temperatures and pressures cause gas to move outward radially in a thin, dense shell called "the hydrodynamic front." The front acts like a piston that pushes against and compresses the surrounding medium to make a spherically expanding shock wave. At first, this shock wave is inside the surface of the developing fireball, which is created in a volume of air by the X-rays. However, within a fraction of a second the dense shock front obscures the fireball, causing the characteristic double pulse of light seen from a nuclear detonation. For air bursts at or near sea-level between 50-60% of the explosion's energy goes into the blast wave, depending on the size and the yield-to-weight ratio of the bomb. As a general rule, the blast fraction is higher for low yield and/or high bomb mass. Furthermore, it decreases at high altitudes because there is less air mass to absorb radiation energy and convert it into blast. This effect is most important for altitudes above 30 km, corresponding to <1 per cent of sea-level air density.

Much of the destruction caused by a nuclear explosion is due to blast effects. Most buildings, except reinforced or blast-resistant structures, will suffer moderate to severe damage when subjected to overpressures of only 35.5 kilopascals (kPa) (5.15 pounds-force per square inch or 0.35 atm).

The blast wind may exceed one thousand km/h. The range for blast effects increases with the explosive yield of the weapon and also depends on the burst altitude. Contrary to what one might expect from geometry the blast range is not maximal for surface or low altitude blasts but increases with altitude up to an "optimum burst altitude" and then decreases rapidly for higher altitudes. This is due to the nonlinear behaviour of shock waves. If the blast wave reaches the ground it is reflected. Below a certain reflection angle the reflected wave and the direct wave merge and form a reinforced horizontal wave, the so-called Mach stem (named after Ernst Mach). For each goal overpressure there is a certain optimum burst height at which the blast range is maximized. In a typical air burst, where the blast range is maximized for 5 to 20 psi (34 to 140 kPa), these values of overpressure and wind velocity noted above will prevail at a range of 0.7 km for 1 kiloton (kt) of TNT yield; 3.2 km for 100 kt; and 15.0 km for 10 megatons (Mt) of TNT.

Two distinct, simultaneous phenomena are associated with the blast wave in air:

- Static overpressure, i.e., the sharp increase in pressure exerted by the shock wave. The overpressure at any given point is directly proportional to the density of the air in the wave.
- Dynamic pressures, i.e., drag exerted by the blast winds required to form the blast wave. These winds push, tumble and tear objects.

Most of the material damage caused by a nuclear air burst is caused by a combination of the high static overpressures and the blast winds. The long compression of the blast wave weakens structures, which are then torn apart by the blast winds. The compression, vacuum and drag phases together may last several seconds or longer, and exert forces many times greater than the strongest hurricane. Acting on the human body, the shock waves cause pressure waves through the tissues. These waves mostly damage junctions between tissues of different densities (bone and muscle) or the interface between tissue and air. Lungs and the abdominal cavity, which contain air, are particularly injured. The damage causes severe hemorrhaging or air embolisms, either of which can be rapidly fatal. The overpressure estimated to damage lungs is about 70 kPa. Some eardrums would probably rupture around 22 kPa (0.2 atm) and half would rupture between 90 and 130 kPa (0.9 to 1.2 atm).

Blast Winds: The drag energies of the blast winds are proportional to the cubes of their velocities multiplied by the durations. These winds may reach several hundred kilometers per hour.

Thermal Radiation

Nuclear weapons emit large amounts of thermal radiation as visible, infrared, and ultraviolet light. The chief hazards are burns and eye injuries. On clear days, these injuries can occur well beyond blast ranges. The light is so powerful that it can start fires that spread rapidly in the debris left by a blast. However, the high winds following the blast wave will put out almost all such fires, unless the yield is very high. This is because the intensity of the blast effects drops off with the third power of distance from the explosion, while the intensity of radiation effects drops off with the second power of range. However, in urban areas, the extinguishing of fires ignited by thermal radiation matters little, as fires will be started anyway by electrical shorts, gas pilot lights, overturned stoves, and other ignition sources. The range of thermal effects increases markedly with weapon yield. Thermal radiation accounts for between 35-45% of the energy released in the explosion, depending on the yield of the device.

There are two types of eye injuries from the thermal radiation of a weapon: Flash blindness is caused by the initial brilliant flash of light produced by the nuclear detonation. More light energy is received on the retina than can be tolerated, but less than is required for irreversible injury. The retina is particularly susceptible to visible and short wavelength infrared light, since this part of the electromagnetic spectrum is focused by the lens on the retina. The result is bleaching of the visual pigments and temporary blindness for up to 40 minutes.

A retinal burn resulting in permanent damage from scarring is also caused by the concentration of direct thermal energy on the retina by the lens. It will occur only when the fireball is actually in the individual's field of vision and would be a relatively uncommon injury. Retinal burns, however, may be sustained at considerable distances from the explosion. The apparent size of the fireball, a function of yield and range will determine the degree and extent of retinal scarring. A scar in the central visual field would be more debilitating. Generally, a limited visual field defect, which will be barely noticeable, is all that is likely to occur.

When thermal radiation strikes an object, part will be reflected, part transmitted, and the rest absorbed. The fraction that is absorbed depends on the nature and color of the material. A thin material may transmit a lot. A light colored object may reflect much of the incident radiation and thus escape damage. The absorbed thermal radiation raises the temperature of the surface and results in scorching, charring, and burning of wood, paper, fabrics, etc. If the material is a poor thermal conductor, the heat is confined to the surface of the material. Actual ignition of materials depends on how long the thermal pulse lasts and the thickness and moisture content of the target. Near ground zero where the energy flux exceeds 125 J/cm^2, what can burn, will. Farther away, only the most easily ignited materials will flame. Incendiary effects are compounded by secondary fires started by the blast wave effects such as from upset stoves and furnaces.

In Hiroshima, a tremendous firestorm developed within 20 minutes after detonation and destroyed many more buildings and homes. A firestorm has gale force winds blowing in towards the center of the fire from all points of the compass. It is not, however, a phenomenon peculiar to nuclear explosions, having been observed frequently in large forest fires and following incendiary raids during World War II. Because thermal radiation travels more or less in a straight line from the fireball (unless scattered) any opaque object will produce a protective shadow. If fog or haze scatters the light, it will heat things from all directions and shielding will be less effective, but fog or haze would also diminish the range of these effects.

Indirect Effects

Electromagnetic Pulse

Gamma rays from a nuclear explosion produce high energy electrons through Compton scattering. These electrons are captured in the Earth's magnetic field, at altitudes between twenty and forty kilometers, where they resonate. The oscillating electric current produces a coherent electromagnetic pulse (EMP) which lasts about one millisecond. Secondary effects may last for more than a second. The pulse is powerful enough to cause long metal objects (such as cables) to act as antennas and generate high voltages when the pulse passes. These voltages, and the associated high currents, can destroy unshielded electronics and even many wires. There are no known biological effects of EMP. The ionized air also disrupts radio traffic that would normally bounce off the ionosphere.

One can shield electronics by wrapping them completely in conductive material such as aluminum foil, however the effects of the EMP can penetrate any shielding depending on the thickness of the metal shielding, the density of the material (lead offers close to the best due to its relative density) and of course the proximity of the blast. This shielding can also be rather ineffective if proper grounding of the shielding is not employed, consequent re-radiation inside the shielding can occur. Semiconductors are extremely susceptible to the effects of EMP due to the close proximity of the PN junctions, this is not the case with thermionic tubes or valves which use stimulated electron emission and are therefor immune. All American and Russian backup communications systems are valve operated to ensure effective operation during or after a nuclear incident. A Faraday cage doesn't offer protection from the effects of EMP unless the mesh was designed to have holes no bigger than the smallest wavelength emitted from a nuclear explosion, in practice this is impossible as a nuclear explosion emits all known wavelengths, some smaller than the atomic bonds of some metals. A Faraday cage was designed to protect from electrical discharges only. Additionally radios cannot operate whilst shielded, because broadcast radio waves cannot reach them.

Ionizing Radiation

About 5% of the energy released in a nuclear air burst is in the form of ionizing radiation: neutrons, gamma rays, alpha particles, and electrons moving at speeds up to the speed of light. Gamma rays are high energy light waves; the others are particles that move slower than light. The neutrons result almost exclusively from the fission and fusion reactions, while the initial gamma radiation includes that arising from these reactions as well as that resulting from the decay of short-lived fission products. The intensity of initial nuclear radiation decreases rapidly with distance from the point of burst because the radiation spreads over a larger area as it travels away from the explosion. It is also reduced by atmospheric absorption and scattering.

The character of the radiation received at a given location also varies with distance from the explosion. Near the point of the explosion, the neutron intensity is greater than the gamma intensity, but with increasing distance the neutron-gamma ratio decreases. Ultimately, the neutron component of initial radiation becomes negligible in comparison with the gamma component. The range for significant levels of initial radiation does not increase markedly with weapon yield and, as a result, the initial radiation becomes less of a hazard with increasing yield. With larger weapons, above 50 kT (200 TJ), blast and thermal effects are so much greater in importance that prompt radiation effects can be ignored.

The neutron radiation serves to transmute the surrounding matter, often rendering it radioactive. When added to the dust of radioactive material released by the bomb itself, a large amount of radioactive material is released into the environment. This form of radioactive contamination is known as nuclear fallout and poses the primary risk of exposure to ionizing radiation for a large nuclear weapon.

Details of nuclear weapon design also affect neutron emission: the gun-type assembly Hiroshima bomb leaked far more neutrons than the implosion type 21 kt Nagasaki bomb because the light hydrogen nuclei (protons) predominating in the exploded TNT molecules (surrounding the core of the Nagasaki bomb) slowed down neutrons very efficiently while the heavier iron atoms in the steel nose forging of the Hiroshima bomb scattered neutrons without absorbing much neutron energy.

Earthquake

The pressure wave from an underground explosion will propagate through the ground and cause a minor earthquake. Theory suggests that a nuclear explosion could trigger fault rupture and cause a major quake at distances within a few tens of kilometres from the shot point.

Other Phenomena

As the fireball rises through still air, it takes on the flow pattern of a vortex ring with incandescent material in the vortex core as seen in certain photographs. At the explosion of nuclear bombs lightning discharges sometimes occur. Not related to the explosion itself, often there are smoke trails seen in photographs of nuclear explosions. These are formed from sounding rockets emitting smoke launched before detonation. The smoke trails are used to determine the position of the shockwave, which is invisible, in the milliseconds after detonation through the refraction of light, which causes an optical break in the smoke trails as the shockwave passes.

The heat and airborne debris created by a nuclear explosion can cause rain. After the Hiroshima explosion, these drops of water were recorded to have been about the size of a marble. A *fizzle* occurs if the nuclear chain reaction is not sustained long enough to cause an explosion, or if the explosion is of much less energy than expected. This can happen if, for example, the yield of the fissile material used is too low, the compression explosives around fissile material misfire or the neutron initiator fails.

Survivability

This is highly dependent on factors such as proximity to the blast and the direction of the wind carrying fallout. Death is highly likely and radiation poisoning is almost certain if one is close enough within the radius of the blast (for example 3 to 4 miles for a 1 megaton atmospheric blast).

Effects of Nuclear Explosions on human health

The medical effects of a nuclear blast upon humans can be put into four categories:

- Initial stage — the first 1–2 weeks, in which are the greatest amount of deaths, with 90% due to thermal injury and or blast effects and 10% due to superlethal radiation exposure
- Intermediate stage — from 3–8 weeks. The deaths in this period are from ionization radiation in the median lethal range
- Late period — lasting from 8–20 weeks. This period has some improvement in survivors condition.
- Delayed period — from 20+ weeks. Characterized by "numerous complications, mostly related to healing of thermal and mechanical injuries coupled with infertility, subfertility and blood disorders caused by radiation." Also, ionizing radiation from fallout can cause genetic effects, birth defects, cancer, cataracts and other effects in organs and tissue.

Blast Effects-The Initial Stage

Immediate Post-attack Period

The main causes of death and disablement in this state are thermal burns and the failure of structures resulting from the blast effect. Injury from the pressure wave is minimal in contrast because the human body can survive up to 2 bar (30 psi) while most buildings can only withstand a 0.8 bar (12 psi) blast. Therefore, the fate of humans is closely related to the survival of the buildings around them.

Fate within Certain Peak Overpressure

- over 0.8 bar (12 psi)-98% dead 2% injured
- 0.3-0.8 bar (5-12 psi)-50% dead 40% injured 10% safe
- 0.14-0.3 bar (2-5 psi)-5% dead 45% injured 50% safe

Types of Radioactive Exposure after a Nuclear Attack

In a Nuclear explosion the human body can be irradiated by at least three processes. The first (the major cause of burns) is not caused by ionizing radiation.

- Thermal burns from infrared heat radiation.
- Beta burns from shallow ionizing beta radiation (this would be from fallout particles; the largest particles in local fallout would be likely to have very high radioactivity because they would be deposited so soon after detonation; it is likely that one such particle upon the skin would be able to cause a localised burn). However, these decay particles are very weakly penetrating and have a short range.
- Gamma burns from highly penetrating gamma radiation. This would likely cause deep gamma penetration within the body, which would result in uniform whole body irradiation rather than only a surface burn. In cases of whole body gamma irradiation (*circa* 10 Gy) due to accidents involving medical product irradiators, some of the human subjects have developed injuries to their skin between the time of irradiation and death.

In the picture on the right, the normal clothing that the woman was wearing would have been unable to attenuate the gamma radiation and it is likely that any such effect was evenly applied to her entire body. Beta burns would be likely all over the body due to contact with fallout, but thermal burns are often on one side of the body as heat radiation does not penetrate the human body. In addition, the pattern on her clothing has been burnt into the skin. This is because white fabric reflects more infra-red light than dark fabric. As a result, the skin underneath dark fabric is burned more than the skin covered by white clothing. There is also the risk of internal radiation poisoning by ingestion of fallout particles.

Radiation Poisoning

Radiation poisoning, also called "radiation sickness" or a "creeping dose", is a form of damage to organ tissue due to excessive exposure to ionizing radiation. The term is generally used to refer to acute problems caused by a large dosage of radiation in a short period, though this also has occurred with long term exposure to low level radiation. Many of the symptoms of radiation poisoning occur as ionizing radiation interferes with cell division. There are numerous lethal radiation syndromes including prodromal syndrome, bone marrow death, central nervous system death and gastrointestinal death.

Prodromal Syndrome

In prodromal (initial) syndrome, a dose of 1.5 gray or less is not lethal, but causes gastrointestinal distress such as anorexia, nausea, fatigue and possibly diarrhea.

Bone Marrow Death

Bone marrow death is caused by a dose of radiation between 2 and 10 gray and is characterized by the part of the bone marrow that makes the blood being broken down. Therefore production of red and white blood cells and platelets is stopped by division of precursor stem cells ceasing (4.5 gray kills 95% of stem cells). The loss of platelets greatly increases the chance of fatal hemorrhage. While the lack of white blood cells causes septicemia infections, the fall in red blood cells is minimal and only causes mild anemia.

The exposure to 4.5 gray of penetrating gamma rays has many effects that occur at different times:

In 24 hours:

- vomiting
- diarrhea

These will usually abate after 6–7 days.

Within 3–4 weeks there is a period of extreme illness.

- severe bloody diarrhea, indicating intestinal disorders causing fluid imbalance
- extensive internal bleeding
- septicemia infections

The peak incidence of acute BM death corresponds to the 30 day nadir in blood cell numbers. The number of deaths then falls progressively until it reaches 0 at 60 days after irradiation. The amount of radiation greatly affects the probability of death. For example over the range of 2 to 6 gray the probability of death in untreated adults goes from about 1% to 99%, but these figures are for healthy adults. Therefore results may differ because of the thermal and mechanical injuries and infectious conditions.

Gastrointestinal Death

Gastrointestinal death is caused by a dose of radiation between 10 and 50 gray. Whole body doses cause damage to epithelial cells lining the gastrointestinal tract and this combined with the bone marrow damage is fatal. All symptoms become increasingly severe causing exhaustion and emaciation in a few days and death within 7–14 days from loss of water and electrolytes.

The symptoms of gastrointestinal death are:

- gastrointestinal pain
- anorexia
- nausea
- vomiting
- diarrhea

Central Nervous System Death

Central nervous system death is the main cause of death in 24–48 hours among those exposed to 50 gray.

The symptoms are:

- vomiting
- nausea
- diarrhea
- drowsiness
- lethargy
- tremors
- delirium
- frequent seizures
- convulsions
- prostration
- coma
- respiratory failure
- death

Short Term Effects (6-8 weeks)

Skin: First of all the skin, which is susceptible to beta-emitting radioactive fallout. The principal site of damage is the germinal layer, and often the initial response is erythema (reddening) due to blood vessels congestion and edema. Erythema lasting more than 10 days occurs in 50% of people exposed to 5-6 gray.

Other effects with exposure include:

- 2-3 gray—temporary hair loss
- 7 gray—permanent epilation occurs
- 10 gray—itching and flaking occurs
- 10-20 gray—weeping blistering and ulceration will occur

Lungs: The lungs are the most radiosensitive organ, and radiation pneumonitis can occur leading to pulmonary insufficiency and death (100% after exposure to 50 gray of radiation), in a few months.

Radiation pneumonitis is characterized by:

- Loss of epithelial cells
- Edema
- Inflammation
- Occlusions of airways, air sacs and blood vessels
- Fibrosis

The Ovaries

A single dose of 1-2 gray will cause temporary sterility and suppress menstruation for periods up to 3 years; a dose of 4 gray will cause permanent sterility.

The Testicles

A dose of 0.1 gray will cause low sperm count for up to a year; 2.5 grays will cause sterility for 2 to 3 years or more. 4 grays will cause permanent sterility.

Long Term Effects

Cataract Induction

The timespan for developing this symptom ranges from 6 months to 30 years to develop but the median time for developing them is 2–3 years.

- 2 gray of gamma rays cause opacities in a few percent
- 6-7 gray can seriously impair vision and cause cataracts

Cancer induction

Cancer induction is the most significant long term risk of exposure to a nuclear bomb. Approximately 1 out of every 80 people exposed to 1 gray will die from cancer and 1 in 40 people will get cancer. Different types of cancer take different times for them to appear:

- 2 years for leukemia to appear
- 20 or more years for skin cancer or lung cancer

In Utero Effects

1 gray dose of radiation will cause between 0 and 20 extra cases of perinatal mortality, per 1,000 births and 0-20 cases of severe mental sub normality. 0.05 gray will increase death due to cancer 10 times, to 5 per 1,000. An antenatal dose of 1 gray in the first trimester causes the risk of fatal cancer will increase to 100%.

5

Nuclear Warfare: The Future of Military Organization

Ours is the age of the network. Whether framed in socio-economic, technological or ideological terms, our present times are increasingly seen as characterized by the rise and spread of fluid, decentralized forms of social organization in which information and telecommunication devices play key roles. For Manuel Castells, author of the seminal *Network society* trilogy, the network constitutes nothing less than 'the new social morphology of our societies' whose 'logic substantially modifies the operation and outcomes in the processes of production, experience, power and culture'.

Business enterprises are seen to be moving towards more flexible and open organizational arrangements as they alternately cooperate and compete with other companies on specific projects, flatten their hierarchical structures by cutting out layers of middle management, and outsource and subcontract large areas of their activities in order to increase their reactivity and adaptability to changing economic environments. In many sectors, the large bureaucratic centres of production which once dominated the industrial era no longer appear suited to competing with their more nimble counterparts within a fast-paced global economy.

Within civil society, non-governmental organizations have proliferated, representing a bewildering range of agendas and political stances but capable of forming powerful ad hoc coalitions to lobby, demonstrate and campaign for or against specific issues. The anti-(or alter-)globalization movement has been perhaps the most spectacular manifestation yet of the disparate yet highly effective transnational social groupings, capable of coalescing and acting worldwide without any formal overarching organizational structure, that seem to be eclipsing mass-membership trade unions and political parties as vehicles of social contestation.

In the criminal underworld, the loose confederation of organizations pursuing illicit activities which mushroomed in Russia after the collapse of the Soviet Union inaugurated a broader trend away from large, centralized criminal associations. In the aftermath of the successful dismantling of the Cali and Medellín cartels in the 1990s, the Colombian drugs trade has shifted towards a decentralized network of several hundred smaller groups, spreading its activities more widely and rendering its operations far less vulnerable to traditional decapitation strikes aimed at taking out key leaders. Likewise, the disruption of the Sicilian Cosa Nostra has seen ownership of the majority of the Italian drug trade pass to the 'Ndrangheta criminal organization from Calabria, which employs a more horizontal structure in which autonomous elements are held together by a common perspective and interests but do not form a single vertical organization.

The internet is of course the most celebrated manifestation of this network era, but we can find a wide array of information and telecommunication technologies and infrastructures deployed within all these burgeoning forms of social organization. Faced with these remarkable transformations occurring across the social field, many now believe with Castells that 'networks are proliferating in all domains of the economy and society, outcompeting and outperforming vertically organized corporations and centralized bureaucracies'.

War is no exception. At the turn of the century, the Pentagon adopted the doctrine of network-centric warfare and set out its vision of autonomous 'swarming' and 'self-synchronized' warfighting units connected to one another by high-speed data links and superior battlefield awareness. Of course, the actors that have truly excelled at adopting loose, decentralized organizational structures are the jihadist networks and insurgent movements that have tied down the net-enabled US army in Afghanistan and Iraq. The recently retired head of US Central Command responsible for operations in the Gulf and Central Asia, General John Abizaid, is in no doubt that 'the enemy is in fact more networked, more decentralized, and operates within a broader commander's intent than any twentieth century foe we've ever met. In fact, this enemy is better networked than we are.' The lesson is clear, however: 'It takes a network to beat a network, and our network must be better.'

The widespread availability of information and telecommunication technologies has no doubt contributed to empowering such organizational arrangements; but is it in itself a sufficient explanation for the present emergence of the network society and its impact on military thinking and practice? While technology certainly contributes to defining the space of possible social formations and practical organizational arrangements, it remains nonetheless primarily a tool which is given meaning and put to specific uses within a broader sociocultural setting. The aeroplane may have made strategic bombing possible, but the latter's implementation required the adoption of a whole set of organizational, tactical and normative commitments. Nor does technology appear *ex nihilo*: it is the product of a particular human engagement with the world. As Martin van Creveld has observed, 'behind military hardware there is hardware in general, and behind that there is technology as a certain kind of know-how, as a way of looking at the world and coping with its problems'.

In the present age, it is science that provides the dominant way of looking at the world, whether as a methodological disposition to problem-solving or in informing our conceptions of how the world works. Our present understanding of the social world in terms of information and networks is directly reflected in the central preoccupations of contemporary science. Indeed, the genealogy of the concepts of swarming and self-synchronization dear to network-centric warfare can be traced back to the scientific theories of chaos and complexity which have emerged over the past few decades. Where technology has played a role, it is in conjunction with the scientific conceptual frameworks that have accompanied its development and diffusion. From the very introduction of the term 'network-centric warfare' in 1998, military doctrine and scientific theory were being explicitly linked by its proponents: 'Military operations are enormously complex, and complexity theory tells us that such enterprises organize best from the bottom-up.' Nor is this a novel phenomenon. In fact, scientific concepts and theoretical frameworks have been influencing military thought and practice since the inception of the scientific revolution in the late sixteenth century. Moreover, the traffic between science and warfare has not been all one way: military imperatives have stimulated both technological and scientific discoveries. From the earliest synergies between the study of the motion of bodies and military ballistics, science and the military art have been inextricably bound, long before the scientific breakthrough of the Manhattan project yielded the atomic weapon.

This article will argue that a *scientific way of warfare*, understood as the application of the methodological and theoretical frameworks of science to the exercise of military force, established itself at the beginning of the modern era and has since grown in influence to become one of the dominant lenses through which armed conflict is contemplated. Inspired by the formidable successes of modern technoscience, military men in search of certainty on the battlefield have turned to the intellectual tools that have proved so effective in predicting and dominating the natural world. The specific ideas brought to bear on military affairs have evolved alongside the theoretical developments of science, and four distinct regimes of the scientific way of warfare will be distinguished here: mechanistic, thermodynamic, cybernetic and chaoplexic warfare. Each of these regimes is closely associated to a paradigmatic technology which dominated the contemporaneous historical period both as a tool and as a general explanatory model for the essential workings of the world—respectively the clock, the engine, the computer and the network.

The Scientific and Military Quests for Order

Throughout the ages, military leaders have sought to organize and direct their armies as to best preserve their order and coherence when faced with the centrifugal forces of chaos unleashed on the battlefield. In this way they have tried to avert for as long as possible the state of disorganized free-for-all which threatens all armies under the stress of battle. The forces that have succeeded in remaining organized while precipitating their adversaries into disarray have almost invariably prevailed. Hence, for van Creveld, the history of command in war consists essentially of an endless quest for certainty— certainty about the state and intentions of the enemy's forces; certainty about the manifold factors that together constitute the environment in which the war is fought, from the weather and the terrain to radioactivity and the presence of chemical warfare agents; and last, but definitely not least, certainty about the state, intentions, and activities of one's own forces.

Likewise, John Keegan notes that the fundamental purpose of training 'is to reduce the conduct of war to a set of rules and a system of procedures—and therefore to make orderly and rational what is essentially chaotic and instinctive'.9 The practice of warfare can thus be understood as the attempt to impose order over chaos, to exert control where it most threatens to elude, and to find predictability in the midst of uncertainty.

States, along with other political entities, seek to employ organized violence in order to attain certain political objectives. As only one of the instruments of statecraft, rational and measured employment of military force must be commensurate with the overall objective to which it is intended to contribute. This is the meaning of Clausewitz's oft-repeated dictum that war is the continuation of policy by other means, strategic thinking being the exercise of judgement over the appropriate means to be deployed in the pursuit of a given political end. However, the formulation of strategy and the assessment of the role of military force within it require an understanding of the likely effects of any course of action. Hence, for Gray, 'if the essence of strategy is instrumentality, the essence of instrumentality is predictability'. Strategic thought and behaviour are therefore necessarily accompanied by a rationalization of military force as an instrument of broader political objectives and a theorization of the potential and limits of the use of organized violence, all in an effort to bring order and predictability to activities which would otherwise be governed by chance and contingency.

A clear parallel can be drawn between the ordering processes inherent in military organization and the instrumental application of armed force, on the one hand, and scientific endeavour, on the other. Indeed, scientists continuously strive to extract patterns from 'noise', to identify regularities in the fog of randomness, to uncover the 'laws' governing the behaviour of nature and reveal the hidden order behind its apparent chaos. For the scientist Norbert Wiener, the 'highest destiny' of mathematics, the universal language of science, was 'the discovery of order among disorder'. Alfred North Whitehead expressed the same idea, albeit in more poetic fashion, when he proposed that the pursuit of mathematics was 'a divine madness of the human spirit, a refuge from the goading urgency of contingent happenings'.

With the discovery and formulation of regularities comes greater predictability of phenomena and an enhanced control over the natural world, notably through the technical devices assembled to exploit such constancies in nature. Auguste Comte, the founder of positivism, explicitly made this link: 'from science comes prevision; from prevision comes control.' The scientific project is thus inextricably connected to the drive for greater control and power over the world, as originally formulated by one of its earliest expositors, Francis Bacon: *scientia potentia est* ('knowledge is power').

The successes of modern science in uncovering seemingly eternal laws of nature and developing or perfecting technological contraptions to take advantage of them has unsurprisingly proved highly attractive to military thinkers and practitioners seeking to dominate the battlefield and render their activity as predictable as possible. Many, in the image of Jomini, have thus been persuaded that 'all strategy is controlled by invariable scientific principles' only awaiting discovery by the rational mind, and have thus sought to emulate the achievements of the natural sciences. Along with the adoption of a scientific disposition in the study of military problems, the resulting scientific way of warfare has entailed the espousal of the successively dominant theoretical frameworks of the sciences, shaping four distinct orientations to the exercise of armed force throughout the modern era.

Mechanistic Warfare and the Clock

Dominant in European thought throughout the seventeenth and eighteenth centuries, the ideas of mechanism constituted the first major body of scientific discourse of the modern epoch. Under it the universe became understood as an entirely mechanical system composed wholly of matter in motion under a complete and regular set of laws of nature. Central to mechanism were the laws of motion as formulated by Newton, the concomitant notions of force, gravity, mass and the reversibility of time, and the belief that any whole could be understood through the analysis of its individual parts.

Within the mechanistic world-view, clockwork acted not only as a model for the order, regularity and predictability of the universe and its diverse natural bodies but also as a mechanism serving scientific enquiry as an instrument and object of study. By embodying a general concept of operation and model of organization enmeshed in wider cultural discourses, clockwork came to represent simultaneously the unveiled order of the physical world and a prescribed ideal in human affairs. Chaos was exorcized by the invocation of divine clockwork behind all phenomena and the promise of complete predictability and control.

A clockwork universe also implied a divine watchmaker who had constructed its mechanism and set it in motion. This vision resonated with the enlightened absolutism of the day, its faith in the rational and orderly organization of government, and the position of the monarch as uncontested divine representative and sole seat of power.

Mechanistic warfare subscribed to the same vision, with its armies emphasizing rehearsed, synchronous movements and characterized by the lack of autonomy of their parts and their unflinching obedience to the predetermined sequence of battle decided upon by their commanders. Geometry and the newly discovered laws of motion were widely applied to improve fortifications and ballistics, but in the field the tendency was towards shaping armies into giant clockwork mechanisms. In an age in which the state of firearms technology meant its effects on the battlefield were maximized through coordinated volleys, and with the possibility of communications highly restricted once engagement with the enemy had begun, troops were heavily drilled into marching in step according to rigid tactical deployments and performing synchronized firing and reloading cycles at the highest possible tempo.

Mechanistic warfare attempted to maintain order and ward off chaos through a preprogrammed and centralized routine devoid of any capacity for reactivity to the actions of the opposing army. With virtually all initiative removed from individual soldiers, success required that the commanding officers meticulously plan ahead the course of the battle and dictate in advance the series of manoeuvres to be carried out. Although this model was the product of lengthy developments which can be traced back to the Dutch armies of Maurice of Nassau at the turn of the seventeenth century, Frederick the Great's Prussian army embodies best the principles and practices of mechanistic warfare.

Thermodynamic Warfare and the Engine

With thermodynamics and the engine, science gained an understanding of the energy that drove the previously studied mechanisms of motion. As the study of heat derived from the engineering prowess that produced the steam engine, nineteenth-century thermodynamics revolutionized the scientific world-view through the discovery of both the convertibility of all forms of energy (chemical, electrical, kinetic or other) and their inevitable dissipation into randomness through entropy (the inherent tendency towards the dissipation of useful energy). No longer appearing reversible but acquiring direction, time was said to have found its arrow, one leading to the inevitable heat death of the universe in an inevitable progression from order to chaos. With the formulation of entropy in particular came a probabilistic approach to scientific problems, undermining the tidy linearity and precise predictability of mechanistic models.

The thermodynamic world was one of instability and change in which the cultivated stability of the *ancien régime* was swept away by revolutionary and nationalistic fervour. But if time found its arrow, it was not always from order to chaos. Ideologies of progress also proclaimed a direction to history, at the end of which lay a liberal, socialist or national paradise. From the chaos of the age, a final and immutable order would emerge, even if more disorder would first be required in the form of war or revolution, those great 'engines' of history. Narratives of optimistic progress and fearful decline alternated in the cultural imagination of nineteenth-and early twentieth-century Europe. But if there were conflicting accounts of the direction time was taking, what remained undisputed was the new impermanence of the world and the uncertainty it brought with it. As the founder of 'scientific socialism' Karl Marx famously put it, 'all that is solid melts into the air' in the foundry of the new industrial world. The engine, the device that put to work the sources of motive power and was central to industrialization, replaced clockwork as the dominant mechanical model, and became the theoretical and practical nexus for the new scientific world-view.

Thermodynamic warfare saw the channelling into war of ever greater flows of energy, whether of a ballistic, motorized, industrial or moral nature, as nationstates clashed in ever wider conflicts that drew on all the resources at their disposal. Entire societies were mobilized as war became total. Beginning with the feverish *élan* of the French Revolution and Napoleonic wars of conquest, thermodynamic warfare culminated in the ultimate paroxysm of the Second World War and the detonation of the atom bomb. If the logistical requirements of industrial warfare brought whole economies under unprecedented centralized control, the chaos of the battlefield imposed some tactical decentralization, notably through the German army's *Auftragstaktik*, the mission-oriented tactics successfully experimented with by stormtrooper units during the First World War and subsequently developed into *Blitzkrieg*.

Thermodynamic thought also expressed itself in the writings of Clausewitz, who recognized the essentially dynamic and irreducibly unpredictable nature of Antoine Bousquet war, and theorized the inevitable friction and fog inherent in military operations. Chaos was here understood as intrinsic to the practice of warfare, a constant threat to the best laid plans: something that military commanders should be able to recognize and adapt to, rather than engaging in self-defeating attempts to banish it.

Cybernetic Warfare and the Computer

As the intensity and breadth of the battlefield grew along with its logistical requirements, new communication technologies became necessary to achieve the required integration and coordination of increasingly large and intricate military systems. The harnessing of electromagnetic forces for telecommunication purposes proceeded with telegraphy and telephony, simultaneously stimulating growing scientific interest in the concept of information. Cybernetics emerged from the unprecedented technological and industrial effort of the Second World War, in particular the work on the automation of anti-aircraft defences. The selfproclaimed 'science of communications and control' promised to manage chaos and disruption through self-regulating mechanisms of negative information feedback. By being defined in terms of negative entropy (negentropy), information became conceptualized as the source of all order. The computer, also developed during the war for the purposes of code-breaking and the computation of nuclear physics, emerged as the new dominant technology and abstract model through which the world came to be understood chiefly in terms of information processing.

The drive for complete predictability and centralized control over armed conflict was renewed under cybernetic warfare with the deployment of computers and automated control technologies, and the widespread application of the analytical tools of operations research and systems analysis. The Cold War and the constant threat of nuclear annihilation required ever greater levels of automation and centralization of the war machine; and cybernetics, with its promise of stability in the face of perturbation, appeared best suited to the containment and management of a conflict of potentially apocalyptic proportions. Vast command and control architectures were established to organize the global projection of armed force and the rapid mobilization of military systems within the shrinking windows of opportunity afforded by nuclear weaponry. Scientific methodology was applied to warfare more systematically than ever, with operations research and systems analysis applied comprehensively to both tactical and strategic questions. The first two decades of the postwar era saw the rise of the defence intellectuals and their analytical tools in the United States, culminating in the nomination of Robert McNamara as Secretary of Defence.

In its most pristine form, cybernetic warfare fuelled wild yet enduring fantasies of omniscience and omnipotence on the battlefield. In 1969 General William Westmoreland, commander-in-chief of US forces in Vietnam, formulated his vision of the military's future, encapsulating this cybernetic ideal:

On the battlefield of the future, enemy forces will be located, tracked, and targeted almost instantaneously through the use of data links, computer assisted intelligence evaluation, and automated fire control. With first round kill probabilities approaching certainty, and with surveillance devices that can continually track the enemy, the need for large forces to fix the opponent becomes less important.

Towards Chaoplexic Warfare

Since the mid-1970s, the cybernetic mode of warfare has come under increasing challenge from the military reversal for US forces in Vietnam, geopolitical transformation following the end of the Cold War, and novel scientific developments growing out of the original corpus of cybernetics. The increasing application of computers to the study of scientific problems, the exploration of non-linear mathematics, and an extension of the cybernetic analysis of systems to questions of self-organization opened the way for novel scientific approaches which eventually crystallized into the theories of chaos and complexity (here referred to together as *chaoplexity*). Information remains the central concept, and in this sense chaoplexity is an outgrowth of cybernetics; but the focus on change, evolution and positive feedback breaks with the cybernetic pioneers' concern for stability. Chaos is seen no longer as simply a threat to order which must be averted at all costs, but as the very condition of possibility of order. The key notions here are those of non-linearity, self-organization and emergence, and the pivotal technological figure is that of the network, the distributed model of information exchange perhaps best embodied by the internet.

The Science of Chaoplexity

Although still firmly set in the informational paradigm, chaos theory and complexity science departed from cybernetics in shifting the focus away from the stabilizing self-regulation (or homeostasis) underlying the persistence of existing systems towards runaway processes of change leading to the emergence of new systems or patterns of behaviour. Non-linear dynamics and positive feedback processes, whereby small causes can amplify into large effects, are crucial here. Chaos theorists have used computer simulations of non-linear systems to reveal how initially minute variations can ramp up into dramatic changes in the long-term behaviour of the system. The popular image invoked to illustrate this phenomenon is the 'butterfly effect': the notion that a butterfly flapping its wings in (say) Tokyo can cause a tornado in (say) California. While chaos theory has imposed serious limits on the ability to predict the long-term behaviour of systems, it has also provided new insights, uncovering a subtle order and structure to phenomena previously believed to be completely devoid of recognizable patterns, such as the turbulence of fluids or plate tectonics.

Building on the original insights of chaos theory, complexity scientists turned to the interactions of the different component parts of living systems, and particularly to the new properties and behaviours constituted through the networked selforganization of autonomous agents. Self-organization is the process by which the autonomous interaction of individual entities results in the bottom-up emergence of complex systems, systems composed of many parts which are connected in a non-linear fashion. The notion of the network is central to describing the patterns of interaction which are constituted by the interplay of entities in a complex system: 'The first and most obvious property of any network is its non-linearity— it goes in all directions. Thus the relationships in a network pattern are non-linear relationships. In particular, an influence, or message, may travel along a cyclical path, which may become a feedback loop. The concept of feedback is intimately connected with the network pattern.'

Of special interest are the 'complex adaptive systems' which display the ability to change and learn from experience. Complexity theorist John Holland defines a complex adaptive system as a dynamic network of many agents acting simultaneously, constantly both acting and reacting to what the other agents are doing. Since the control of a complex adaptive system tends to be highly dispersed and decentralized, any coherent behaviour in the system arises from competition and cooperation among the agents themselves. It is the accumulation of all the individual decisions taken by the multitude of agents which produces the overall behaviour of the system, which can thus be said to be emergent. Complex adaptive systems include living organisms, insect colonies, bird flocks, ecosystems, businesses, stock markets and other forms of social organization; the constituent agents may be cells, species, individuals, firms or nations. From the perspective of chaoplexity, the most successful systems are those that retain flexibility and openness in the interaction and organization of their parts within environments which elude complete predictability. No longer is order to be sought in a natural tendency towards equilibrium. On the contrary, it is with non-equilibrium that order emerges from chaos, at the point where instability and creative mutation allow for the genesis of new forms and actions. As Ian King puts it, 'networking [is] a way of maintaining a low-level chaotic substrate so that—as in the brain—the chaos will from time to time give birth to an intellectual self-organizing structure'.

Decentralized self-organizing systems are inherently better equipped than centralized systems to deal with limited predictability and contingency. According to the biologist Christopher Langton, 'since it's effectively impossible to cover every conceivable situation, top-down systems are forever running into combinations of events they don't know how to handle. They tend to be touchy and fragile, and they all too often grind to a halt in a dither of indecision.' In contrast, decentralized systems of quasi-autonomous units can operate more effectively and with a greater degree of adaptability on the basis of the local calculations of the networked agents constituting them. For Stuart Kauffman, 'networks in the regime near the edge of chaos—this compromise between order and surprise—appear best able to coordinate complex activities and best able to evolve as well'.

Chaoplexity has challenged some of the most deeply held scientific convictions about the natural world and opened up whole new areas of research. It is now also increasingly weighing on the debates about military organization, heralding a new era in the scientific way of warfare.

The Dawn of Chaoplexic Warfare

Cybernetic warfare experienced its first serious reversal with the Vietnam War, where its analytical techniques and military systems foundered in the conditions of a low-intensity conflict. James Gibson has written persuasively about the failure in the jungles of South-East Asia of 'technowar', an approach to military conflict in which war was viewed as 'a production system that can be rationally managed and warfare as a kind of activity that can be scientifically determined by constructing computer models'. The conduct of the war was blighted by the attempts of the military and political hierarchy to micro-manage the conflict and by an obsession with statistical evaluation and information-gathering which frequently created assessments of the war that were completely at variance with the reality on the ground. Despite the deployment of an unprecedented telecommunications network in the field of operations, command and control technologies failed to perform as expected, with saturation and bottlenecks preventing information on Vietcong positions and movements from arriving in time to be actionable. Perhaps most seriously, a misguided faith in the powers of technoscience to grant military omnipotence led policy-makers to embrace armed force more willingly as the means to solve complex strategic problems. Such hubris was perfectly encapsulated by Henry Kissinger's claim in 1968 that 'a scientific revolution has, for all practical purposes, removed technical limits from the exercise of power in foreign policy'.

The debacle in Vietnam provoked some soul-searching among strategists and military men but did not result in an immediate abandonment of the central principles of cybernetic warfare, which continued to dominate military thinking through the 1980s. All the early contributions to the debate on the revolution in military affairs were premised on the idea that computers, telecommunication links and precision-guided munitions would finally deliver the frictionless, automated battlefield promised by Westmoreland. However, new thinking drawing on the emerging non-linear sciences did begin to penetrate military theory, at first espoused only by isolated individuals but entering the mainstream at the turn of the century.

The late US air force colonel John Boyd is perhaps the most prominent pioneer of chaoplexic warfare, and increasingly is considered to be one of the most important military thinkers of recent times. Boyd is best known for his formulation of the OODA loop (observe–orient–decide–act), describing the decision-making process of the warfighter engaged in combat. Although this is at first sight reminiscent of a typical cybernetic feedback loop, whereby a system adjusts its behaviour to incoming information from its environment in order to meet a desired objective, Boyd was insistent on the need for the analytical frameworks used during the orientation phase to be continually challenged and reinvented through a perpetual process of 'destruction and creation'. No predetermined automated response can prevail for long in a world that is 'uncertain, everchanging, unpredictable'. Boyd went on to contribute to US Marine Corps doctrine, which displays clear signs of the influence of chaoplexity in asserting that 'the best we can hope for is to impose a general framework of order on the disorder, to prescribe the general flow of action rather than to try to control each event', and that 'like a living organism, a military organization is never in a state of stable equilibrium but is instead in a continuous state of flux—continuously adjusting to its surroundings'. If the earlier proclamations of an imminent revolution in military affairs remained firmly tributary to cybernetic conceptions, the ascent of network-centric warfare (NCW) marked the onset of a shift towards chaoplexic notions on the centre ground of debates over military doctrine. With its ideas couched in the language and concepts of the non-linear sciences, NCW first appeared on the scene within the US navy in the late 1990s before rapidly rising to become the new official Pentagon gospel under the agenda of 'Transformation' with the founding of the Office of Force Transformation in 2001 under the stewardship of its original formulator Vice Admiral Arthur Cebrowski. According to Cebrowski, networkcentric warfare views war as a 'complex, adaptive system where non-linear variables continuously interact'. Since 'coordination from the top down inevitably results in delays and errors in force dispositions', the military should seek to acquire 'the ability of a well-informed force to organize and coordinate complex warfare activities from the bottom up'. For Cebrowski, what is being proposed is nothing less than a 'new theory of war'.

Such a new theory can emerge only by breaking with the command and control principles that governed cybernetic warfare during the Cold War, as suggested by Alberts and Hayes:

Control Theory requires both prediction and the existence of an adequate set of levers of control ... [But] having effective, centrally managed levers that can control or even predictably influence a complex, adaptive system is far from guaranteed ... In the Information Age, control needs to be thought about and approached differently. Control is not something that can be imposed on a complex adaptive system, particularly when there are many independent actors. Control, that is, ensuring that behavior stays within or moving to within acceptable bounds, can only be achieved indirectly. The most promising approach involves establishing, to the extent possible, a set of initial conditions that will *result* in the desired behavior. In other words, control is not achieved by imposing a parallel process, but rather emerges from influencing the behaviors of independent agents. NCW theorists claim that through the distribution of information across the battlefield and the constitution of a common operational picture via an overarching 'Global Information Grid', command and control will be decentralized and individual troops will be freed to act on their own initiative, leading to self-synchronization, a clear nod to the chaoplexic notion of self-organization. New tactical schemes denied to their hierarchical counterparts are seen as the emergent properties that will be unlocked by fully networked self-synchronizing forces. Drawing further from the writings of complexity theorists and deploying biological metaphors, military theorists appeal to the 'swarm', the networks of distributed intelligence that enable bees, ants and termites to evolve complex forms of collective behaviour on the basis of the simple rules of interaction of their individual members. Of particular interest are the resilience and flexibility of these swarms as amorphous ensembles whose continued existence and successful operation is not critically dependent on any single individual. Military swarms promise not only more adaptable and survivable forces but also new offensive and defensive tactics better suited to the contemporary battlespace.

According to Alberts and Hayes, decentralization and information-sharing will permit military platforms to 'evolve from being networked entities to being nodes in the network, to organizing efforts resembling "packs" and "swarms"'. The ensembles of different entities making up fighting forces, whether human or robotic, will 'ultimately become dynamically reconfigurable packs, swarms, or other organizations of highly specialized components that work together like the cells of our bodies' and will be 'less mechanical and more organic, less engineered and more "grown"'.

Beyond the flexibility and evolutionary capability that are attributed to military swarms, it is also claimed that they will be able to bring force to bear in a new manner. Rather than throwing themselves onto the enemy in 'waves', forces will be able to converge on their target from all directions in offensive bursts, thereby maximizing the shock effect. For Arquilla and Ronfeldt, the full effects of swarming are achieved when the dispersed nodes of a network of small (and also perhaps some large) forces can converge on an enemy from multiple directions, through either fire or maneuver. The overall aim should be *sustainable pulsing*—swarm networks must be able to coalesce rapidly and stealthily on a target, then dissever and redisperse, immediately ready to recombine for a new pulse. A swarm network should have little to no mass as a rule (except perhaps during a pulse), but it should have a high energy potential—like a swarm of bees that can fell a mighty beast, or a network of antibodies that can attack a spreading virus.

Troops that can disperse swiftly after an attack or 'pulse' also have the advantage of being less vulnerable to enemy attacks, particularly in the context of the high lethality and precision characteristic of contemporary and future battlefields. The promises of network-centric warfare are bold and, for all its deployment of chaoplexic language, the doctrine suffers from a number of potentially critical weaknesses. In several respects it has not significantly broken with cybernetic warfare and therefore may not in fact implement all the features of a truly chaoplexic way of warfare.

While 'decentralization' is the order-word of the day, the networking of troops may in fact provide the technological infrastructure for greater micro-management than ever by a military brass which will have access to data feeds from anywhere in the battlespace. Second, dependence on a unified 'Global Information Grid' could both create a critical vulnerability likely to be targeted by competent adversaries and deprive troops of the skills required to respond creatively to situations in which only limited local information is available (as most of the complex adaptive systems studied are found to do). Furthermore, NCW advocates fall back all too often on impoverished conceptions of Boyd's OODA loop which substitute speed of execution of predetermined responses for creative thinking and adaptability to the unforeseen. Finally, there persists a tendency to see information technology as the panacea which will permanently lift the friction and fog of war which has plagued all past militaries, when in fact chaoplexity points to the irreducible contingency and unpredictability of war and the need to organize so as to tolerate and even take advantage of this uncertainty.

Ultimately chaoplexic warfare will depend more on doctrinal and organizational commitments than on any particular information technologies, which are liable to be employed to quite contrary purposes. The full arrival of chaoplexic warfare may therefore still lie ahead; but the debates around network-centric warfare clearly show an impetus towards greater decentralization and the use of the network form of organization within armed forces. NCW now has its counterparts in most major western militaries, including Network Enabled Capabilities (NEC) in the United Kingdom, NATO Network Enabled Capabilities (NNEC), and Network Enabled Operations (NEOps) in Canada. Where such militaries have encountered recent setbacks, for example in Iraq, Afghanistan or Lebanon, it has been against opponents that have employed decentralized networks to good effect against better-equipped forces, thereby further stimulating discussion about their merits and underlining the limitations of established modes of operation. Just as the ideas of mechanism, thermodynamics and cybernetics inspired past military thought and practice in association with their respective paradigmatic technologies, a new set of scientific theories are now occupying a central role within the doctrinal and organizational changes of the armies of the early twenty-first century. Our network age is therefore also that of chaoplexity.

6

Modern Nuclear Warfare and Time Value of Military Force

Introduction

This chapter is about time; more specifically it is about the tensions generated by conflicting considerations of time. As the opening statement from a 1936 Command and General Staff School manual illustrates, time-induced tensions between political and military imperatives have long characterized warfare. Even as political and military leaders have recognized the problem of these tensions, they have searched for ways to mitigate and overcome their effects. From the first moment man began to grasp the military implications of airpower, it has had a special appeal as a potential solution, but it was only the potential about which theorists could speculate. In addition to conquering the third dimension of elevation, airpower's special characteristics seemed to hold promise as well for conquering the fourth dimension of time. Now that airpower has advanced and matured to realize some of this potential, as demonstrated in recent wars, one can better appraise the extent to which airpower has succeeded in this regard.

Overview

In examining some of these recent wars from the perspective of time, this study concentrates on that central tension which often appears in war and goes one step further by seeking to answer the question: "How can airpower help resolve time-induced tensions between political and military imperatives in the conduct of modern warfare?" The question is important, if for no other reason than the implications it has for the congruence of political and military objectives. If one accepts Carl von Clausewitz's characterization of war as the "continuation of political intercourse, with the addition of other means," then that congruence is vital to the success of any military operation. In seeking to answer this important question, this study defines the terms and limits of the argument.

Methodology

Although theory will serve as a guide to organize a coherent framework and derive a paradigm, the primary evidence for illustrating and analysing the problem will come from three historical studies: the Arab-Israeli War of 1967, the Falklands War, and the Gulf War. Not only did airpower figure prominently in each of these cases, but airpower had also developed enough by the time of these cases to realize a great deal of its potential capability. In other words, there is less tendency in these cases to excuse a lack of airpower effectiveness with the explanation that airpower was still in its infancy. Additionally, these cases meet the following criteria:

1. There was a demonstrable tension between political and military imperatives.
2. There is evidence to support the interpretation that a significant component of this tension related to time.
3. The time-induced tension had operational consequences.
4. Airpower had a real or potential role in resolving the tensions.

Definitions

Before proceeding with the argument, it is appropriate to define the major terms which compose the question, that is, what one means specifically by the terms *time, war, airpower, political imperative*, and *military imperative*.

Time is the "nonspatial continuum in which events occur in apparently irreversible succession from the past through the present to the future." Time, in this sense, is an objective phenomenon that has both physical and psychological aspects. Other assumptions about time are that it can be observed, measured, manipulated, and exploited.

For the purposes of this study, war is defined as organized social conflict between defined actors that involves direct violent action. This overlapping of conflict and war is consistent with the idea that conflict is a precondition for war, that there can be conflict without war but no war without conflict. The primacy of violence in the conflict as a condition for war is consistent with Clausewitz's idea that "War is thus an act of force to compel our enemy to do our will."

One can define airpower as the ability to exploit the third dimension to affect a situation or adversary. Since the idea of exploiting the third dimension would include space, it follows that space power is part of airpower. *Aerospace power* might be a more technically correct term since airpower in this definition implies the ability to do something through space (space power), as well as the ability to do something through the air (airpower). Although the term *airpower* may sound awkward in a literal sense when used to encompass the two, it is less cumbersome and embodies the history and tradition of thought on the subject better than the term *aerospace power*.

Political imperatives are distinguished from military imperatives by defining them as those imperatives that stem from governmental interaction with citizens, organizations, and other governments which interaction does not include the application of force in the pursuit of objectives. Military imperatives, on the other hand, relate directly to the application of force, the management of violence, and the accomplishment of specific tasks in the execution of the military strategy sanctioned by political authority.

Limits of the Argument

This study is limited in that it concentrates on situations more appropriately characterized as war, even if limited, which featured military force as the prominent instrument of national power in pursuing objectives. It also focuses on three cases where time was a constraining factor, a situation which is not always the case. Therefore, the results of this study are limited in application to cases where such pressures are present.

Time in the Theory of War

Viewing time as a nonspatial continuum in which events occur in a sequential, irreversible order as determined by time is the first step in conceiving of time as the fourth dimension. One can describe and define something fairly accurately through the spatial dimensions of length, width, and height, but to place it in its complete context, one must also describe its place in time. Since such a description usually involves a measurement, it is also consistent with the assumption that time can be observed and measured. Because time constitutes a fourth dimension, it is also a perspective from which one can view events. Just as one could view a series of buildings from the perspective of relative elevation—the third dimension—one can also view the same buildings from the perspective of relative time, that is, when they were built. As is always the case when one selects a particular perspective as the primary reference from which to examine a phenomenon, viewing things from that perspective brings certain aspects into focus which might not otherwise be visible and obscures others. Looking at things in this manner is also part of the process of deciphering their meaning. To continue with the previous example, knowing when one building was constructed would go a long way toward explaining why it looks the way it does as well as why its appearance differs or does not differ from the other buildings. Focusing on a certain dimension as a point of perspective, therefore, has significant value in understanding a phenomenon and relating it to other phenomena.

The idea that the reality of everything is rooted in the time continuum and that time thus links past, present, and future has led some to conclude the temporal perspective is not only a valuable perspective but the dominant and most important perspective. The purpose in mentioning these writers and their views here is not to support an argument that time is the most important dimension, rather it is the more limited aim of simply dramatizing how important many feel it is to view war from the time perspective. In *War and Anti-War*, Alvin and Heidi Toffler described how a US Army officer borrowed from their philosophy of time to write new military doctrine because he believed the military had to recognize time as the primary dimension. In their view, the US won the Gulf War because it used a "fast-cycle, time-based competitive strategy." Robert R. Leonhard, another US Army officer, has written an entire book on the importance of time in war. Its thesis is simple: "the most effective way to perceive, interpret, and plan military operations is in terms of time, rather than space." He too insists that time is the dominant dimension in war. Although they have not been as obvious in their declared intention as the aforementioned authors, war theorists of all eras have done just that. A review of their thoughts on the subject will contribute to understanding what time in war means.

War Theorists on Time

Carl von Clausewitz thought the time factor important enough to devote a chapter of *On War* to the "Unification of Forces in Time." In this chapter, Clausewitz argues against the piecemeal commitment of forces overtime and advances an early idea of parallel warfare by arguing that "the simultaneous use of all means intended for a given action appears as an elementary law of war." In viewing the use of force from the time perspective and proposing time as the unifying element, Clausewitz seems also to appreciate the fact that such simultaneous use will have an effect beyond the mere cumulative addition of individual strengths.

Time emerges again in Clausewitz when he considers the effect of its passage on events in war, a concept he calls "duration." Clausewitz recognizes that time is important in tactical engagements because forces weaken overtime in battle. At a higher level, he sees this weakening effect of time as something which "is less likely to bring favour to the victor than to the vanquished." This view leads him to characterize a defensive war as a "waiting war," in which one counts on time to improve one's prospects. Clausewitz recognizes, however, that the passage of time does not necessarily ensure that the strong will grow weaker and the weak will grow stronger. On the contrary, he allows for situations where the passage of time may also assist the conqueror, especially those where there is little chance of the defender receiving outside help.

Having outlined the problems caused by the passage of time, particularly to the conqueror, Clausewitz offers advice about overcoming them. In proposing "The Plan of a War Designed to Lead to the Total Defeat of the Enemy," Clausewitz emphasizes the necessity of speed to the point of enunciating it as a principle.

"The second principle is the rapid use of our forces," writes the theorist, "Any unnecessary expenditure of time, every unnecessary detour, is a waste of strength and thus abhorrent to strategic thought." Also important in his estimation was surprise, which he viewed in temporal terms as a question of timing whose advantage was increased by the speed of such an attack.

Other theorists echo many of these same themes in their works. Antoine Henri Jomini also emphasizes speed and its force-multiplying effect when he writes, "The system of rapid and continuous marches multiplies the effect of an army, and at the same time neutralizes a great part of that of the enemy's, and is often sufficient to insure success...." Speed in destruction is the foundation of the basic principle laid out by Giulio Douhet: "*Inflict the greatest damage in the shortest possible time.*" Douhet was one of the first to realize the potential for airpower to accomplish this task and achieve the desired surprise in doing so. For B. H. Liddell Hart, the more timing increased the measure of surprise, the more it reduced the amount of force required to achieve an objective; in other words, speed in action had a force component all its own.

Another temporal characteristic that Liddell Hart emphasized was tempo. In studying the French defeat by the Germans in 1940, Liddell Hart theorized that their loss turned on the time factor because they were unable to keep up with the tempo of German operations and became paralyzed as a result. A more recent theorist who seizes on this idea and makes it the heart of his work is John Boyd. Boyd emphasized rapid tempo as the key to maintaining initiative. In Boyd's world, the speed at which one could perform the cycle of observing, orienting, deciding, and acting (OODA loop) determined tempo. By performing this cycle of events faster than one's opponent, one could cause psychological dislocation similar to that described by Liddell Hart, achieve surprise, and maintain initiative.

Running somewhat counter to this emphasis on speed is Mao Tse-tung's thought on the idea of protracted war. In this concept of a war named for its temporal orientation, Mao expands on Clausewitz's idea of a waiting war but makes the concept his own by providing the details to turn it into a viable strategy. Writing with a view to the specific case of China, Mao assumes that the balance of forces will change with the passage of time, thus making protraction of war at the strategic level the way to victory. Waiting, however, is not sufficient in itself to ensure victory, and Mao proposes maintaining the initiative at the operational level through rapid mobile warfare across a broad front until the balance of forces favour a strategic counteroffensive. Through this creative strategy, Mao manages to use the passage of time as a weapon (protraction), while still gleaning the advantages of rapid tempo at a lower, sustainable level. One suspects that both Clausewitz and Boyd would approve.

Characteristics of Time in War

Emerging from this review of how time has figured in various theorists' view of war is a picture of how various characteristics of time figure in enduring concepts of warfare. As one studies the picture, one first distinguishes the characteristics of time in general before beginning to see how these characteristics underpin much of what passes for "principles" and "laws" of war.

The five characteristics of time which appear in this review are duration, tempo, timing, sequence, and synchronization. Duration involves the passage of time, and theorists have concentrated on the effects of this passage. Both Clausewitz's idea of a waiting war and Mao's concept of protracted war center on this characteristic. Tempo describes the frequency or pace of events in the time continuum. One can relate the concepts of speed and initiative to tempo as well as the principle of the offensive since it embraces the necessity of initiative. As discussed previously, tempo and initiative were inextricably linked in John Boyd's world. Timing has to do with opportunity and the choice of a particular moment in time for action or inaction. Timing is at the heart of the principle of surprise which bids one to "strike the enemy at a time or place or in a manner for which he is unprepared," and it figures prominently in the writings of all theorists. Sequence involves the order of events in time. The ability to understand this order and perhaps predict how it will unfold in the future is key to the concepts of genius and coup d'oeil which Clausewitz emphasizes. Sequence and order also figure highly in Boyd's orientation phase of the OODA loop. Finally there is the characteristic of synchronization which implies the ability to orchestrate events so that they occur at appropriate points in time. To remain true to the principle of mass, which call for the concentration of forces at the proper time and place, one must synchronize forces. In fighting a parallel war, synchronization of forces is also paramount to achieving the desired effects.

Physical and Psychological Aspects of Time

This review of time's prominence in the works of war theorists and the characteristics which emerge from their ideas leads one to the question of time's physical and psychological aspects. To the extent that this study has considered time as an objective phenomenon, one can assume certain physical aspects exist. Such a concept is consistent with the previously advanced ideas that time can be measured and that the reality of events is rooted in the time continuum. For example, both ideas find expression in the historical record that the Japanese attacked Pearl Harbor on 7 December 1941. Indeed, even the temporal characteristics of duration, tempo, timing, sequence, and synchronization are expressions of time's physical aspect. Time's physical aspect is only part of its character, however, for it has a psychological aspect as well, which stems from human perception. The perception of time primarily determines its psychological aspect. Depending on the conditions, one might view time's passage or duration as either fast or slow. In unfavorable conditions, for example, time might seem to drag. One can view surprise as the psychological aspect of unexpected timing. Synchronization can allow one to achieve shock effect through parallel attack, and psychological dislocation can result from rapid tempo. None of this is revelatory, but it does emphasize that time has both physical and psychological aspects.

One can exploit or manipulate time to achieve one's ends by capitalizing on these physical and psychological aspects. In this construction, exploiting time would involve taking advantage of time's enduring physical aspects, such as a fixed duration of an event, for a particular gain. For example, if one knows that it will take three weeks for an enemy force to reach one's position, one can exploit the time by making defensive preparations. Manipulating time, on the other hand, might imply taking an action with the aim of changing the way one perceives time. Some possibilities for manipulation lie in the ability to compress or expand time frames (e.g., by accelerating or slowing the pace of activities), shorten or lengthen intervals, accelerate or decelerate tempo, and control timing. As for changing time to make it pass slowly or quickly or even to stop, affecting the perception of time, a psychological aspect, would seem the only way.

Political and Military Dynamics of Time

The meaning and implications of time in war usually spawn different considerations for political and military decision makers. Although there is wide agreement with Clausewitz's statement that "war is simply a continuation of political intercourse, with the addition of other means," there remain differences between the political and military imperatives that affect time considerations. In fact, Clausewitz seemed to recognize those differences and sought mainly to warn the student of war that one should not make the mistake of dividing the political and military realms into two worlds with no connection. It is, of course, well known that the only source of war is politics—the intercourse of governments and peoples; but it is apt to be assumed that war suspends that intercourse and replaces it by a wholly different condition, ruled by no law but its own. We maintain, on the contrary, that war is simply a continuation of political inter-course, with... other means.

Although war is not a disconnected, autonomous world, the addition of other means introduces different imperatives. In the domain of war, a military leader finds himself not only trying to satisfy the wishes of the political authorities, he also must address specific military problems which have time considerations all their own. For example, moving a military force from one location to another might require a certain number of days or weeks. Optimizing the timing of an attack to ensure success may dictate that it take place at a certain moment.

Political imperatives, on the other hand, derive from the relations between a government and its people, as well as between a government and other governments. The circumstances of these relations often differ markedly from the circumstances of the military situation and so produce different time considerations. A government may hasten or postpone an action simply because domestic public opinion demands that it do so. International political pressure or considerations may have a similar effect. Seen in this light, the political sphere appears much more fluid and unstable, characteristics which account for some of the time disconnects with the more static and stable features of the military sphere.

A significant problem occurs when political imperatives and military imperatives come into conflict because of differing time considerations. Political imperatives may require a quick military response in a situation where distances, force readiness, logistical factors, and other military considerations might counsel postponing an attack. In another situation, the prudent military action might be an immediate attack, while a lack of domestic or international support forces political leaders to postpone any military move. Gen Charles G. Boyd described a similar predicament in the North Atlantic Treaty Organization (NATO):

Thus at the very point when military intervention carries both the greatest potential pay off and the lowest risk, diverse national cultures and political structures can delay agreement on a course of action. Thus the differences between the meaning of time to the military and political decision makers center around the different demands of their specific situations and the tension between the physical and psychological aspects of time in those situations. The result of these differences is often, though not always, time-induced tensions between political and military imperatives.

Resolving these tensions in some way is essential to success. Unless these tensions are resolved, there can be no congruence of political and military operations, a situation which will likely result in failure to achieve the desired objective. Political considerations will remain primary, for "if war is part of policy, policy will determine its character"; however, the primacy of politics does not relieve the political leader of responsibility for seeking a way to resolve these time-induced tensions. It is incumbent upon both political and military decision makers to find a way to achieve congruence in this regard, and airpower may be an appropriate means to solve this problem.

The Arab-Israeli War of 1967

The dramatic Israeli air strike that began the Six-Day War of 1967 seized the public imagination and remains to this day an enduring image that leaps to mind when one brings up the war. The persistence of that image is in many ways proper, for it was through these initial air strikes that the Israelis achieved air superiority and paved the way for the quick victory which followed in a matter of days. Given the strength of that picture and the seemingly simple beauty of what happened, it is tempting to admire the Israeli achievement briefly, make a few appropriate comments about the importance of air superiority, and move on to more intractable and vexing problems. It would be easy to take such an approach—it would also be a mistake. Although the Israeli Air Force achieved air superiority, they accomplished more than they dreamed or were even aware of at the time. As they won air superiority, they also succeeded in temporarily paralysing their most dangerous enemy through physical and psychological dislocation as well as satisfactorily resolving the tension between time-induced political and military imperatives. Yet even as they demonstrated this tremendous potential of airpower, they failed to exploit fully the opportunities created by air superiority and thus leave modern airmen a lesson about taking full advantage of such a situation. Given such nuances and complexities, the event deserves more than cursory attention.

The Course of the War

The proximate events leading up to the Six-Day War began in April 1967, when Israelis responded to Syrian artillery attacks with an air strike. This strike led to an air battle in which the Israelis shot down six Syrian aircraft. Tensions in the region were already taut and escalated quickly in the weeks following the incident, primarily through the actions of the Egyptian President Gamal Abdel Nasser. In quick succession,

Nasser moved 100,000 troops into the Sinai along Israel's border, demanded and obtained the withdrawal of United Nations (UN) peacekeeping forces, and closed the Straits of Tiran to Israeli shipping. Other Arab nations rallied to Nasser's call; and Israel soon found itself surrounded by a hostile Arab force which included 328,000 troops, 2,330 tanks, and 682 fighters and bombers. The Israelis had 250,000 troops, 1,000 tanks, and 286 combat aircraft available to counter this threat. Given the Arab actions and particularly the closure of the straits, a belligerent act in itself, war seemed inevitable in spite of international efforts to pacify the situation. In the face of this threat, Israel decided to seize the initiative and launch a massive preemptive attack against Arab airpower on 5 June 1967. Penetrating Arab radar defenses at low altitude, the Israeli Air Force succeeded in destroying the air forces of Egypt, Jordan, and Syria in short order, catching many of the targeted aircraft on the ground. Having achieved air superiority, the Israeli Air Force turned to supporting the ground forces which had begun advancing minutes after the Israeli aircraft struck their first targets. Using rapid maneuver by armor, Israeli ground forces destroyed Egyptian armored forces as they captured the Sinai in a series of battles. Within three days another Israeli force secured the West Bank of the Jordan River and took the ancient city of Jerusalem. A final Israeli thrust encountered stiffer resistance from Syrian forces in the North but, with the help of Israeli airpower, succeeded in breaking through on 10 June and capturing the Golan Heights before a United Nations cease-fire took effect.

Political Imperatives

In the weeks of May leading up to the war, many political factors, including doubt about their own military capabilities, drove the Israelis to put off a decision for war. There was also hope that international efforts by the UN, the United States, Great Britain, and France might defuse the situation and convince Egypt to lift the blockade. Concern about the political cost of striking first worried Israelis as well. The US had consistently cautioned Israel against attacking and had warned Israel it would remain alone if it chose to attack first. In spite of these pressures not to go to war, Israel had to concern itself with survival, and that issue overrode all other considerations. Rather than face slow strangulation followed by a coup de grâce from encircling Arab forces, Israel might survive and perhaps even progress by seizing the initiative, striking first, and taking out the Arab threat in a quick war. Conquering strategic areas to improve its future security would be an important goal of such a limited war.

Military Imperatives

Although war might be the only way out of its predicament,

the Israeli military faced a monumental task if the nation chose that course. Internal lines of communication and unity of command seemed their only advantages as the Israelis surveyed a threat that surrounded them and outnumbered them in every category of men and equipment. In this situation, the primary military imperative was to defend Israel and not give up precious ground. It would also be important to keep the Arab forces from achieving unity of effort. One way to accomplish this task would be to seize and maintain the initiative while applying mass judiciously and quickly against divided Arab forces. In such a move, destroying Arab combat capability would be paramount so that the Israelis could shift forces to heighten the effect of mass without worrying about security. As a final concern, the Israeli military had to worry about controlling key terrain such as the Sinai, the West Bank of the Jordan River, and the Golan Heights.

The Time Problem

It is worthwhile at this point to examine the time-induced tensions between political and military imperatives that characterized this situation. In the time leading up to the commencement of hostilities, political imperatives generated by international considerations put off going to war while military imperatives of time argued that Israel act sooner rather than later in order not to lose the initiative or allow the forces aligned against it to gain any more advantage in preparation or numbers. Once the war began, however, the situation reversed itself. The political situation of Israel demanded that the war be short, decisive, relatively cheap in terms of lives and materiel, and lead to peace (perhaps by trading land). Because there was a good chance the superpowers might intervene early to stop the war, the Israelis needed to accomplish their political objectives quickly. Moshe Dayan, the Israeli Minister of Defence, was particularly concerned about such intervention and told his generals the duration of any campaign would be limited as a result. Although the military commanders might welcome a quick and painless war, their imperatives were more concerned with doing the job of destroying Arab combat capability, particularly the Egyptian Army, and taking strategic objectives, such as the Golan Heights, however long that might take. No matter how good their performance, falling short of these objectives would be viewed as a failure. A short war scenario taxed their ability to solve the military problem of achieving these objectives given that Arab forces encircled Israel. If Israel divided its forces to meet each threat separately, it meant less mass on each front which might lead to less momentum, a slower advance, and longer time for operations. Taking a sequential approach to defeating the individual Arab forces would allow greater concentration of force but also threatened to prolong operations in the time it would take to swing the main effort from one area to another. In either situation, Israel's commanders had a difficult military problem which seemed to require more time than the political circumstances might allow.

Operational Consequences and Risk

The operational consequences of this situation were that the Israel Defence Forces (IDF) had to find a way to go on the offensive with numerically inferior ground and air forces, destroy Arab combat capability, and seize strategic territory all in a brief time frame. Faced with this difficult situation and its time conflicts, the Israeli military forces would turn to a plan which emphasized a smashing blow for air superiority as a way to deal with these consequences, but it was a plan which entailed risk.

The men who would employ Israeli airpower perceived the role of air superiority in a way that was little different doctrinally from the way US forces express it today. Joint Publication 1-02 defines air superiority as "that degree of dominance in the airbattle of one force over another which permits the conduct of operations by the former and its related land, sea, and air forces at a given time and place without prohibitive interference by the opposing force." In their particular situation, the Israelis gave top priority to air superiority primarily to achieve freedom of action for their air forces and freedom of action for their ground forces, which might assist them in countering the numerical superiority of the opposing ground forces. The small size of the Israeli Air Force and the fact it would depend upon many of its aircraft to swing between the air superiority and ground support missions made the initial battle for air superiority all the more critical to achieving these objectives. Israel's plan, Operation Moked, was based in its broad outline on the Luftwaffe's initial strike during Operation

Barbarossa. It also owed a debt to Douhet's general principle that "it is easier and more effective to destroy the enemy's aerial power by destroying his nests and eggs on the ground than to hunt his flying birds in the air." The basic idea was to catch enemy aircraft on the ground, hold them there by bombing the runways, then destroy them with rockets, missiles, and cannons on subsequent passes. The plan proved particularly prescient in the way it incorporated considerations for force composition, training, intelligence, timing, and targeting. Operation Moked was first of all a *living* plan which began in 1963 but was continually updated as intelligence and lessons from training required. Gen Ezer Weizmann was the architect of its first pillar, an air force composed of fighter bombers that could both defeat an enemy air force and support Israeli ground forces. Weizmann was also relentless in his emphasis on training; "We always went on the assumption that we would be fighting the finest air force in the world, then set out to show that this was not the case." The plan called for this well-trained but small force to accomplish the formidable task of destroying the enemy air force in a short span of time. Given the scale of that effort, each plane would have to fly four to five sorties each day with only a few minutes turn between each sortie. Because the ideal of simultaneous attack was impossible, Operation Moked gave priority to destroying MiG-21s, the primary air-to-air threat, and Tu-16s, the strategic bombing threat to Israel's cities, as well as their bases; these were the first targets to be hit.

A final feature of Moked was its daring acceptance of operational risk: during the initial strike only 12 aircraft would defend Israel, eight in the air and four on strip alert. So shaky was the government's faith in Moked that Maj Gen Moti Hod, the new Israeli Air Force commander never directly told his political superiors that the air defenses would be so lean for fear that Israel's leaders might not accept such a risk. Instead, he only promised that the capital would not be subjected to "massive bombings."

Airpower's Role

Had the Israeli government known how successful Operation Moked would be, it might not have been so hesitant in approving the preemptive strike. As it turned out, the results of Moked's execution exceeded the hopes and dreams of even its true believers in the Israeli Air Force, for it achieved not only air superiority but temporarily paralyzed Egyptian commanders with its shock effect as it successfully resolved the time-induced tensions between political and military imperatives. Nevertheless, a review of the follow-up support of ground forces reveals missed opportunities for fully exploiting air superiority and the potential of the Israeli Air Force.

Although they were unaware of it at the time, the Israeli plan for using airpower to achieve air superiority would help resolve time-induced tensions by using a weapon which could be drawn at the chosen time and wielded with quick, devastating results. The Israeli Air Force executed Moked almost flawlessly, achieving complete surprise as it did so. Taking off at 7:00 a.m. (Israeli time) so as to attack at 7:45 a.m. (8:45 a.m., Egyptian time), the first 40 aircraft struck the 10 most critical Egyptian airfields almost simultaneously. They caught the Egyptians at the most vulnerable time when their morning patrols had just landed and commanders were en route to work. Only 10 minutes separated waves of aircraft, and each flight of four had seven minutes to work its target, which was time enough for a bomb run and a few more passes for strafing, missiles, and rockets. With ground crews working feverishly to turn around aircraft in less than eight minutes, some Israeli aircraft were off on another sortie less than an hour they had taken off. Through the initial concentration on Egypt and the fast turnaround of aircraft, Israel was able to mass its air force in time and space to achieve its maximum potential.

The targeting aspects of the plan proved as sound as the timing. Fortunately for the Israelis, the Egyptian facilitated the task of attacking specific aircraft by concentrating types at particular bases. Such an arrangement made it easier for the Israelis to attack the MiG-21s and Tu-16s as a first priority. An additional advantage of the timing chosen by the Israelis was the opportunity it presented to target the Egyptian pilots as well as destroy their aircraft. The Egyptians lost 100 of their 350 qualified pilots in the first attacks, many of them killed by Israeli strafing. The Israeli Air Force repeated its pattern of employment as it turned toward the other Arab air forces: By the end of the war's first day, Jordan's air force was totally destroyed, Egypt's had suffered heavy losses, and

Syria's was severely stunned. Altogether, 25 Arab air bases had been attacked, and Israeli pilots claimed more than 300 aircraft destroyed. Virtually flawless execution of a brilliant plan gave Israel air superiority by the end of the first day. Although the Israeli Air Force continued some attacks against airfields the second day, they had already begun to turn their main effort toward supporting ground forces.

Although they were probably unaware of it, the Israelis had achieved more than air superiority with Operation Moked. The speed and intensity of the initial attacks delivered such a shock to the Egyptian General Headquarters and especially the commander, Fieldmarshal H. 'Amer, that the Egyptian forces were unable to react with any coherent response. Things fell apart; the center did not hold. The original plan to advance was forgotten, and Amer issued confusing orders. When he finally did react, he ordered an unplanned withdrawal which he was later convinced to stop but not before the damage was done. Egyptian forces were in disarray and thus easy prey for the Israeli ground and air forces. In inflicting such a shocking blow, the air superiority campaign had gone beyond its objectives and achieved important psychological as well as physical effects.

The success of the air superiority campaign and its dramatic effects contributed substantially to meeting the political imperative of finishing the war quickly, decisively, and with little loss of life or treasure. Although historians of the war typically separate the air and ground campaigns and linger long over the details of the latter, the speed with which military objectives were achieved was due in large part to air superiority and air support. Unfortunately, the Israeli plan did not take full advantage of airpower to support maneuver warfare; otherwise, the advance might have been even faster. Once it had switched roles to support ground forces, the Israeli Air Force lost much of its initiative to target and attack because the system worked on the basis of demands from ground units. Some commanders did not make full use of the availability and potential of air support in their scheme, so sortie rates actually dropped in response to slowing demand.

IDF ground units conducted three separate operations, one against the Egyptian army in the Sinai, another against the Jordanian army on the West Bank, and a third against the Syrian army in the Golan Heights. Flying both interdiction and close air support (CAS) sorties in support of the ground war, the Israeli Air Force had turned the bulk of its might against the Arab armies by the second day. Israeli aircraft achieved great success in attacking vehicles and blocking key points such as the Mitla Pass, which was choked with over 150 abandoned or destroyed vehicles. Had the Israelis employed a push, instead of demand, CAS system with provision for alternate interdiction targets if CAS were not needed, they could have made more effective use of their available airpower and perhaps shortened battles even more. Such a failure take advantage of airpower's ability to achieve synergetic effects in combination with ground forces represented a lost opportunity on the part of the IDF. Nevertheless, this shortcoming did not impede the Israelis significantly enough to keep them from attaining their military objectives in the time allowed by political constraints, although the Israelis had to race to secure the Golan Heights in time to accept the UN imposed cease-fire, effective at 6:30 P.M. on 10 June.

The Falklands War

In the Falklands War, Great Britain unexpectedly found itself stretching its NATO-oriented air and sea power to the limit in an effort to recover a group of islands which, although much closer to Argentina, nevertheless lay at the limits of Argentine air and sea power. Distance translated into time, and time remained a problem for both sides throughout the war. For the British, the problem consisted of deploying a task force thousands of miles to accomplish a limited, but daunting objective in the brief time that international and domestic political support afforded.

It was a mission fraught with risk, and tolerance for risk by the British military commanders would play an important role in events. The Argentines, on the other hand, had to outlast the British politically and militarily in order to preserve their gains. Although airpower would figure prominently in the attempts of both sides to satisfy their imperatives, numbers, training, technical sophistication, operational risk, and the extreme demands of the situation would work to limit airpower's contribution in significant ways.

The Course of the War

Surprised by the Argentine invasion of the Falkland Islands on 2 April 1982, the British government hurriedly assembled a task force which included two aircraft carriers, destroyers, frigates, and other support ships. Air assets included 20 Sea Harriers and a variety of helicopters. The British based tanker and transport aircraft at Ascension Island which was more than 4,000 miles from Port Stanley in the Falklands. The Argentine Air Force which faced this threat was a modern one that counted 180 fighter-bombers, including Mirage IIIs and A-4 Skyhawks, as well as nine squadrons of transports, auxiliary aviation, and trainers among its 450 aircraft. Naval aviation assets supplemented this force with 130 aircraft of their own, the most formidable being six Super Etendards, which were capable of firing

Exocet antiship missiles. As far as the ground order of battle was concerned, the British initially dispatched a commando brigade, which was joined by an infantry brigade in early June. They would go up against a reinforced Argentine force in the Falklands, which, although scattered, numbered near 10,000.

While the British task force steamed toward the islands, the US tried to no avail to negotiate a peace between the two countries. Combat began in earnest with the British recapture of South Georgia on 25 April. The first air attack on the Falklands proper came shortly after on 1 May when a British Vulcan bomber attacked the runway at Port Stanley.

The fighting escalated throughout the month of May in spite of international peace efforts, as the Argentines tried to thwart the British invasion and succeeded in sinking five British ships at the high cost of 23 Argentine aircraft. In spite of their ship losses, the British established a foothold after their 21 May landing on San Carlos, a presence which they began to expand by 27 May in response to political pressure.

Despite a scare in the close battle at Goose Green, the British made steady progress. With the exception of a devastating attack against landing craft on 8 June, Argentine air pressure on British operations subsided after the May onslaught, and the British secured the surrender of all Argentine forces on the islands by 14 June.

Political Imperatives

For the casual observer, the Falklands War was an unlikely contest that sent him scurrying for an atlas and history book to figure out where and why these events were unfolding. Great Britain had claimed the Falkland Islands since 1833 and absorbed them into its empire. The dissolution of the British Empire after World War II did not affect the status of these islands in ways it affected other colonies. Instead, the Falklands and Gibraltar persisted as British possessions inhabited by persons of British descent, but claimed by neighboring countries. Negotiations with Argentina about the status of the islands had dragged on since 1965 and had become part of the routine business handled by the British Foreign Office.

When business as usual suddenly turned to war, the British found themselves in an ambiguous situation. True, they were fighting about the violation of British sovereignty and the rights of British subjects of British descent, but there were less than 2,000 of these subjects on islands of questionable strategic value, which were a legacy of British colonialism and which lay 8,000 miles away. On one extreme, there were those who asked whether recapturing these islands was worth the loss of even one British life, while there were many closer to the middle who pushed for a political solution before and during the war. On 29 April 1982, a member of Parliament asked during debate, "Will the Prime Minister tell the House how many British and Argentine soldiers, and how many Falklanders, she is prepared to see killed... to establish the sovereignty that she will later concede in negotiations." Leaders of the Labor opposition were more moderate in tone but still anxious, as Michael Foot demonstrated in his questions on 26 April 1982:

When will we return to the Security Council on these matters? In the meantime, how are we to ensure—indeed, to be absolutely sure—that there will be no dangerous escalation of the crisis in any way? What is the form of political control over military operations? In present circumstances that political control must be absolute and there must be no possibility of any mistakes whatever. Foot's questions point to the fact that Prime Minister Margaret Thatcher could only count on the Labor party's support in this crisis if the war remained strictly limited and tightly controlled.

International political support for the British cause was also shaky. Although the UN Security Council had passed a resolution demanding an Argentine withdrawal and the European Economic Community (EEC) had initially voted economic sanctions against Argentina, this support eroded over time. During May some members of the EEC dropped their sanctions. By June, Britain would have to veto a UN Security Council motion which called for a cease-fire. This weak international base of support would combine with domestic political pressures to limit Britain's objectives and the time in which she could accomplish them. Rather fighting a general war with Argentina, Britain would limit her operations and objectives to retaking the Falklands themselves. Military operations in support of these objectives would have to be rapid, otherwise support could evaporate.

The Falkland Islands were a much more emotional issue for the Argentines, who still viewed the Malvinas as their stolen heritage. The military junta under Gen Leopoldo Galtieri, who was sworn in as president of Argentina in 1981, had decided to make 1982 "the year of the Malvinas." The junta's intent was to reestablish Argentine sovereignty of the islands before the 150th anniversary of British rule, and they began to consider military options in case diplomatic efforts failed. An international incident involving Argentine workers on South Georgia Island accelerated events and forced the junta to act quickly in order to preserve the element of surprise. The price of this quick action was the lack of a coherent plan and the extensive military preparation required to execute it.

The Organization of American States (OAS) was really the only formal source of international support the Argentines found in the wake of this action, although it found sympathy among nations diverse as Israel and China as well. Domestic support in Argentina, on the other hand, was overwhelming: "a wave of indescribably joy and contagious festivity spread like wildfire throughout the land." The junta, of course, was counting on this support to sustain its own fortunes at a time when the government was straining to hold control. Only days before the invasion, critics of the regime had staged the largest demonstrations since 1976. In such a situation, Argentina's only political option was to fight a waiting war in hopes that domestic support would sustain it until a combination of military reversals and international pressure forced Great Britain to back away from its objectives.

Military Imperatives

Although the Falklands are closer to Argentina than to Britain, distance would still pose a significant military problem to both sides, and that distance translated into time, whether it was time to get there, time to get supplies there, time over target, or time on station. The Falklands were 8,000 nautical miles (nm) from Great Britain and 4,225 nm from Ascension Island, Britain's nearest logistical base. The islands lie only 400 nm from the Argentine mainland, a fact that was to their advantage, but other factors—such as limited aerial refueling assets, an unwillingness to risk its aircraft carrier, and failure to build up airfields on the Falklands to support fighters—would make the distance every bit as critical to the Argentine side. Some have speculated that had the islands been 100 miles closer to Argentina, the Argentines might have prevailed in their efforts to take the Falklands.

The overwhelming distance confronted Great Britain's military with a power projection problem. Although once a maritime power, Britain had been focusing on its NATO role to the detriment of its expeditionary capability. Fortunately for the British, the timing of the Argentine attack worked in their favour; 18 months later and the Royal Navy would have retired and sold the *Hermes* and *Invincible* aircraft carriers that were the heart of the British task force. As it turned out, the British were able to put together a joint task force with air, sea, and land components capable of undertaking the daunting operation. In deploying this force, the British military leaders had to find a way to take advantage of their technical sophistication and training to overcome the problems of distance, security, sustainment, and numerical inferiority. With limited resources of men and materiel, the British had to be careful lest they blow the operation with a rash move which could cost them dearly.

Military common sense dictated that the Argentines prey upon these factors of distance, limited resources, and caution which characterized the British operation. The primary task facing the Argentine military forces was strengthening their defence of the Falklands to make any British move against them too costly to sustain. Given Argentine numerical superiority in air and ground forces, reinforcing the Falklands with more troops, preparing defenses there, and increasing the capability of airpower to strike the British task force were obvious ways to accomplish this end. The air strategy in particular appealed to the Argentines, for it seemed that "the best way to stop the invasion was to sink the ships in the hope of either killing the troops before they went ashore or making the cost to Britain so high that Whitehall would opt to withdraw or negotiate."

The Time Problem

A comparison of these political and military imperatives reveals some significant conflicts brought on by the demands of time. As far as Great Britain's political interests were concerned, the Falklands War had to be a quick one. Not only should it end quickly before international political pressure mounted against the British, but timely victories should punctuate its progress in order to shore up domestic support and send signals to the Argentines that continued resistance was hopeless. Military imperatives, on the other hand, counseled a cautious pace for British numerical inferiority and stretched lines of communication meant that its military commanders had to be deliberate and careful about each move. If the British lost an aircraft carrier or even a battalion in their haste to succeed, they might lose the war.

Politically, time seemed to be on the Argentine side. The longer they could hold on to the Falklands and plead their case to the international community, the greater the chance they might come away with a victory of some sort even if it meant initially withdrawing their troops. Therefore it was in the Argentines' interest to prolong the war in hopes that the British could not sustain the war politically or militarily. A prolonged war of exhaustion seemed the proper military strategy to accomplish this goal, but it was easier to articulate than to execute for the Argentine military. In spite of numerical superiority in most areas, the training and technical sophistication of the Argentine military did not compare favorably to the British in many areas and would hinder their efforts to carry out the strategy. Such were the primary time-induced tensions between political and military imperatives which faced the British and Argentine forces in the Falklands War. More important than the tensions themselves were the operational consequences they wrought, for Clausewitz's view of war would hold. Political considerations would remain primary and often dictate moves whose timing and scheme were not optimal from a military point of view.

Operational Consequences and Risk

The political sense of urgency on the British side caused the British military commanders to move more quickly than they might have liked and to divide forces when it was not prudent. This operational consequence manifested itself early in the war in the retaking of South Georgia, as Admiral Woodward, commander of the British naval task force noted:

> Politically, it was clearly expedient to provide an early demonstration of force to support declared resolve, in the hope that a political solution might result. The plan to retake South Georgia as soon as possible and to push our surface and S/M [submarine] forces as far south as possible were driven by political need—which committed me to splitting my assets and denying myself my prime military requirement, a work-up of the full battle group.

This would not be the last time that a British commander would find himself moving sooner than he would have liked and splitting his forces as he did so. In the battle for Goose Green, Brig Gen Julian Thompson would have to make the same sacrifices for political reasons, only this time the risks and costs would be much higher.

Political pressure determined the move on Goose Green in response to the events of the week prior. From 21 to 25 May, in the course of the San Carlos landing and establishment of a beachhead, the Argentines had sunk four British ships, including the *Atlantic Conveyor* which had contained vital lift helicopters for ground operations beyond the beachhead. By 26 May, the British War Cabinet, in the wake of these dire events and a new UN peace initiative, was questioning the lack of movement by British ground forces. London needed a sign of progress, and Northwood, Great Britain's military headquarters, transmitted this requirement to General Thompson in specific terms:

The radio-telephone was as clear as if the call had been coming from next door. As clear and unequivocal were the orders from Northwood. The Goose Green operation was to be re-mounted and more action was required all around. Plainly the people at the back-end were getting restless.

In selecting the time and place of battle, General Thompson's political masters forced him to move before logistical preparations on the beachhead were complete and to divide his forces in the face of an enemy who outnumbered him. As it turned out, the battle was a close one decided by a British flank attack which, along with a timely close air support strike by Harriers, broke a stalemate. The British battalion commander died trying to regain the initiative in what some would call a politician's battle. In spite of these tactical shortcomings, the battle for Goose Green accomplished the political purpose of sustaining public support by giving the British a badly needed victory.

The British success at Goose Green marked a turning point in many ways, most significantly perhaps in that it represented the failure of the Argentines to thwart the establishment and expansion of a beachhead. The Argentines had counted on achieving at least a stalemate through air attacks and ground defenses, if not prevent a landing altogether. The furious air attacks of 21 to 25 May which had claimed four British ships had been part of that effort, but they had failed to stop the landing in spite of the heavy toll they took.

One of the main reasons why the Argentines were able to inflict such losses on the British had to do with the level of operational risk the British were willing to tolerate. Rather than risk losing either or both of his carriers, Admiral Woodward had placed them well to the east of the Falklands after the first British ship was sunk. In Admiral Woodward's view, "the loss of one, much less both, carriers would immediately and seriously prejudice the whole operation and probably kill any thought of longer term operations." The disadvantage of this decision was that it would significantly limit the Harriers' already precious combat air patrol time and restrict their ability to intercept aerial attacks. Admiral Woodward was caught between Scylla and Charybdis: while staying further away limited his ability to protect other ships, he might lose that very ability altogether if he moved closer. The lack of complete air superiority over the landing area also meant that the British only had six hours each evening in which to move in and unload cargo and amphibious ships, a situation made worse by the shortage of heavy lift helicopters. These conditions seriously slowed the logistics buildup and ultimately affected the tempo of ground operations. Although many criticized Admiral Woodward's decision, General Thompson, the ground commander whom he supported, thought it was a wise one:

> The policy of keeping the Carriers so far from the Falkland Islands was criticized by the ill-informed at the time and subsequently. Max Hastings was right to say that Admiral Woodward was the only person who could have lost the war in an after-noon. Admiral Woodward's skillfull handling of the Carrier Battle Group kept them safe and thus our air support intact.

That air support would be vital in the battle for Goose Green and thus instrumental in pushing operations along in accordance with political imperatives, and subsequent events would prove the wisdom of Admiral Woodward in managing this operational risk.

The Role of Airpower

Although airpower in the Falklands War did not have the dramatic effect it did in the Arab-Israeli War of 1967, it nevertheless played a prominent role and contributed to overcoming some of the time-induced tensions between political and military imperatives. For the British, airpower functioned as one of the arms which struck first, as the arm which provided an important degree of security and freedom of action for all forces, and as the arm of a combined arms team which helped accelerate progress on the ground. Airpower for the Argentines was the key to prolonging and possibly preventing British operations around the islands. Ultimately the British made the best use of their airpower resources to solve time problems, although there was unrealized potential on both sides. The attack on Port Stanley airfield by a Vulcan bomber on 1 May was another early demonstration of force and political resolve in addition to the retaking of South Georgia. Although it was a small attack, it was a classic use of airpower to strike first across large distances and achieve effects beyond the immediate and obvious ones. Damage to the runway was limited, but the attack probably ended any notions the Argentines might have of recovering fighter aircraft there after ship attacks. Additionally, the British had demonstrated an ability to bomb distant airfields and thus threaten mainland Argentina. In reaction, the Argentines moved Mirage interceptors from the south to cover more of the mainland and its airfields. This move created more problems for the Argentines and handicapped their ability to contest air superiority over the Falklands.

Providing air superiority to protect the British task force became the top airpower objective for the British as the Argentines focused on destroying the British ships. Stationing the carriers to the east made the job more difficult for the Harriers, who already had limited range, but they made up some of the disadvantage through their air combat skills, the technological edge of their aircraft, and the prowess of their launch crews in generating sorties. Although they were outnumbered three-to-one in aircraft, the British generated 2,000 sorties while the Argentines could only muster 455 sorties during combat operations. In aerial engagements, the British took advantage of their air combat skills and the all-aspect kill capability of the US-supplied AIM-9L Sidewinder to claim 20 Argentine aircraft with no British losses in air combat. In spite of these impressive numbers, Argentine aircraft were still able to inflict substantial losses on the British task force through 26 May; however, the attrition caused by British air defenses kept the Argentines from posing a significant threat to land operations after that date. That degree of air superiority provided a freedom of action to British forces which helped accelerate the pace of operations, although a threat still remained.

Air support to ground operations also helped move things along, especially during the battle for Goose Green. A Harrier close air support strike was instrumental in breaking the stalemate during the battle and helping the British to regain the initiative. This strike silenced Argentinian air defence guns and artillery while boosting British morale at a critical juncture. It also had a role in wearing down Argentine resistance. The promise of more

Harrier attacks helped precipitate a surrender during negotiations with the Argentine defenders. Unfortunately, the vulnerability of British carriers to attack by land-based airpower that resulted in moving them further east also limited the role British airpower could play in supporting ground operations.

In spite of these British advantages in the air, the Argentines pressed the attack against the British landings with their own airpower. With their fleet restricted from the exclusion zone by the submarine threat and the bulk of their army concentrated around Port Stanley, the Argentine air arm bore the burden of repulsing the British landing at San Carlos. From 21 to 25 May, the Argentine pilots gallantly conducted mass attacks on the British task force which succeeded in sinking four ships and damaging at least 10 others. Greater results might have been possible but for the limited number of Exocet missiles available to the Argentines and their problems with getting bombs to fuse. The attrition of British ships was insufficient to stop the landing and expansion of the beachhead, however, and Argentine losses were too high to sustain. By the end of May, the mass attacks were no longer possible and the Argentines could launch only three or four pairs of aircraft a day. In the end, Argentine airpower by itself could neither prevent the landing nor make its cost so high and prolonged as to be prohibitive.

The Gulf War

The Gulf War resembled the Falklands War in that the US found itself in an unexpected military confrontation which would require it to employ its forces in a theatre thousands of miles away on very short notice. As in the Falklands War, political pressure would force action before military leaders were ready, and airpower would play a prominent role as a result. The Gulf War, however, was fought on a scale which would dwarf the Falklands War, and airpower's contribution to overcoming the problem of time was appropriate to that scale. In the Gulf War, airpower would strike before coalition land power had finished its preparations, and its effect on Iraq's fielded forces and ability to command them would allow the coalition ground forces to complete this devastation in a matter of days. Airpower's success in this regard would lead some to proclaim that airpower was the decisive force and had finally realized the potential Giulio Douhet and others had prophesied. In the ensuing arguments, participants in the debate would often lose sight of what may have been incontrovertible: that airpower had acted first as a single instrument and later as part of a combined force after setting a standard for tempo and effects that would ultimately ensure the congruence of political and military operations in regard to time.

The Course of the War

The events of the Gulf War were set in motion by Iraq's invasion of Kuwait on 2 August 1990. By the following day, Iraq's forces had swept through the emirate and were poised on the Kuwaiti-Saudi border. Iraq's dictator, Saddam Hussein used disputes between Iraq and Kuwait over territory and economic issues, including the amelioration of Iraqi debt, to justify his actions which culminated in the annexation of Kuwait on 8 August. International reaction to the invasion was strongly negative and would grow from unilateral condemnations to action by regional organizations as well as the UN. As the standoff continued, forces poured into Saudi Arabia to contain the Iraqi threat even as Saddam began to reinforce Iraqi divisions in Kuwait with an additional 250,000 troops. A containment strategy complemented with economic sanctions gradually gave way to the conviction that offensive military action would be required to eject Iraq from Kuwait; and on 29 November 1990, the UN authorized the use of such force if Iraq did not withdraw by 15 January 1991. Diplomatic efforts to avert war failed, and the US-led coalition began offensive operations with air attacks on 17 January 1991.

Rather than engage the dug-in Iraqi forces in ground battle immediately, coalition commanders chose instead to use air attacks to blind and weaken Iraqi defenses while continuing their preparations for the land war. Air operations would continue unaccompanied by significant ground action until late February, in spite of Iraqi attempts, such as the attack on Khafji and Scud missile attacks, to draw the coalition into a premature land war. Gaining air superiority within days, coalition aircraft targeted the entire range of Iraqi military capability with relentless operations around the clock. Although bad weather prolonged air operations, the coalition had achieved air supremacy and had reduced the combat effectiveness of Iraqi units enough to commence ground operations on 24 February 1991. Assisted by close air support and interdiction missions, coalition ground forces rapidly overcame Iraqi defenses and routed Iraqi ground forces. In full retreat and still unable to prevent the destruction wrought by coalition forces, the Iraqi forces agreed to a cease-fire and UN terms on 28 February 1991, 100 hours after the ground offensive began.

Political Imperatives

Coming as it did at the end of the cold war, the Iraqi invasion of Kuwait challenged the US to define its post-cold-war foreign policy and assert its world leadership in a new environment. Although the US was quick to condemn the invasion, it was not immediately clear what action the US would take in response. After consultation with allies and a particularly invigorating conversation with British Prime Minister Margaret Thatcher, US President George Bush declared on 5 August 1990 that the "naked aggression" of the Iraqi invasion "shall not stand." President Bush went on to outline the objectives which the US would pursue:

- immediate, complete, and unconditional withdrawal of all Iraqi forces from Kuwait;
- restoration of Kuwait's legitimate government;
- security and stability of Saudi Arabia and the Persian Gulf; and
- safety and protection of the lives of American citizens abroad.

With this forceful declaration, Bush made it clear that the US would be aggressive and vigorous in leading the international opposition to Iraq's invasion. What was unclear was could he command the international and domestic support necessary to achieve these objectives. The breadth and variety of international response was simultaneously a strength and weakness for the US-led coalition. Ultimately, almost 50 countries made some form of contribution to the effort, and 38 of those actually supplied forces of some sort. Although the strength of this response would permit the marshaling of enormous force as well as the clout of a UN mandate, its disparate nature would demand careful leadership lest Iraq exploit its diversity to create divisions. In the same vein, it was questionable whether such a disparate coalition could survive the strain of war, particularly one that produced many casualties and pitted Arab against Arab.

It was also questionable whether American political support at home could endure such a war. Early on even a senator of the Bush's own party urged caution, "Mr. President, I hope you will resist the calls that are being made for an offensive action," said Sen William S. Cohen (R-Maine). As the US committed more forces in spite of public skepticism reflected in the opinion polls, Democrats grew more vocal. "It's as if the great armed force which was created to fight the Cold War is at the President's own disposal for any diversion he may wish, no matter what it costs," railed democratic Sen Daniel Patrick Moynihan of New York, "He will wreck our military." Moynihan's colleague, Sen Sam Nunn (D-Ga.), conducted Senate hearings in December which featured many witnesses critical of Bush's policy. Nunn himself interrupted Gen Colin L. Powell, chairman of the Joint Chiefs of Staff, to say, "That's the major point here; I mean, the way you find out whether sanctions work or not is to—is to give them enough time to work." A congressional vote in January that narrowly authorized the use of force underscored how tentative this support could be.

The Bush administration had to be sensitive to the fragility of this domestic and international support as it went about forming a viable strategy. Given the objectives Bush had articulated, war might be inevitable, but that war would have to be short and relatively bloodless, or support might crumble. Saddam Hussein, on the other hand, could be expected to exploit these weaknesses fully. As he had told the American ambassador to Baghdad before the invasion, "Yours is a society which cannot accept 10,000 dead in one battle." In addition to haunting Americans with the ghost of Vietnam by promising a long, bloody war, Saddam also sought to divide Arabs from the rest of the coalition by appealing to pan-Arab sentiments and linking Kuwait's fate with the Palestinian issue. Success in either of these ploys would strengthen his chances for surviving the coalition's attempt to wrest Kuwait from his grasp.

Military Imperatives

Coalition military imperatives shifted quickly from a defensive orientation to an offensive orientation in response to changing political objectives. When the decision was first taken to send forces, the emphasis was on containing the Iraqi thrust to Kuwait and protecting the Saudi oil fields. Such a mission required quick response in order to deter and fast follow-up to make the deterrent force credible. Though challenging, such a defensive mission was a tractable problem given US capabilities. Rolling back the invasion was another thing, a task whose difficulty was orders of magnitude greater. Such an undertaking could well require a ground offensive as part of a combined operation and thus significantly more troops; traditional wisdom had proposed a 3-to-1 advantage in numbers when attacking prepared defenses. Planning also had to be creative, detailed, and comprehensive, as one can see when considering the six military objectives in the operations order for Desert Storm:

1. attack Iraqi political/military leadership and command and control,
2. gain and maintain air superiority,
3. sever Iraqi supply lines,
4. destroy chemical, biological, and nuclear capability,
5. destroy Republican Guard Forces, and
6. liberate Kuwait City. In order to accomplish these objectives, coalition forces would target three Iraqi centres of gravity:
    - Iraqi National Command Authority;
    - Iraq's nuclear, chemical, and biological capability; and
    - The Republican Guard Forces Command.

Given the size of forces needed to accomplish these objectives and the fact that more than 30 countries would make up the coalition supplying the forces, the task would be even more daunting, especially in terms of coordinating actions in time and space as well as maintaining unity of command and effort.

Iraq's military imperative was to delay any coalition offensive operations for as long as possible and to raise the cost of those operations to unacceptable levels. Adding troops was an important dimension of that strategy. By January 1991, estimates of Iraqi troop strength ranged as high as 540,000, a number which represented 42 to 43 divisions in theatre. By steadily fortifying these troops and their equipment, the Iraqis hoped to survive any air attack and remain ready to bleed the coalition's ground forces white when they launched an offensive. The Iraqi defenses sought to achieve this goal by channeling coalition forces into killing zones with their defenses, as they had done with some success in the Iran-Iraq War. As a way of dividing those forces by bringing Israel into the fray, Iraq held its Scud missiles ready to attack Israel.

The Time Problem

What made the coalition's military problems even more daunting were the ambitious time constraints the political leaders imposed. While deploying and sustaining an enormous force capable of conducting offensive operations represented a time challenge in itself, planning their employment took time as well. At a point when he felt he still had a couple of months work to do in shoring up his defenses, General Schwarzkopf was told to begin offensive planning for an operation he had told Bush in August would not be possible for 8 to 12 months. He would later complain:

Not only was the plan expected to be ready to execute quickly, it was expected to achieve its objectives quickly once it was in motion, as Bush made clear in a meeting with Schwarzkopf on 11 November 1990:

He listened attentively as I explained the battle plan for the ground campaign. After a moment, he looked at me and asked pointedly, "What is the shortest ground war you can visualize?"

This political sense of urgency would soon manifest itself in the form of an actual deadline for Iraqi compliance, a deadline that also implied a date for the beginning of offensive operations. UN Security Council Resolution 678 of 29 November 1990 authorized the use of "all necessary means" if Iraq did not comply with previous UN resolutions by midnight, 15 January 1991. Whether those means would be ready to use at that time seemed a secondary consideration. Lt Gen Calvin Waller told reporters that the ground forces would not be ready until some time in February, confirming that a significant time-induced tension existed between political and military imperatives. As for the Iraqis, playing the long game was still the politically correct move, but there remained the question of whether they were militarily capable of staying in the game long enough to win it or emerge with something they could call a victory. The enormity and sophistication of the coalition military resources arrayed against the Iraqi commanders might have given them pause to wonder if there was not a tension between what was expected of them in terms of how long they were to survive and still inflict heavy losses and their capability to fulfil that political time objective.

Operational Consequences and Risk

The most significant operational consequence of these time-induced tensions was that US forces would have to attack Iraqi forces shortly after 15 January 1991, whether military preparations for a ground offensive were complete or not. Although he understood the political reasons for acting early, General Schwarzkopf knew that his ground forces would not be ready for another month after the deadline. This situation meant that air operations would have to begin early and run alone until such time as the ground forces were ready. The British commander, Gen Sir Peter de la Billière, recalled how the situation worried the coalition commander:

> He was very frank about the conflicting pressures under which he found himself working.... This meant that the air war was going to have to run for several weeks and, even if it had to start early for political reasons, it would have to continue until he was ready on the ground. On this point he was adamant: nothing would induce him to start the land war until he was fully prepared. "Peter," he said, "if there's one matter I'll resign on, this is it. If they don't give me the time I need, I'll quit."

Although political imperatives would force him to accept this situation, General Schwarzkopf obviously understood the operational risk it entailed. By beginning offensive operations with airpower alone and before ground preparations were ready, he was starting a war which he was not ready to fight with all the means at his disposal. As he already realized, he might be prodded into striking before he was ready if air operations did not go well. Another possibility was that air offensive might trigger an Iraqi ground attack which could also force him into premature action as well as disrupt his preparations. In either case, it was a risk he would have to accept and which he could only reduce by ensuring the soundness of his defensive preparations and urging along the pace of his offensive preparations. Finally, he would depend on the success of airpower in the opening phases to make that risk tolerable and worthwhile.

The Role of Airpower

The military leadership of the coalition ultimately turned to airpower as the solution to their operational dilemma. Airpower proved a ready force which could fulfil both political and military imperatives by commencing offensive military operations, defending and masking coalition ground forces as they prepared for offensive operations, making significant progress toward the accomplishment of theatre military objectives, and degrading the tactical and operational effectiveness of Iraqi ground formations, particularly the Republican Guard. In addition to achieving quick results and paralysing many Iraqi units, airpower combined with ground and naval forces to achieve synergistic effects, accelerate the decision on the ground, and minimize friendly casualties. As a direct result of airpower's important role, the coalition was able to commence operations shortly after the 15 January deadline and end them after achieving its objectives only six weeks later, thus resolving time conflicts between political and military imperatives.

At the outset of the crisis, airpower proved its value as a ready force which could respond quickly to deter and defend. Within 24 hours of notification, air resources began deploying to the region; roughly 500 fighter attack aircraft had arrived in theatre by 23 August. At the same time fighters were arriving, airlift was bringing in combat personnel, 99 percent of whom would ultimately fly into theatre, as well as supplies. In addition to serving in this defensive capacity, airpower employed according to the plan of Instant Thunder represented the only offensive possibility available to commanders in the early days.

With the commencement of offensive air operations on 17 January 1991, coalition airpower set the tone and tempo of operations which would help preserve the initiative for the coalition throughout the war. In an effort to achieve nearly simultaneous attack, coalition planners orchestrated an intense first two days of attacks that tore apart Iraqi air defenses and struck the whole range of targets. They took advantage of every capability, from F-117s to Tornados to helicopters to drones, and launched over 2,700 sorties the first day. Even more amazing was the coalition's ability to sustain this high tempo of between 2,000 to 3,000 sorties a day; by the beginning of the ground war, they had flown nearly 100,000 sorties. In achieving air supremacy by 27 January 1991, coalition airpower had removed the Iraqi Air Force from the fight and provided a freedom of action for coalition ground forces which allow preparations to proceed unmolested.

The same freedom of action left coalition airpower free to attack Iraq's political and military leadership, command and control, supply lines, weapons of mass destruction, and its ground forces, particularly the Republican Guard. The record of these attacks indicate effects beyond those annotated by the thousands of troops who deserted or were killed, or the numbers of tanks which were destroyed. The cumulative effect of constant attack, the loss of equipment and supplies, and the loss of life sapped the Iraqi soldier's will to fight:

At least as important as the destructive force of airpower were its consequential effects: particularly dislocation and demoralization. It was the combination of all these effects which wrecked the Iraqi army as an effective and cohesive fighting force and paved the way for the rapid—and for the Allies relatively bloodless—liberation of Kuwait.

Airpower also made an important contribution in keeping Saddam from drawing the coalition into ground operations prematurely in an effort to force a prolonged war of attrition. The Iraqi move on Khafji was an attempt to achieve this goal, but the movement then and immediately thereafter only increased Iraqi ground forces' exposure to air attack, and attrition of Iraqi equipment increased dramatically during that week. Air operations during the Khafji battle also illustrated the coalition air commander's ability to shift effort and mass forces quickly in response to a need. Essential to this capability were the coalition's massive inflight refueling resources (432 refueling sorties were flown the first day) and its flexible command and control system.

Although airpower alone did not bring about the rapid and complete defeat of Iraqi forces, it provided integral support to the combined arms effort which finally did. The success of air operations prior to the land offensive was the major factor in ensuring the speed with which the ground forces accomplished their objectives. In addition to reducing the combat effectiveness of Iraqi units, air attacks blinded the Iraqi forces and thus masked the movement of ground forces to the west. Airpower in the form of theatre airlift and helicopters assisted in expediting that move. Once ground operations began, a continuous "push" flow of CAS and interdiction sorties ensured the Iraqi divisions could not move or fight effectively, because airpower had either physically incapacitated them or psychologically demoralized them. Airpower integrated effectively with ground maneuver and fires to achieve synergistic effects and thus enabled coalition forces to conclude the final phase with lightning speed (four days) and minimum casualties.

In contrast to the dramatic success of the coalition's use of airpower to overcome time conflicts, Iraq chose to let its air force languish in shelters before trying to find a safe haven for it in Iran. With the exception of Scud missile attacks, Iraq made little attempt, other than some air defence sorties, to use airpower to prolong the war and inflict attrition on the coalition. The Scud attacks, however, proved to be a cheap and effective way to divert coalition airpower from its preferred employment while also threatening to divide the coalition by bringing Israel into the war.

The Mechanism

Time-induced tensions between political and military imperatives were evident in the Arab-Israeli War of 1967, the Falklands War, and the Gulf War. Analysis to this point has also indicated that airpower played a role in resolving these tensions. Although the study has elaborated in detail on how airpower resolved these tensions, it has yet to offer a general explanation of how airpower overcomes such conflicts; however, a unified analysis of the evidence can assist in identifying this mechanism. This chapter offers such an analysis as well as defines the mechanism which emerges from it. In this study, a global view of the evidence suggests that a time-based strategy was the mechanism through which airpower accomplished this task. Having identified the mechanism, this chapter defines what characterizes a time-based strategy as well as discusses its particular elements and considerations.

Identifying the Mechanism

Although none of the parties to the conflicts discussed in this study ever announced the use of a time-based strategy, the evidence suggests that some form of a time-based strategy was responsible for success in overcoming time conflicts between political and military imperatives. Israel, Britain, and the coalition all had significant political factors that pressured them to end their respective wars quickly. In other words, time became a paramount or extremely significant consideration in the accomplishment of their objectives. The very survival of the state was at stake in Israel's case, a situation which created a compelling sense of political urgency. Israel found itself surrounded by hostile Arab nations who seemed content to wait until Israel had been weakened by economic pressure (closure of the Straits of Tiran and pressure of maintaining mobilization) before striking. In these circumstances, Israel chose to seize the initiative and begin the war itself; however, doing so meant Israel would stand alone and depend on its own political and economic resources to sustain its war effort. Therefore, the war had to be short and decisive.

Time pressures were also strong in the Gulf War, although Saudi Arabia was perhaps the only member of the coalition motivated by the core security interest of survival. Given the number and diversity of the coalition's members, one had to wonder how long the coalition could hold together, even with strong US leadership and UN authority. This time pressure soon manifested itself in the UN Security Council resolution which established an actual deadline for Iraqi withdrawal. A quick war was one way to minimize the exposure to this pressure. In addition to international political urgency, US domestic political considerations also argued for a short war.

In the Falklands War, on the other hand, time was an extremely significant but not a paramount consideration. International interest in resolving the conflict and domestic questions as to whether the Falklands were worth the price in British blood and treasure put pressure on British leaders to finish the war quickly; however, the urgency was not as pressing as it was in the other two cases. In the Falklands War, time pressure was more evident in the demand for signs of continued progress, as seen in the political prompting to break out from the beachhead, which resulted in the battle of Goose Green.

Given that "war is simply a continuation of political intercourse," military commanders had to respect the importance of political time imperatives in formulating employment options no matter how daunting their military tasks were. To a greater or lesser extent depending on the specific circumstances, their strategy became time-based in essence, if not in name. Israel's commanders knew they had a narrow window of time in which to conduct their operations. At the same time they had the formidable task of defeating Arab armies on several fronts. A defensive war was not likely to defeat those armies or improve the security of Israel in the time required, so the Israeli strategy had to become offensive and time-based in order to satisfy political and military imperatives. British military commanders also bowed to time pressures in shaping strategy, as the early move on South Georgia and the battle for Goose Green illustrate; however, the hazards of risking his precious carriers made Admiral Woodward resistant to letting time imperatives completely govern his moves. Political time imperatives weighed much more heavily on General Schwarzkopf during the Gulf War. Time and again he had to shape his strategy with time as a paramount consideration whether he was considering the moment at which he would attack or the manner in which he would attack. His meetings with political leaders such as President Bush underscored the necessity of attacking soon after the deadline and making the ensuing war as short as possible.

Even as military commanders shaped their strategies with time as a primary consideration, evaluation of operational risks and benefits also had profound implications for their plans. Since the survival of Israel hung in the balance, Israeli military commanders were willing to take enormous risks with the expectation of reaping equally great benefits. They divided their ground forces and left only 12 aircraft to defend Israel during the initial strike of Operation Moked. In the Falklands War, the British had to be more cautious. Security of the British Isles was not in jeopardy, but the British task force commander had to worry about the safety of his carriers. Losing a carrier might mean losing the war for lack of ability to prosecute it. As a result, Admiral Woodward balanced operational risk and benefits in placing the carriers east of the Falklands. In doing so he achieved a compromise between keeping them safely out of Argentine aircraft range and putting them close enough to make use of their airpower. The trade-off was not without cost, however, for it reduced the effectiveness of British air cover and lengthened the logistics buildup. Starting offensive air operations before ground preparations were complete constituted the chief operational risk General Schwarzkopf had to take in the Gulf War. Although he risked triggering an Iraqi attack which might disrupt his preparations and precipitate a premature ground war, he reaped the benefits of complying with political time constraints and having the air attack mask his movements.

A unified analysis of the evidence thus indicates a time-based strategy was the mechanism through which military commanders resolved time-induced tensions between political and military imperatives. In fashioning these strategies, military leaders sought to satisfy political time imperatives while also striking an acceptable balance between operational risk and benefits. In the British case, the acceptable level of operational risk limited the extent to which time considerations could dominate the strategy.

Defining a Time-based Strategy

Having identified a time-based strategy is the mechanism, the next logical step is to define a time-based strategy. Before attempting that task, however, it makes sense to explore briefly whether the conditions obtained in these cases are likely to be encountered in the future. More specifically, one must speculate time conflicts between political and military imperatives will characterize future wars. The short answer is that trends favour the reemergence of these time-induced tensions. In light of continued advances in communications and the integration of global interests, one can expect future wars to attract international attention and involvement just as the three wars that were discussed. International political considerations will, therefore, hold for the national political leaders even as they marshal domestic political support for their actions. The latter will obviously be more crucial for a democracy, but even more authoritarian governments cannot afford to ignore it. The speed of these interactions will continue to increase as information technology advances and will affect military leaders as well as political leaders. The implications for theatre warfare are significant:

With time compressed over extended space and with that immense space rendered comprehensible by a technological *coup d'oeil*, an entire theatre can become a simultaneous battlefield where events, as in the days of Napoleon, may determine national destinies. In addition, the horizontal, real-time communication link to the vertical continuum of war only reinforces the interaction of the people with the other two thirds of the Clausewitzian trinity.

Even as they respond to political imperatives for action, military commanders will face daunting time-space problems whose resolution challenges even the latest technology. In other words, there are still likely to be situations where there is tension between political and military imperatives, a significant component of which has to do with time. One can also expect that commanders will have to analyze and manage operational risk well in order to overcome these tensions.

If time-induced tensions are likely to characterize future wars, then the mechanism of a time-based strategy is useful to those who will have to deal with those situations as well as to those endeavoring to understand past wars where these conflicts were present. With that double utility in mind, this study defines a time-based strategy as one in which time is a paramount or extremely significant consideration. Commanders form such strategies in response to situations where time-induced tensions between political and military imperatives are present. The aim of a time-based strategy is to resolve these tensions and make military operations congruent with political considerations. As it outlined a plan for employing forces, a time-based strategy would do so with time as the governing consideration. Such a plan would recognize the particular capabilities of specific forms of military power, airpower for example, in this regard and integrate them into a combined arms scheme which takes advantage of those capabilities. By appreciating the physical and psychological effects obtainable and their effect on time considerations, a time-based strategy seeks to use military force to accomplish political objectives. In doing so, a time-based strategy also weighs the operational risks and benefits in terms of time with the aim of balancing them to achieve the greatest time benefit at the lowest risk.

Implications

In addition to revealing a time-based strategy as the mechanism for overcoming time conflicts between political and military imperatives, the evidence also points to the prominence of airpower's role in that strategy. This link between time-based strategies and airpower has important implications for both the airpower theorist and the airpower strategist. It is the job of the airpower theorist to plumb the meaning and relevance of this relationship between airpower and time-based strategy and to continue interpreting its implications for airpower as well as its utility in guiding future action. Evaluating the usefulness of the time perspective, interpreting the relationship between airpower and time, and considering the idea of a four-dimensional model of warfare are among the worthwhile tasks for the airpower theorist. While the airpower theorist concerns himself with the implications for airpower doctrine and theory, the airpower strategist has the more pressing problem of determining the immediate utility of time-based strategies and airpower's role in them. Among the issues the airpower strategist must consider are the appropriateness of a time-based strategy, airpower's role in that strategy, and balancing the operational risks and benefits associated with the use of airpower.

Implications for Airpower Theory

Just as there is value in viewing war from the perspective of time, there is value in examining airpower from the temporal perspective as well. Although theorists have tended to concentrate on airpower's ability to exploit the third dimension as its defining feature, the importance of time in war as suggested by this study urges a consideration of airpower's ability to exploit the fourth dimension, which is time. An exploration of this ability to exploit the fourth dimension would contribute to a more complete understanding of airpower's nature. This shift in perspective demands a fundamental reexamination of airpower in the same manner that the advent of airpower forced a reexamination of warfare from the aerial perspective. Unfortunately, airpower theorists have tended to remain fixed on airpower's progress in exploiting the third dimension (elevation) while ignoring its potential to conquer the fourth dimension (time). Some viewed the Gulf War as the apotheosis of airpower's utility as an instrument of war, and one airpower theorist was inspired to call for a "three-dimensional model of warfare... based on a unique capability that defines the essence of airpower. That capability is the quick concentration of great power over any spot on the surface of the globe." Although his idea of a three-dimensional model has merit, it is interesting to note that his use of the word *quick* brings time into model. Indeed, a four-dimensional model of warfare might describe the phenomenon more accurately and also encompass airpower's role and effects better in that it would include time as well as space. As demonstrated in this study, understanding how airpower can work to resolve time-induced tensions between political and military imperatives is one step toward forming such a unified view and comprehending the full potential of airpower as a force in war.

Implications for Airpower Strategy

While the airpower theorist ponders the larger questions about time and the very nature of airpower, the airpower strategist must put these ideas about airpower and time-based strategies to immediate use. The first step is to decide whether a time-based strategy is appropriate. In making this decision, the airpower strategist has to consider the political goals and the political conditions, both international and domestic, which form the context in which those goals are pursued. He must then evaluate the theatre military goals as well as the theatre conditions which will affect the accomplishment of those goals. By comparing the political and military imperatives which emerge from this analysis, he can determine if any tensions between the two relate to time. If such time-induced tensions are present, he must evaluate how prominent they are and whether they argue for accelerating or decelerating results. If time is a paramount or extremely significant consideration, then a time-based strategy is appropriate and the airpower strategist can begin to determine what role airpower can play in it.

In planning this role, an airpower strategist must appreciate the potential airpower has to overcome time-induced tensions. A superficial analysis would simply point to airpower's speed and range as the characteristics which enable it to overcome these tensions. Although these traits are important to airpower's potential, they are insufficient to describe the full potential of airpower to resolve time problems. Airpower's efficacy in this regard ultimately has to do with effects achieved and the way it achieves them.

In each of the situations described, airpower constituted a ready force, one which could be brought to bear quickly over long distance. A. G. B. Vallance aptly describes this characteristic as "responsiveness":

In each structure terms, responsiveness demands quick-reacting combat air forces, supported by tankers and air transports to provide them with strategic and operational reach. It demands a procurement system which is as responsive as the front line it supports, one which is capable of providing the equipment enhancements needed to match the existing operational situation. And finally, responsiveness requires high levels of operational proficiency.

In addition to readiness and training, flexibility is an important dimension of airpower's responsiveness because it implies that airpower is capable of responding to a variety of situations by performing a variety of actions with a variety of effects. If airpower is truly responsive, it will not only strike first, it will achieve significant results as it does so. The earlier in the conflict such action takes place, the greater the chance the results will be significant:

There is yet another reason to reach for an airpower solution. In every culture there is a direct relationship between time and the effectiveness of employing force. In essence, there is a "time value of war." The greatest likelihood of achieving objectives—with the lowest potential for casualties and collateral damage—exists at the beginning of a contingency.

Another characteristic of airpower which helps overcome time problems is its ability to provide freedom of action in the form of air superiority or air supremacy. The Israelis and the coalition made it the foundation of their operations, while the British battled for it as best they could under the circumstances. Such freedom of action assists in ensuring security of forces. It also helps accelerate the tempo of operations, whether air or ground, and high tempo will characterize well-executed air operations which seek to maintain initiative. Both operational proficiency and technical sophistication contribute to airpower's ability to achieve high tempo as Israeli, British, and coalition forces proved by their operations. For the Israelis and British, high tempo also served as a force multiplier.

Airpower's advantage in achieving mass by concentrating tremendous force quickly at any place and time is also the key to the effects it can achieve. Israel's Operation Moked masterfully exploited this capability as did the coalition's plan for the first two days of the air war. While the coalition effort came close to achieving simultaneous attack, the Israeli example shows that numbers, while nice to have, are not absolutely necessary to exploit this capability. Through airpower the Israelis concentrated force at diverse places in a narrow time frame and thus achieved effects similar to those obtained by simultaneous attack.

Synchronization that ultimately coordinates such effects is also important. Such synchronization is evident in the synergy which occurs when airpower is integrated properly with other forces. Whether it was the Israelis in the last three days of the 1967 war, the British at Goose Green, or the coalition in the 100-hour ground offensive, this synergy sped up operations and increased the destruction and demoralization wrought by the attack. In the final analysis, these physical and psychological effects that airpower achieves with speed, responsiveness, mass, high tempo, synchronization, and synergy are what allows it to overcome time conflicts between political and military imperatives.

In addition to understanding how airpower works to overcome time conflicts, the airpower strategist must also appreciate the operational risks and benefits associated with the use of airpower. As he evaluates the operational risks and benefits in terms of time for a given airpower option, he should aim for the greatest time benefit at the lowest operational risk. Such choices are rarely easy, particularly when numbers of airpower resources are limited, as the Israeli and British situations illustrate.

7

Nuclear Proliferation and Non-Proliferation Treaty

Nuclear proliferation is a term now used to describe the spread of nuclear weapons, fissile material, and weapons-applicable nuclear technology and information, to nations which are not recognized as "Nuclear Weapon States" by the *Treaty on the Nonproliferation of Nuclear Weapons*, also known as the Nuclear Nonproliferation Treaty or NPT.

Proliferation has been opposed by many nations with and without nuclear weapons, the governments of which fear that more countries with nuclear weapons may increase the possibility of nuclear warfare (up to and including the so-called "countervalue" targeting of civilians with nuclear weapons), de-stabilize international or regional relations, or infringe upon the national sovereignty of states.

Four nations besides the five recognized Nuclear Weapons States, none of which signed or ratified the NPT, have acquired, or are presumed to have acquired, nuclear weapons: India, Pakistan, North Korea, and Israel. One critique of the NPT is that it is discriminatory in recognizing as nuclear weapon states only those counties that tested nuclear weapons before 1968 and requiring all other states joining the treaty to forswear nuclear weapons.

Nuclear Proliferation

Research into the development of nuclear weapons was undertaken during World War II by the United States, the United Kingdom, Germany, Japan, and the USSR. The United States was the first and is the only country to have used a nuclear weapon in war, when it used two bombs against Japan in August 1945. With their loss during the war, Germany and Japan ceased to be involved in any nuclear weapon research. In August 1949, the USSR tested a nuclear weapon. The United Kingdom tested a nuclear weapon in October 1952. France developed a nuclear weapon in 1960. The People's Republic of China detonated a nuclear weapon in 1964. India exploded a nuclear device in 1974, and Pakistan tested a weapon in 1998. In 2006, North Korea conducted a nuclear test.

Non-proliferation Efforts

Early efforts to prevent nuclear proliferation involved intense government secrecy, the wartime acquisition of known uranium stores (the Combined Development Trust), and at times even outright sabotage—such as the bombing of a heavy-water facility thought to be used for a German nuclear program. None of these efforts were explicitly public, owing to the fact that the weapon developments themselves were kept secret until the bombing of Hiroshima.

Earnest international efforts to promote nuclear non-proliferation began soon after World War II, when the Truman Administration proposed the Baruch Plan of 1946, named after Bernard Baruch, America's first representative to the United Nations Atomic Energy Commission. The Baruch Plan, which drew heavily from the Acheson-Lilienthal Report of 1946, proposed the verifiable dismantlement and destruction of the U.S. nuclear arsenal (which, at that time, was the only nuclear arsenal in the world) after all governments had cooperated successfully to accomplish two things: (1) the establishment of an "international atomic development authority," which would actually own and control all military-applicable nuclear materials and activities, and (2) the creation of a system of automatic sanctions, which not even the U.N. Security Council could veto, and which would proportionately punish states attempting to acquire the capability to make nuclear weapons or fissile material.

Although the Baruch Plan enjoyed wide international support, it failed to emerge from the UNAEC because the Soviet Union planned to veto it in the Security Council. Still, it remained official American policy until 1953, when President Eisenhower made his

"Atoms for Peace" proposal before the U.N. General Assembly. Eisenhower's proposal led eventually to the creation of the International Atomic Energy Agency (IAEA) in 1957. Under the "Atoms for Peace" program thousands of scientists from around the world were educated in nuclear science and then dispatched home, where many later pursued secret weapons programs in their home country.

Efforts to conclude an international agreement to limit the spread of nuclear weapons did not begin until the early 1960s, after four nations (the United States, the Soviet Union, Britain and France) had acquired nuclear weapons. Although these efforts stalled in the early 1960s, they renewed once again in 1964, after China detonated a nuclear weapon. In 1968, governments represented at the Eighteen Nation Disarmament Committee (ENDC) finished negotiations on the text of the NPT. In June 1968, the U.N. General Assembly endorsed the NPT with General Assembly Resolution 2373 (XXII), and in July 1968, the NPT opened for signature in Washington, DC, London and Moscow. The NPT entered into force in March 1970.

Since the mid-1970s, the primary focus of non-proliferation efforts has been to maintain, and even increase, international control over the fissile material and specialized technologies necessary to build such devices because these are the most difficult and expensive parts of a nuclear weapons program. The main materials whose generation and distribution is controlled are highly enriched uranium and plutonium. Other than the acquisition of these special materials, the scientific and technical means for weapons construction to develop rudimentary, but working, nuclear explosive devices are considered to be within the reach of industrialized nations.

Since its founding by the United Nations in 1957, the International Atomic Energy Agency (IAEA) has promoted two, sometimes contradictory, missions: on the one hand, the Agency seeks to promote and spread internationally the use of civilian nuclear energy; on the other hand, it seeks to prevent, or at least detect, the diversion of civilian nuclear energy to nuclear weapons, nuclear explosive devices or purposes unknown. The IAEA now operates a safeguards system as specified under Article III of the

Nuclear Non-Proliferation Treaty (NPT) of 1968, which aims to ensure that civil stocks of uranium, plutonium, as well as facilities and technologies associated with these nuclear materials, are used only for peaceful purposes and do not contribute in any way to proliferation or nuclear weapons programs.

Dual use Technology

Dual use technology refers to the possibility of military use of civilian nuclear power technology. The enriched uranium used in most nuclear reactors is not concentrated enough to build a bomb. Most nuclear reactors run on 4% enriched uranium; Little Boy used 80% enriched uranium; while lower enrichment levels could be used, the minimum bomb size would rapidly become unfeasibly large as the level was decreased. However, the same plants and technology used to enrich uranium for power generation can be used to make the highly enriched uranium needed to build a bomb. In addition, the plutonium produced in power reactors, if separated from spent fuel through chemical reprocessing (much less technically challenging than isotopic separation), can be used for a bomb. While the plutonium resulting from normal reactor fueling cycles is less than ideal for weapons use because of the concentration of Pu-240, a usable weapon can be produced from it. If the reactor is operated on very short fueling cycles, bomb-grade plutonium can be produced. However, such operation would be virtually impossible to camouflage in many reactor designs, as the frequent shutdowns for refueling would be obvious, for instance in satellite photographs. Fast breeder reactors require reprocessing, generate more plutonium than they consume (and more than non-breeders), and can produce better than weapons-grade plutonium. New technology for breeder reactors, like SSTAR, may lessen the risk of nuclear proliferation by providing sealed reactors with a limited self-contained fuel supply that could be remotely shut down in case of tampering.

International Cooperation

Nuclear Non-Proliferation Treaty

At present, 189 countries are States Parties to the *Treaty on the Nonproliferation of Nuclear Weapons*, more commonly known as the

Nuclear Nonproliferation Treaty or NPT. These include the five Nuclear Weapons States (NWS) recognized by the NPT: the People's Republic of China, France, Russian Federation, the UK, and the United States.

Notable non-signatories to the NPT are Israel, Pakistan, and India (the latter two have since tested nuclear weapons, while Israel is considered by most to be an unacknowledged nuclear weapons state). North Korea was once a signatory but withdrew in January 2003. The legality of North Korea's withdrawal is debatable but as of 9 October 2006, North Korea clearly possesses the capability to make a nuclear explosive device.

International Atomic Energy Agency

The IAEA was established on 29 July 1957 to help nations develop nuclear energy for peaceful purposes. Allied to this role is the administration of safeguards arrangements to provide assurance to the international community that individual countries are honouring their commitments under the treaty. Though established under its own international treaty, the IAEA reports to both the United Nations General Assembly and the Security Council.

The IAEA regularly inspects civil nuclear facilities to verify the accuracy of documentation supplied to it. The agency checks inventories, and samples and analyses materials. Safeguards are designed to deter diversion of nuclear material by increasing the risk of early detection. They are complemented by controls on the export of sensitive technology from countries such as UK and United States through voluntary bodies such as the Nuclear Suppliers Group. The main concern of the IAEA is that uranium not be enriched beyond what is necessary for commercial civil plants, and that plutonium which is produced by nuclear reactors not be refined into a form that would be suitable for bomb production.

Scope of Safeguards

Traditional safeguards are arrangements to account for and control the use of nuclear materials. This verification is a key element in the international system which ensures that uranium in particular is used only for peaceful purposes.

Parties to the NPT agree to accept technical safeguard measures applied by the IAEA. These require that operators of nuclear facilities maintain and declare detailed accounting records of all movements and transactions involving nuclear material. Over 550 facilities and several hundred other locations are subject to regular inspection, and their records and the nuclear material being audited. Inspections by the IAEA are complemented by other measures such as surveillance cameras and instrumentation.

The inspections act as an alert system providing a warning of the possible diversion of nuclear material from peaceful activities. The system relies on;

1. Material Accountancy-tracking all inward and outward transfers and the flow of materials in any nuclear facility. This includes sampling and analysis of nuclear material, on-site inspections, and review and verification of operating records.
2. Physical Security-restricting access to nuclear materials at the site.
3. Containment and Surveillance-use of seals, automatic cameras and other instruments to detect unreported movement or tampering with nuclear materials, as well as spot checks on-site.

All NPT non-weapons states must accept these full-scope safeguards. In the five weapons states plus the non-NPT states (India, Pakistan and Israel), facility-specific safeguards apply. IAEA inspectors regularly visit these facilities to verify completeness and accuracy of records.

The terms of the NPT cannot be enforced by the IAEA itself, nor can nations be forced to sign the treaty. In reality, as shown in Iraq and North Korea, safeguards can be backed up by diplomatic, political and economic measures.

While traditional safeguards easily verified the correctness of formal declarations by suspect states, in the 1990s attention turned to what might not have been declared. While accepting safeguards at declared facilities, Iraq had set up elaborate equipment elsewhere in an attempt to enrich uranium to weapons grade. North Korea attempted to use research reactors (not commercial electricity-generating reactors) and a reprocessing plant to produce some weapons-grade plutonium. The weakness of the NPT regime lay in the fact that no obvious diversion of material was involved. The uranium used as fuel probably came from indigenous sources, and the nuclear facilities were built by the countries themselves without being declared or placed under safeguards. Iraq, as an NPT party, was obliged to declare all facilities but did not do so. Nevertheless, the activities were detected and brought under control using international diplomacy. In Iraq, a military defeat assisted this process. In North Korea, the activities concerned took place before the conclusion of its NPT safeguards agreement. With North Korea, the promised provision of commercial power reactors appeared to resolve the situation for a time, but it later withdrew from the NPT and declared it had nuclear weapons.

Additional Protocol

In 1993 a program was initiated to strengthen and extend the classical safeguards system, and a model protocol was agreed by the IAEA Board of Governors 1997. The measures boosted the IAEA's ability to detect undeclared nuclear activities, including those with no connection to the civil fuel cycle.

Innovations were of two kinds. Some could be implemented on the basis of IAEA's existing legal authority through safeguards agreements and inspections. Others required further legal authority to be conferred through an Additional Protocol. This must be agreed by each non-weapons state with IAEA, as a supplement to any existing comprehensive safeguards agreement. Weapons states have agreed to accept the principles of the model additional protocol.

Key elements of the model Additional Protocol:

- The IAEA is to be given considerably more information on nuclear and nuclear-related activities, including R & D, production of uranium and thorium (regardless of whether it is traded), and nuclear-related imports and exports.
- IAEA inspectors will have greater rights of access. This will include any suspect location, it can be at short notice (e.g., two hours), and the IAEA can deploy environmental sampling and remote monitoring techniques to detect illicit activities.

- States must streamline administrative procedures so that IAEA inspectors get automatic visa renewal and can communicate more readily with IAEA headquarters.
- Further evolution of safeguards is towards evaluation of each state, taking account of its particular situation and the kind of nuclear materials it has. This will involve greater judgement on the part of IAEA and the development of effective methodologies which reassure NPT States.

As of 9 October 2008, 127 countries have signed Additional protocols, and 88 have brought them into force. The IAEA is also applying the measures of the Additional Protocol in Taiwan. Among the leading countries that have not signed the Additional Protocol are Egypt, which says it will not sign until Israel accepts comprehensive IAEA safeguards, and Brazil, which opposes making the protocol a requirement for international cooperation on enrichment and reprocessing, but has not ruled out signing.

Limitations of Safeguards

The greatest risk from nuclear weapons proliferation comes from countries which have not joined the NPT and which have significant unsafeguarded nuclear activities; India, Pakistan, and Israel fall within this category. While safeguards apply to some of their activities, others remain beyond scrutiny.

A further concern is that countries may develop various sensitive nuclear fuel cycle facilities and research reactors under full safeguards and then subsequently opt out of the NPT. Bilateral agreements, such as insisted upon by Australia and Canada for sale of uranium, address this by including fallback provisions, but many countries are outside the scope of these agreements. If a nuclear-capable country does leave the NPT, it is likely to be reported by the IAEA to the UN Security Council, just as if it were in breach of its safeguards agreement. Trade sanctions would then be likely.

IAEA safeguards, together with bilateral safeguards applied under the NPT can, and do, ensure that uranium supplied by countries such as Australia and Canada does not contribute to nuclear weapons proliferation. In fact, the worldwide application of those safeguards and the substantial world trade in uranium for nuclear electricity make the proliferation of nuclear weapons much less likely.

The Additional Protocol, once it is widely in force, will provide credible assurance that there are no undeclared nuclear materials or activities in the states concerned. This will be a major step forward in preventing nuclear proliferation.

Other Developments

The Nuclear Suppliers Group communicated its guidelines, essentially a set of export rules, to the IAEA in 1978. These were to ensure that transfers of nuclear material or equipment would not be diverted to unsafeguarded nuclear fuel cycle or nuclear explosive activities, and formal government assurances to this effect were required from recipients. The Guidelines also recognised the need for physical protection measures in the transfer of sensitive facilities, technology and weapons-usable materials, and strengthened retransfer provisions. The group began with seven members – the United States, the former USSR, the UK, France, Germany, Canada and Japan – but now includes 46 countries including all five nuclear weapons states.

According to Kenneth D. Bergeron's *Tritium on Ice: The Dangerous New Alliance of Nuclear Weapons and Nuclear Power*, tritium is not classified as a 'special nuclear material' but rather as a 'by-product'. It is seen as an important litmus test on the seriousness of the United States' intention to nuclear disarm. This radioactive super-heavy hydrogen isotope is used to boost the efficiency of fissile materials in nuclear weapons. The United States resumed tritium production in 2003 for the first time in 15 years. This could indicate that there is a potential nuclear arm stockpile replacement since the isotope naturally decays.

In May 1995, NPT parties reaffirmed their commitment to a Fissile Materials Cut-off Treaty to prohibit the production of any further fissile material for weapons. This aims to complement the Comprehensive Test Ban Treaty of 1996 and to codify commitments made by the United States, the UK, France and Russia to cease production of weapons material, as well as putting a similar ban on China. This treaty will also put more pressure on Israel, India and Pakistan to agree to international verification.

On 9 August 2005, Ayatollah Ali Khamenei issued a fatwa forbidding the production, stockpiling and use of nuclear weapons. Khamenei's official statement was made at the meeting of the International Atomic Energy Agency (IAEA) in Vienna. As of February 2006 Iran formally announced that uranium enrichment within their borders has continued. Iran claims it is for peaceful purposes but the United Kingdom, France, Germany, and the United States claim the purpose is for nuclear weapons research and construction.

Unsanctioned Nuclear Activity

Non-signatory States

India, Pakistan and Israel have been "threshold" countries in terms of the international non-proliferation regime. They possess or are quickly capable of assembling one or more nuclear weapons. They have remained outside the 1970 NPT. They are thus largely excluded from trade in nuclear plant or materials, except for safety-related devices for a few safeguarded facilities. In May 1998 India and Pakistan each exploded several nuclear devices underground. This heightened concerns regarding an arms race between them, with Pakistan involving the People's Republic of China, an acknowledged nuclear weapons state. Both countries are opposed to the NPT as it stands, and India has consistently attacked the Treaty since its inception in 1970 labeling it as a lopsided treaty in favour of the nuclear powers.

Relations between the two countries are tense and hostile, and the risks of nuclear conflict between them have long been considered quite high. Kashmir is a prime cause of bilateral tension, its sovereignty being in dispute since 1948. There is persistent low level military conflict due to Pakistan backing an insurgency there and the disputed status of Kashmir. Both engaged in a conventional arms race in the 1980s, including sophisticated technology and equipment capable of delivering nuclear weapons. In the 1990s the arms race quickened. In 1994 India reversed a four-year trend of reduced allocations for defence, and despite its much smaller economy, Pakistan was expected to push its own expenditures yet higher. Both have lost their patrons: India, the former USSR, and Pakistan, the United States.

But it is the growth and modernization of China's nuclear arsenal and its assistance with Pakistan's nuclear power programme and, reportedly, with missile technology, which exacerbate Indian concerns. In particular, Pakistan is aided by China's People's Liberation Army, which operates somewhat autonomously within that country as an exporter of military material.

India

Nuclear power for civil use is well established in India. Its civil nuclear strategy has been directed towards complete independence in the nuclear fuel cycle, necessary because of its outspoken rejection of the NPT. This self-sufficiency extends from uranium exploration and mining through fuel fabrication, heavy water production, reactor design and construction, to reprocessing and waste management. It has a small fast breeder reactor and is planning a much larger one. It is also developing technology to utilise its abundant resources of thorium as a nuclear fuel. India has 14 small nuclear power reactors in commercial operation, two larger ones under construction, and ten more planned. The 14 operating ones (2548 MWe total) comprise:

- two 150 MWe BWRs from the United States, which started up in 1969, now use locally-enriched uranium and are under safeguards,
- two small Canadian PHWRs (1972 & 1980), also under safeguards, and
- ten local PHWRs based on Canadian designs, two of 150 and eight 200 MWe.
- two new 540 MWe and two 700 MWe plants at tarapore (known as TAPP :Tarapore Atomic Power Project)

The two under construction and two of the planned ones are 450 MWe versions of these 200 MWe domestic products. Construction has been seriously delayed by financial and technical problems. In 2001 a final agreement was signed with Russia for the country's first large nuclear power plant, comprising two VVER-1000 reactors, under a Russian-financed US$3 billion contract. The first unit is due to be commissioned in 2007. A further two Russian units are under consideration for the site. Nuclear power supplied 3.1% of India's electricity in 2000 and this was expected to reach

10% by 2005. Its industry is largely without IAEA safeguards, though a few plants are under facility-specific safeguards. As a result India's nuclear power programme proceeds largely without fuel or technological assistance from other countries.

Its weapons material appears to come from a Canadian-designed 40MW "research" reactor which started up in 1960, well before the NPT, and a 100MW indigenous unit in operation since 1985. Both use local uranium, as India does not import any nuclear fuel. It is estimated that India may have built up enough weapons-grade plutonium for a hundred nuclear warheads.

It is widely believed that the nuclear programs of India and Pakistan used CANDU reactors to produce fissionable materials for their weapons; however, this is not accurate. Both Canada (by supplying the 40 MW research reactor) and the United States (by supplying 21 tons of heavy water) supplied India with the technology necessary to create a nuclear weapons program, dubbed CIRUS (Canada-India Reactor, United States). Canada sold India the reactor on the condition that the reactor and any by-products would be "employed for peaceful purposes only.". Similarly, the United States sold India heavy water for use in the reactor "only... in connection with research into and the use of atomic energy for peaceful purposes". India, in violation of these agreements, used the Canadian-supplied reactor and American-supplied heavy water to produce plutonium for their first nuclear explosion, Smiling Buddha. The Indian government controversially justified this, however, by claiming that Smiling Buddha was a "peaceful nuclear explosion."

The country has at least three other research reactors including the tiny one which is exploring the use of thorium as a nuclear fuel, by breeding fissile U-233. In addition, an advanced heavy-water thorium cycle is under development. India exploded a nuclear device in 1974, the so-called Smiling Buddha test, which it has consistently claimed was for peaceful purposes. Others saw it as a response to China's nuclear weapons capability. It was then universally perceived, notwithstanding official denials, to possess, or to be able to quickly assemble, nuclear weapons. In 1997 it deployed its own medium-range missile and is now developing a long-range missile capable of reaching targets in China's industrial heartland. In 1995 the United States quietly intervened to head off a proposed nuclear test. However, in 1998 there were five more tests in Operation Shakti. These were unambiguously military, including one claimed to be of a sophisticated thermonuclear device, and their declared purpose was "to help in the design of nuclear weapons of different yields and different delivery systems".

Indian security policies are driven by:

- its determination to be recognized as a dominant power in the region
- its increasing concern with China's expanding nuclear weapons and missile delivery programmes
- its concern with Pakistan's capability to deliver nuclear weapons deep into India

It perceives nuclear weapons as a cost-effective political counter to China's nuclear and conventional weaponry, and the effects of its nuclear weapons policy in provoking Pakistan is, by some accounts, considered incidental. India has had an unhappy relationship with China. After an uneasy ceasefire ended the 1962 war, relations between the two nations were frozen until 1998. Since then a degree of high-level contact has been established and a few elementary confidence-building measures put in place. China still occupies some territory which it captured during the aforementioned war, claimed by India, and India still occupies some territory claimed by China. Its nuclear weapon and missile support for Pakistan is a major bone of contention.

American President George W. Bush met with India Prime Minister Manmohan Singh to discuss India's involvement with nuclear weapons. The two countries agreed that the United States would give nuclear power assistance to India.

Pakistan

Pakistan is believed to have produced the material for its weapons using Chinese help.

In Pakistan, nuclear power supplies only 1.7% of the country's electricity. It has one small (125 MWe) Canadian PHWR nuclear power reactor from 1971 which is under international safeguards, and a 300 MWe PWR supplied by China under safeguards, which started up in May 2000. A third one, a Chinese PWR, is planned.

Enriched fuel for the PWRs will be imported from China. It also has a 9 MW research reactor of 1965 vintage, and there are persistent reports of another "multipurpose" reactor, a 50 MW PHWR near Khushab, which is presumed to have potential for producing weapons plutonium.

Pakistan's concentration is on weapons technology, particularly the production of highly enriched uranium suitable for nuclear weapons, utilising indigenous uranium. It has at least one small centrifuge enrichment plant. In 1990 the U.S. Administration cut off aid because it was unable to certify that Pakistan was not pursuing a policy of manufacturing nuclear weapons. This was relaxed late in 2001. In 1996 the United States froze export loans to China because it was allegedly supplying centrifuge enrichment technology to Pakistan. Indian opinion is in no doubt about Pakistan's nuclear weapons capability. Pakistan has made it clear since early 1996 that it had done the basic development work, and that if India staged a nuclear test, Pakistan would immediately start assembling its own nuclear explosive device. It is assumed to now have enough highly-enriched uranium for up to forty nuclear warheads.

In April 1998 Pakistan test fired a long-range missile capable of reaching Madras in southern India, pushing home the point by naming it after a 12th century Muslim conqueror. This development removed India's main military advantage over Pakistan. Pakistan's securitv concerns derive from India's possession of a nuclear weapons capability. In May 1998 Pakistan announced that they had conducted six underground tests in the Chagai Hills, five on the 28th and one on the 30th of that month. Seismic events consistent with these claims were recorded.

Pakistan-North Korea Nuclear Proliferation and Missile Cooperation

Pakistan and North Korea's efforts to acquire nuclear weapons have had some similarities. Both countries first attempted the plutonium route to acquire such weapons and, when this was thwarted, turned towards uranium enrichment.

Pakistan

In the 1970s, Pakistan first focused on the plutonium route.

They expected to obtain the fissile material from a reprocessing plant provided by France. This plan failed due to U.S. intervention. Pakistan, not wanting to give up, redoubled its efforts to obtain uranium enrichment technology. The main efforts towards this direction were done under Dr. Abdul Qadeer Khan. Dr. Khan had earlier worked with Fysisch Dynamisch Onderzoekslaboratorium (FDO). FDO was a subsidiary of the Dutch firm VMF-Stork based in Amsterdam. From 1972 to 1975 Dr. Khan had access to classified data used to enrich ordinary uranium to weapons grade concentrations. FDO was working on the development of ultra high-speed centrifuges for URENCO.

In 1974 while he was on secondment for 17 days as a translator to the URENCO plant in Almelo, he obtained photographs and documents of the plant. Dr. Khan returned to Pakistan in 1976 and initiated the Uranium enrichment program on the basis of the technology he had stolen from his previous employer. Dr. Khan relied on nuclear technology supplied by American, Canadian, Swiss, German, Dutch, British, Japanese and Russian companies. Dr. Khan said of the assistance he got from the Japanese, "Next month the Japanese would come here and all the work would be done under their supervision." After the British Government stopped the British subsidiary of the American Emerson Electric Co from shipping the nuclear technology to Pakistan, Dr. Khan describes his frustration with a supplier from Germany as "That man from the German team was unethical. When he did not get the order from us, he wrote a letter to a Labour Party member and questions were asked in [British] Parliament."

His efforts made Dr. Khan into a national hero. In 1981, as a tribute, the president of Pakistan, General Muhammad Zia-ul-Haq, renamed the enrichment plant the A. Q. Khan Research Laboratories.

In 2003, IAEA unearthed a nuclear black market with close ties to Pakistan. It was widely believed to have direct involvement of the government of Pakistan. This claim could not be verified due to the refusal of the government of Pakistan to allow IAEA to interview the alleged head of the nuclear black market, who happened to be no other than Dr. Khan. Dr. Khan later confessed to his crimes on national television, bailing out the government by taking full responsibility. He confessed to nuclear proliferation from Pakistan to Iran and North Korea. He was immediately given presidential immunity. Exact nature of the involvement at the governmental level is still unclear, but the manner in which the government acted cast doubt on the sincerity of Pakistan.

North Korea

North Korea joined the NPT in 1985 and had subsequently signed a safeguards agreement with the IAEA. However it was believed that North Korea was diverting plutonium extracted from the fuel of its reactor at Yongbyon, for use in nuclear weapons. The subsequent confrontation with IAEA on the issue of inspections and suspected violations, resulted in North Korea threatening to withdraw from the NPT in 1993. This led to negotiations with the United States resulting in the Agreed Framework of 1994, which provided for IAEA safeguards being applied to its reactors and spent fuel rods. These spent fuel rods were sealed in canisters by the United States to prevent North Korea from extracting plutonium from them. North Korea had to therefore freeze its plutonium programme.

During this period Pakistan-North Korea cooperation in missile technology transfer was being established. A high level Pakistani military delegation visited North Korea in August-September 1992, reportedly to discuss the supply of Scud missile technology to Pakistan. In 1993, PM Benazir Bhutto traveled to China and North Korea. The visits are believed to be related to the subsequent acquisition of Ghauri (North Korean No-dong) missiles by Pakistan. During the period 1992-1994, A.Q. Khan was reported to have visited North Korea thirteen times. The missile cooperation program with North Korea was under Dr. A. Q. Khan's Kahuta Research Laboratories. At this time China was under U.S. pressure not to supply the M series of missiles to Pakistan. This forced the latter (possibly with Chinese connivance) to approach North Korea for missile transfers. Reports indicate that North Korea was willing to supply missile sub-systems including rocket motors, inertial guidance systems, control and testing equipment of Scud SSMs for US$ 50 million.

It is not clear what North Korea got in return. Joseph S. Bermudez Jr. in *Jane's Defence Weekly* (27 November 2002) reports that Western analysts had begun to question what North Korea received in payment for the missiles; many suspected it was nuclear technology and components. Khan's KRL was in charge of both Pakistan's uranium enrichment program and also of the missile program with North Korea. It is therefore likely during this period that cooperation in nuclear technology between Pakistan and North Korea was initiated. Western intelligence agencies began to notice exchange of personnel, technology and components between KRL and entities of the North Korean 2nd Economic Committee (responsible for weapons production).

A *New York Times* report on 18 October 2002 quoted U.S. intelligence officials having stated that Pakistan was a major supplier of critical equipment to North Korea. The report added that equipment such as gas centrifuges appeared to have been "part of a barter deal" in which North Korea supplied Pakistan with missiles. Separate reports indicate (*Washington Times*, 22 November 2002) that U.S. intelligence had as early as 1999 picked up signs that North Korea was continuing to develop nuclear arms. Other reports also indicate that North Korea had been working covertly to develop an enrichment capability for nuclear weapons for at least five years and had used technology obtained from Pakistan (Washington Times, 18 October 2002).

Nuclear Arms Control in the Region

The public stance of the two states on non-proliferation differs markedly. Pakistan appears to have dominated a continuing propaganda debate. Pakistan has initiated a series of regional security proposals. It has repeatedly proposed a nuclear free zone in South Asia and has proclaimed its willingness to engage in nuclear disarmament and to sign the Non-Proliferation Treaty if India would do so. It has endorsed a United States proposal for a regional five power conference to consider non-proliferation in South Asia.

India has taken the view that solutions to regional security issues should be found at the international rather than the regional level, since its chief concern is with China. It therefore rejects Pakistan's proposals.

Instead, the 'Gandhi Plan', put forward in 1988, proposed the revision of the Non-Proliferation Treaty, which it regards as inherently discriminatory in favour of the nuclear-weapon States, and a timetable for complete nuclear weapons disarmament. It endorsed early proposals for a Comprehensive Test Ban Treaty and for an international convention to ban the production of highly enriched uranium and plutonium for weapons purposes, known as the 'cut-off' convention.

The United States for some years, especially under the Clinton administration, pursued a variety of initiatives to persuade India and Pakistan to abandon their nuclear weapons programs and to accept comprehensive international safeguards on all their nuclear activities. To this end, the Clinton administration proposed a conference of the five nuclear-weapon states, Japan, Germany, India and Pakistan. India refused this and similar previous proposals, and countered with demands that other potential weapons states, such as Iran and North Korea, should be invited, and that regional limitations would only be acceptable if they were accepted equally by China. The United States would not accept the participation of Iran and North Korea and these initiatives have lapsed.

Another, more recent approach, centres on 'capping' the production of fissile material for weapons purposes, which would hopefully be followed by 'roll back'. To this end, India and the United States jointly sponsored a UN General Assembly resolution in 1993 calling for negotiations for a 'cut-off' convention. Should India and Pakistan join such a convention, they would have to agree to halt the production of fissile materials for weapons and to accept international verification on their relevant nuclear facilities (enrichment and reprocessing plants). It appears that India is now prepared to join negotiations regarding such a Cut-off Treaty, under the UN Conference on Disarmament.

Bilateral confidence-building measures between India and Pakistan to reduce the prospects of confrontation have been limited. In 1990 each side ratified a treaty not to attack the other's nuclear installations, and at the end of 1991 they provided one another with a list showing the location of all their nuclear plants, even though the respective lists were regarded as not being wholly accurate. Early in 1994 India proposed a bilateral agreement for a 'no first use' of nuclear weapons and an extension of the 'no attack' treaty to cover civilian and industrial targets as well as nuclear installations.

Having promoted the Comprehensive Test Ban Treaty since 1954, India dropped its support in 1995 and in 1996 attempted to block the Treaty. Following the 1998 tests the question has been reopened and both Pakistan and India have indicated their intention to sign the CTBT. Indian ratification may be conditional upon the five weapons states agreeing to specific reductions in nuclear arsenals. The UN Conference on Disarmament has also called upon both countries "to accede without delay to the Non-Proliferation Treaty", presumably as non-weapons states.

Israel

Israel is also thought to possess an arsenal of potentially up to several hundred nuclear warheads and associated delivery systems, but this has never been openly confirmed or denied. An Israeli nuclear installation is located about ten kilometers to the south of Dimona, the Negev Nuclear Research Center. Its construction commenced in 1958, with French assistance. The official reason given by the Israeli and French governments was to build a nuclear reactor to power a "desalination plant", in order to "green the Negev". The purpose of the Dimona plant is widely assumed to be the manufacturing of nuclear weapons, and the majority of defence experts have concluded that it does in fact do that. However, the Israeli government refuses to confirm or deny this publicly, a policy it refers to as "ambiguity".

Norway sold 20 tonnes of heavy water needed for the reactor to Israel in 1959 and 1960 in a secret deal. There were no "safeguards" required in this deal to prevent usage of the heavy water for non-peaceful purposes. The British newspaper *Daily Express* accused Israel of working on a bomb in 1960. When the United States intelligence community discovered the purpose of the Dimona plant in the early 1960s, it demanded that Israel agree to international inspections. Israel agreed, but on a condition that U.S., rather than IAEA, inspectors were used, and that Israel would receive advanced notice of all inspections.

Some claim that because Israel knew the schedule of the inspectors' visits, it was able to hide the alleged purpose of the site from the inspectors by installing temporary false walls and other devices before each inspection. The inspectors eventually informed the U.S. government that their inspections were useless due to Israeli restrictions on what areas of the facility they could inspect. In 1969, the United States terminated the inspections. In 1986, Mordechai Vanunu, a former technician at the Dimona plant, revealed to the media some evidence of Israel's nuclear program. Israeli agents arrested him from Italy, drugged him and transported him to Israel, and an Israeli court then tried him in secret on charges of treason and espionage, and sentenced him to eighteen years imprisonment. He was freed on 21 April 2004, but was severely limited by the Israeli government. He was arrested again on 11 November 2004, though formal charges were not immediately filed.

Comments on photographs taken by Mordechai Vanunu inside the Negev Nuclear Research Center have been made by prominent scientists. British nuclear weapons scientist Frank Barnaby, who questioned Vanunu over several days, estimated Israel had enough plutonium for about 150 weapons. Ted Taylor, a bomb designer employed by the United States of America has confirmed the several hundred warhead estimate based on Vanunu's photographs.

Signatory States

Egypt

In 2004 and 2005, Egypt disclosed past undeclared nuclear activities and material to the IAEA. In 2007 and 2008, high enriched and low enriched uranium particles were found in environmental samples taken in Egypt. In 2008, the IAEA states Egypt's statements were consistent with its own findings. In May 2009, *Reuters* reported that the IAEA was conducting further investigation in Egypt.

Iran

In 2003, the IAEA reported that Iran had been in breach of its obligations to comply with provisions of its safeguard agreement. In 2005, the IAEA Board of Governors voted in a rare non-consensus decision to find Iran in non-compliance with its NPT Safeguards Agreement and to report that non-compliance to the UN Security Council, In response, the UN Security Council passed a series of resolutions in response to concerns about the program. Iran's representative to the UN argues sanctions compel Iran to abandon its rights under the Nuclear Nonproliferation Treaty to peaceful nuclear technology. Iran says its uranium enrichment program is exclusively for peaceful purposes and has enriched uranium to "less than 5 percent," consistent with fuel for a nuclear power plant and significantly below the purity of WEU (around 90%) typically used in a weapons program. The director general of the International Atomic Energy Agency, Yukiya Amano, said in 2009 he had not seen any evidence in IAEA official documents that Iran was developing nuclear weapons.

Iraq

Up to the late 1980s it was generally assumed that any undeclared nuclear activities would have to be based on the diversion of nuclear material from safeguards. States acknowledged the possibility of nuclear activities entirely separate from those covered by safeguards, but it was assumed they would be detected by national intelligence activities. There was no particular effort by IAEA to attempt to detect them.

Iraq had been making efforts to secure a nuclear potential since the 1960s. In the late 1970s a specialised plant, Osiraq, was constructed near Baghdad. The plant was attacked during the Iran–Iraq War and was destroyed by Israeli bombers in June 1981. Not until the 1990 NPT Review Conference did some states raise the possibility of making more use of (for example) provisions for "special inspections" in existing NPT Safeguards Agreements. Special inspections can be undertaken at locations other than those where safeguards routinely apply, if there is reason to believe there may be undeclared material or activities.

After inspections in Iraq following the UN Gulf War cease-fire resolution showed the extent of Iraq's clandestine nuclear weapons program, it became clear that the IAEA would have to broaden the scope of its activities. Iraq was an NPT Party, and had thus agreed to place all its nuclear material under IAEA safeguards. But the inspections revealed that it had been pursuing an extensive clandestine uranium enrichment programme, as well as a nuclear weapons design programme. The main thrust of Iraq's uranium enrichment program was the development of technology for electromagnetic isotope separation (EMIS) of indigenous uranium. This uses the same principles as a mass spectrometer (albeit on a much larger scale). Ions of uranium-238 and uranium-235 are separated because they describe arcs of different radii when they move through a magnetic field. This process was used in the Manhattan Project to make the highly enriched uranium used in the Hiroshima bomb, but was abandoned soon afterwards. The Iraqis did the basic research work at their nuclear research establishment at Tuwaitha, near Baghdad, and were building two full-scale facilities at Tarmiya and Ash Sharqat, north of Baghdad. However, when the war broke out, only a few separators had been installed at Tarmiya, and none at Ash Sharqat.

The Iraqis were also very interested in centrifuge enrichment, and had been able to acquire some components including some carbon-fibre rotors, which they were at an early stage of testing.

They were clearly in violation of their NPT and safeguards obligations, and the IAEA Board of Governors ruled to that effect. The UN Security Council then ordered the IAEA to remove, destroy or render harmless Iraq's nuclear weapons capability. This was done by mid 1998, but Iraq then ceased all cooperation with the UN, so the IAEA withdrew from this work. The revelations from Iraq provided the impetus for a very far-reaching reconsideration of what safeguards are intended to achieve.

Myanmar

A report in the *Sydney Morning Herald* and *Searchina*, a Japanese newspaper, report that two Myanmarese defectors saying that the Myanmar junta was secretly building a nuclear reactor and plutonium extraction facility with North Korea's help, with the aim of acquiring its first nuclear bomb in five years. According to the report, "The secret complex, much of it in caves tunnelled into a mountain at Naung Laing in northern Burma, runs parallel to a civilian reactor being built at another site by Russia that both the Russians and Burmese say will be put under international safeguards." In 2002, Myanmar had notified IAEA of its intention to pursue a civilian nuclear programme. Later, Russia announced that it would build a nuclear reactor in Myanmar.

There have also been reports that two Pakistani scientists, from the AQ Khan stable, had been dispatched to Myanmar where they had settled down, to help Myanmar's project. Recently, the David Albright-led Institute for Science and International Security rang alarm bells about Myanmar attempting a nuclear project with North Korean help. If true, the full weight of international pressure will be brought against Myanmar, said officials familiar with developments. But equally, the information that has been peddled by the defectors is also "preliminary" and could be used by the west to turn the screws on Myanmar—on democracy and human rights issues—in the run-up to the elections in the country in 2010. During an ASEAN meeting in Thailand in July 2009, US secretary of state Hillary Clinton highlighted concerns of the North Korean link. "We know there are also growing concerns about military cooperation between North Korea and Burma which we take very seriously," Clinton said.

North Korea

The Democratic People's Republic of Korea (DPRK) acceded to the NPT in 1985 as a condition for the supply of a nuclear power station by the USSR. However, it delayed concluding its NPT Safeguards Agreement with the IAEA, a process which should take only 18 months, until April 1992.

During that period, it brought into operation a small gas-cooled, graphite-moderated, natural-uranium (metal) fuelled "Experimental Power Reactor" of about 25 MWt (5 MWe), based on the UK Magnox design. While this was a well-suited design to start a wholly indigenous nuclear reactor development, it also exhibited all the features of a small plutonium production reactor for weapons purposes. North Korea also made substantial progress in the construction of two larger reactors designed on the same principles, a prototype of about 200 MWt (50 MWe), and a full-scale version of about 800 MWt (200 MWe). They made only slow progress; construction halted on both in 1994 and has not resumed. Both reactors have degraded considerably since that time and would take significant efforts to refurbish.

In addition it completed and commissioned a reprocessing plant that makes the Magnox spent nuclear fuel safe, recovering uranium and plutonium. That plutonium, if the fuel was only irradiated to a very low burn-up, would have been in a form very suitable for weapons. Although all these facilities at Yongbyon were to be under safeguards, there was always the risk that at some stage, the DPRK would withdraw from the NPT and use the plutonium for weapons. One of the first steps in applying NPT safeguards is for the IAEA to verify the initial stocks of uranium and plutonium to ensure that all the nuclear materials in the country have been declared for safeguards purposes. While undertaking this work in 1992, IAEA inspectors found discrepancies which indicated that the reprocessing plant had been used more often than the DPRK had declared, which suggested that the DPRK could have weapons-grade plutonium which it had not declared to the IAEA. Information passed to the IAEA by a Member State (as required by the IAEA) supported that suggestion by indicating that the DPRK had two undeclared waste or other storage sites.

In February 1993 the IAEA called on the DPRK to allow special inspections of the two sites so that the initial stocks of nuclear material could be verified. The DPRK refused, and on 12 March announced its intention to withdraw from the NPT (three months' notice is required). In April 1993 the IAEA Board concluded that the DPRK was in non-compliance with its safeguards obligations and reported the matter to the UN Security Council. In June 1993 the DPRK announced that it had "suspended" its withdrawal from the NPT, but subsequently claimed a "special status" with respect to its safeguards obligations. This was rejected by IAEA.

Once the DPRK's non-compliance had been reported to the UN Security Council, the essential part of the IAEA's mission had been completed. Inspections in the DPRK continued, although inspectors were increasingly hampered in what they were permitted to do by the DPRK's claim of a "special status". However, some 8,000 corroding fuel rods associated with the experimental reactor have remained under close surveillance.

Following bilateral negotiations between the United States and the DPRK, and the conclusion of the Agreed Framework in October 1994, the IAEA has been given additional responsibilities. The agreement requires a freeze on the operation and construction of the DPRK's plutonium production reactors and their related facilities, and the IAEA is responsible for monitoring the freeze until the facilities are eventually dismantled. The DPRK remains uncooperative with the IAEA verification work and has yet to comply with its safeguards agreement. While Iraq was defeated in a war, allowing the UN the opportunity to seek out and destroy its nuclear weapons programme as part of the cease-fire conditions, the DPRK was not defeated, nor was it vulnerable to other measures, such as trade sanctions. It can scarcely afford to import anything, and sanctions on vital commodities, such as oil, would either be ineffective or risk provoking war.

Ultimately, the DPRK was persuaded to stop what appeared to be its nuclear weapons programme in exchange, under the agreed framework, for about US$5 billion in energy-related assistance. This included two 1000 MWe light water nuclear power reactors based on an advanced U.S. System-80 design.

In January 2003 the DPRK withdrew from the NPT. In response, a series of discussions among the DPRK, the United States, and China, a series of six-party talks (the parties being the DPRK, the ROK, China, Japan, the United States and Russia) were held in Beijing; the first beginning in April 2004 concerning North Korea's weapons program. On 10 January 2005, North Korea declared that it was in the possession of nuclear weapons. On 19 September 2005, the fourth round of the Six-Party Talks ended with a joint statement in which North Korea agreed to end its nuclear programs and return to the NPT in exchange for diplomatic, energy and economic assistance. However, by the end of 2005 the DPRK had halted all six-party talks because the United States froze certain DPRK international financial assets such as those in a bank in Macau.

On 9 October 2006, North Korea announced that it has performed its first-ever nuclear weapon test. On 18 December 2006, the six-party talks finally resumed. On 13 February 2007, the parties announced "Initial Actions" to implement the 2005 joint statement including shutdown and disablement of North Korean nuclear facilities in exchange for energy assistance. Reacting to UN sanctions imposed after missile tests in April 2009, North Korea withdrew from the six-party talks, restarted its nuclear facilities and conducted a second nuclear test on 25 May 2009.

Russia

Security of nuclear weapons in Russia remains a matter of concern. According to high-ranking Russian SVR defector

Tretyakov, he had a meeting with two Russian businessman representing a state-created *Chetek* corporation in 1991. They came up with a project of destroying large quantities of chemical wastes collected from Western countries at the island of Novaya Zemlya (a test place for Soviet nuclear weapons) using an underground nuclear blast. The project was rejected by Canadian representatives, but one of the businessmen told Tretyakov that he keeps his own nuclear bomb at his dacha outside Moscow. Tretyakov thought that man was insane, but the "businessmen" (Vladimir K. Dmitriev) replied: "Do not be so naive. With economic conditions the way they are in Russia today, anyone with enough money can buy a nuclear bomb. It's no big deal really".

South Africa

In 1991, South Africa acceded to the NPT, concluded a comprehensive safeguards agreement with the IAEA, and submitted a report on its nuclear material subject to safeguards. At the time, the state had a nuclear power programme producing nearly 10% of the country's electricity, whereas Iraq and North Korea only had research reactors.

The IAEA's initial verification task was complicated by South Africa's announcement that between 1979 and 1989 it built and then dismantled a number of nuclear weapons. South Africa asked the IAEA to verify the conclusion of its weapons programme. In 1995 the IAEA declared that it was satisfied all materials were accounted for and the weapons programme had been terminated and dismantled. South Africa has signed the NPT, and now holds the distinction of being the only known state to have indigenously produced nuclear weapons, and then verifiably dismantled them.

Syria

On September 6, 2007, Israel bombed an officially unidentified site in Syria which it later asserted was a nuclear reactor under construction. The alleged reactor was not asserted to be operational and it was not asserted that nuclear material had been introduced into it. Syria said the site was a military site and was not involved in any nuclear activities. The IAEA requested Syria to provide further access to the site and any other locations where the debris and equipment from the building had been stored. Syria denounced what it called the Western "fabrication and forging of facts" in regards to the incident. IAEA Director General Mohamed ElBaradei criticized the strikes and deplored that information regarding the matter had not been shared with his agency earlier.

United States Cooperation on Nuclear Weapons with the United Kingdom

The United States has given the UK considerable assistance with nuclear weapon design and construction since the 1958 US-UK Mutual Defence Agreement. In 1974 a CIA proliferation assessment noted that "In many cases [Britain's sensitive technology in nuclear and missile fields] is based on technology received from the United States and could not legitimately be passed on without U.S. permission."

The U.S. President authorized the transfer of "nuclear weapon parts" to the UK between at least the years 1975 to 1996. The UK National Audit Office noted that most of the UK Trident warhead development and production expenditure was incurred in the United States, which would supply "certain warhead-related components". Some of the fissile materials for the UK Trident warhead were purchased from the United States. Declassified U.S. Department of Energy documents indicate the UK Trident warhead system was involved in non-nuclear design activities alongside the U.S. W76 nuclear warhead fitted in some U.S. Navy Trident missiles, leading the Federation of American Scientists to speculate that the UK warhead may share design information from the W76.

Under the Mutual Defence Agreement 5.37 tonnes of UK-produced plutonium was sent to the United States in return for 6.7 kg of tritium and 7.5 tonnes of highly enriched uranium over the period 1960-1979. A further 0.47 tonne of plutonium was swapped between the UK and United States for reasons that remain classified. Some of the UK produced plutonium was used in 1962 by the United States for a nuclear weapon test of reactor-grade plutonium.

The United States has supplied nuclear weapon delivery systems to support the UK nuclear forces since before the signing of the NPT. The renewal of this agreement is due to take place through the second decade of the 21st century.

Arguments in Favour of Proliferation

There has been much debate in the academic study of International Security as to the advisability of proliferation. In the late 1950s and early 1960s, Gen. Pierre Marie Gallois of France, an adviser to Charles DeGaulle, argued in books like *The Balance of Terror: Strategy for the Nuclear Age* (1961) that mere possession of a nuclear arsenal, what the French called the *force de frappe*, was enough to ensure deterrence, and thus concluded that the spread of nuclear weapons could increase international stability.

Some very prominent neo-realist scholars, such as Kenneth Waltz, Emeritus Professor of Political Science at UC Berkeley and Adjunct Senior Research Scholar at Columbia University, and John Mearsheimer, R. Wendell Harrison Distinguished Service Professor of Political Science at the University of Chicago, continue to argue along the lines of Gallois (though these scholars rarely acknowledge their intellectual debt to Gallois and his contemporaries). Specifically, these scholars advocate some forms of nuclear proliferation, arguing that it will decrease the likelihood of war, especially in troubled regions of the world. Aside from the majority opinion which opposes proliferation in any form, there are two schools of thought on the matter: those, like Mearsheimer, who favour selective proliferation, and those such as Waltz, who advocate a laissez-faire attitude to programs like North Korea's.

Total Proliferation

In embryo, Waltz argues that the logic of mutually assured destruction (MAD) should work in all security environments, regardless of historical tensions or recent hostility. He sees the Cold War as the ultimate proof of MAD logic – the only occasion when enmity between two Great Powers did not result in military conflict. This was, he argues, because nuclear weapons promote caution in decision-makers. Neither Washington nor Moscow would risk nuclear Armageddon to advance territorial or power goals, hence a peaceful stalemate ensued (Waltz and Sagan (2003)). Waltz believes there to be no reason why this effect would not occur in all circumstances.

Selective Proliferation

John Mearsheimer would not support Waltz's optimism in the

majority of potential instances; however, he has argued for nuclear proliferation as policy in certain places, such as post-Cold War Europe. In two famous articles, Professor Mearsheimer opines that Europe is bound to return to its pre-Cold War environment of regular conflagration and suspicion at some point in the future. He advocates arming both Germany and the Ukraine with nuclear weaponry in order to achieve a balance of power between these states in the east and France/Britain in the west. If this does not occur, he is certain that war will eventually break out on the European continent.

Another separate argument against Waltz's open proliferation and in favour of Mearsheimer's selective distribution is the possibility of nuclear terrorism. Some countries included in the aforementioned laissez-faire distribution could predispose the transfer of nuclear materials or a bomb falling into the hands of groups not affiliated with any governments. Such countries would not have the political will or ability to safeguard attempts at devices being transferred to a third party. Not being deterred by self-annihilation, terrorism groups could push forth their own nuclear agendas or be used as shadow fronts to carry out the attack plans by mentioned unstable governments.

Arguments against both Positions

There are numerous arguments presented against both selective and total proliferation, generally targeting the very neorealist assumptions (such as the primacy of military security in state agendas, the weakness of international institutions, and the long-run unimportance of economic integration and globalization to state strategy) its proponents tend to make. With respect to Mearsheimer's specific example of Europe, many economists and neoliberals argue that the economic integration of Europe through the development of the European Union has made war in most of the European continent so disastrous economically so as to serve as an effective deterrent. Constructivists take this one step further, frequently arguing that the development of EU political institutions has led or will lead to the development of a nascent European identity, which most states on the European continent wish to partake in to some degree or another, and which makes all states within or aspiring to be within the EU regard war between them as unthinkable. As for Waltz, the general opinion is that most states are not in a position to safely guard against nuclear use, that he under-estimates the long-standing antipathy in many regions, and that weak states will be unable to prevent-or will actively provide for-the disastrous possibility of nuclear terrorism. Waltz has dealt with all of these objections at some point in his work; though to many, he has not adequately responded (Betts (2000)).

The Learning Channel documentary Doomsday: "On The Brink" illustrated 40 years of U.S. and Soviet nuclear weapons accidents. Even the 1995 Norwegian rocket incident demonstrated a potential scenario in which Russian democratization and military downsizing at the end of the Cold War did not eliminate the danger of accidental nuclear war through command and control errors. After asking: might a future Russian ruler or renegade Russian general be tempted to use nuclear weapons to make foreign policy? the documentary writers revealed a greater danger of Russian security over its nuclear stocks, but especially the ultimate danger of human nature to want the ultimate weapon of mass destruction to exercise political and military power. Future world leaders might not understand how close the Soviets, Russians, and Americans were to doomsday, how easy it all seemed because apocalypse was avoided for a mere 40 years between rivals, politicians not terrorists, who loved their children and did not want to die, against 30,000 years of human prehistory. History and military experts agree that proliferation can be slowed, but never stopped (technology cannot be uninvented).

Proliferation begets Proliferation

Proliferation begets proliferation is a concept described by Scott Sagan in his article, Why Do States Build Nuclear Weapons? This concept can be described as a strategic chain reaction. If one state produces a nuclear weapon it creates almost a domino effect within the region. States in the region will seek to acquire nuclear weapons to balance or eliminate the security threat. Sagan describes this reaction best in his article when he states, "Every time one state develops nuclear weapons to balance against its main rival, it also creates a nuclear threat to another region, which then has to initiate its own nuclear weapons program to maintain its national security". Going back through history we can see how this has taken place. When the United States demonstrated that it had nuclear power capabilities after the bombing of Hiroshima and Nagasaki, the Russians started to develop their program in preparation for the Cold War. With the Russian military buildup, France and Great Britain perceived this as a security threat and therefore they pursued nuclear weapons.

Nuclear Non-Proliferation Treaty

The Treaty on the Non-Proliferation of Nuclear Weapons, also Nuclear Non-Proliferation Treaty (NPT or NNPT) is a treaty to limit the spread (proliferation) of nuclear weapons. The treaty came into force on 5 March 1970 and currently there are 189 states party to the treaty, five of which are recognized as nuclear weapon states: the United States, Russia, the United Kingdom, France, and China (also the five permanent members of the United Nations Security Council). Four non-parties to the treaty are known or believed to possess nuclear weapons. India, Pakistan and North Korea have openly tested and declared that they possess nuclear weapons, while Israel has had a policy of opacity regarding its own nuclear weapons program. North Korea acceded to the treaty, violated it, and withdrew from it in 2003.

The treaty was proposed by Ireland and Finland and they were the first to sign.

The NPT consists of a preamble and eleven articles. Although the concept of "pillars" appears nowhere in the NPT, the treaty is nevertheless sometimes interpreted as a *three pillar* system, with an implicit balance among them:

1. *non-proliferation,*
2. *disarmament,* and
3. *the right to peacefully use nuclear technology.*

The treaty is reviewed each five years in meetings called Review Conferences of the Parties to the Treaty of Non-Proliferation of Nuclear Weapons. In addition, Sessions of the Preparatory Committee for the Review Conference take place on the intermediate years. Simultaneously, many events organized by independent institutions, groups of experts, think tanks and NGO's take place worldwide in order to provide reports and recommendations that compliment the Preparatory Committees.

Even though the treaty was originally conceived with a limited duration of 25 years, the signing parties decided by consensus to extend the treaty indefinitely and without conditions during the Review Conference in New York City on May 11, 1995.

Treaty "Pillars"

The NPT is commonly described as having three main "pillars": non-proliferation, disarmament, and peaceful use. This "pillars" concept has been questioned by some who believe that the NPT is, as its name suggests, principally about nonproliferation, and who worry that "three pillars" language misleadingly implies that the three elements have equivalent importance.

Non-proliferation

Five states are recognized by the NPT as nuclear weapon states (NWS): China (signed 1992), France (1992), the Soviet Union (1968; obligations and rights now assumed by the Russian Federation), the United Kingdom (1968), and the United States (1968) (The U.S., UK, and Soviet Union were the only states openly possessing such weapons among the original ratifiers of the treaty, which entered into force in 1970). These five nations are also the five permanent members of the United Nations Security Council. These five NWS agree not to transfer "nuclear weapons or other nuclear explosive devices" and "not in any way to assist, encourage, or induce" a non-nuclear weapon state (NNWS) to acquire nuclear weapons. NNWS parties to the NPT agree not to "receive," "manufacture" or "acquire" nuclear weapons or to "seek or receive any assistance in the manufacture of nuclear weapons". NNWS parties also agree to accept safeguards by the International Atomic Energy Agency (IAEA) to verify that they are not diverting nuclear energy from peaceful uses to nuclear weapons or other nuclear explosive devices.

The five NWS parties have made undertakings not to use their nuclear weapons against a non-NWS party except in response to a nuclear attack, or a conventional attack in alliance with a Nuclear Weapons State. However, these undertakings have not been incorporated formally into the treaty, and the exact details have varied over time. The U.S. also had nuclear warheads targeted at North Korea, a non-NWS state, from 1959 until 1991. The previous

United Kingdom Secretary of State for Defence, Geoff Hoon, has also explicitly invoked the possibility of the use of the country's nuclear weapons in response to a non-conventional attack by "rogue states". In January 2006, President Jacques Chirac of France indicated that an incident of state-sponsored terrorism on France could trigger a small-scale nuclear retaliation aimed at destroying the "rogue state's" power centres.

Disarmament

The NPT's preamble contains language affirming the desire of treaty signatories to ease international tension and strengthen international trust so as to create someday the conditions for a halt to the production of nuclear weapons, and treaty on general and complete disarmament that liquidates, in particular, nuclear weapons and their delivery vehicles from national arsenals.

The wording of the NPT's Article VI arguably imposes only a vague obligation on all NPT signatories to move in the general direction of nuclear and total disarmament, saying, "Each of the Parties to the Treaty undertakes to pursue negotiations in good faith on effective measures relating to cessation of the nuclear arms race at an early date and to nuclear disarmament, and on a treaty on general and complete disarmament." Under this interpretation, Article VI does not strictly require all signatories to actually conclude a disarmament treaty. Rather, it only requires them "to negotiate in good faith."

On the other hand, some governments, especially non-nuclear-weapon states belonging to the Non-Aligned Movement, have interpreted Article VI's language as being anything but vague. In their view, Article VI constitutes a formal and specific obligation on the NPT-recognized nuclear-weapon states to disarm themselves of nuclear weapons, and argue that these states have failed to meet their obligation. Some government delegations to the Conference on Disarmament have put forth proposals for a complete and universal disarmament, but no disarmament treaty has emerged from these proposals. Critics of the NPT-recognized nuclear-weapon states sometimes argue that what they view as the failure of the NPT-recognized nuclear weapon states to disarm themselves of nuclear weapons, especially in the post-Cold War era, has angered some non-nuclear-weapon NPT signatories of the NPT.

Such failure, these critics add, provides justification for the non-nuclear-weapon signatories to quit the NPT and develop their own nuclear arsenals.

Other observers have suggested that the linkage between proliferation and disarmament may also work the other way, i.e., that the failure to resolve proliferation threats in Iran and North Korea, for instance, will cripple the prospects for disarmament. No current nuclear weapons state, the argument goes, would seriously consider eliminating its last nuclear weapons without high confidence that other countries would not acquire them. Some observers have even suggested that the very progress of disarmament by the superpowers—which has led to the elimination of thousands of weapons and delivery systems —could eventually make the possession of nuclear weapons more attractive by increasing the perceived strategic value of a small arsenal. As one U.S. official and NPT expert warned in 2007, "logic suggests that as the number of nuclear weapons decreases, the 'marginal utility' of a nuclear weapon as an instrument of military power increases. At the extreme, which it is precisely disarmament's hope to create, the strategic utility of even one or two nuclear weapons would be huge."

Peaceful use of Nuclear Energy

The third pillar allows for and agrees upon the transfer of nuclear technology and materials to NPT signatory countries for the development of civilian nuclear energy programs in those countries, as long as they can demonstrate that their nuclear programs are not being used for the development of nuclear weapons. Since very few of the states with nuclear energy programs are willing to abandon the use of nuclear energy, the third pillar of the NPT under Article IV provides other states with the possibility to do the same, but under conditions intended to make it difficult to develop nuclear weapons.

The treaty recognizes the inalienable right of sovereign states to use nuclear energy for peaceful purposes, but restricts this right for NPT parties to be exercised "in conformity with Articles I and II" (the basic nonproliferation obligations that constitute the "first pillar" of the Treaty). As the commercially popular light water reactor nuclear power station uses enriched uranium fuel, it follows that states must be able either to enrich uranium or purchase it on an international market. Mohamed ElBaradei, Director General of the International Atomic Energy Agency, has called the spread of enrichment and reprocessing capabilities the "Achilles' heel" of the nuclear nonproliferation regime. As of 2007 13 states have an enrichment capability. Because the availability of fissile material has long been considered the principal obstacle to, and "pacing element" for, a country's nuclear weapons development effort, it was declared a major emphasis of U.S. policy in 2004 to prevent the further spread of uranium enrichment and plutonium reprocessing (a.k.a. "ENR") technology. Countries possessing ENR capabilities, it is feared, have what is in effect the option of using this capability to produce fissile material for weapons use on demand, thus giving them what has been termed a "virtual" nuclear weapons program. The degree to which NPT members have a "right" to ENR technology notwithstanding its potentially grave proliferation implications, therefore, is at the cutting edge of policy and legal debates surrounding the meaning of Article IV and its relation to Articles I, II, and III of the Treaty.

Countries that have signed the treaty as Non-Nuclear Weapons States and maintained that status have an unbroken record of not building nuclear weapons. However, Iraq was cited by the IAEA and sanctioned by the UN Security Council for violating its NPT safeguards obligations; North Korea never came into compliance with its NPT safeguards agreement and was cited repeatedly for these violations, and later withdrew from the NPT and tested multiple nuclear devices; Iran was found in non-compliance with its NPT safeguards obligations in an unusual non-consensus decision because it "failed in a number of instances over an extended period of time" to report aspects of its enrichment program; and Libya pursued a clandestine nuclear weapons program before abandoning it in December 2003.

In 1991 Romania reported previously undeclared nuclear activities by the former regime and the IAEA reported this non-compliance to the Security Council for information only. In some regions, the fact that all neighbours are verifiably free of nuclear weapons reduces any pressure individual states might feel to build those weapons themselves, even if neighbours are known to have peaceful nuclear energy programs that might otherwise be suspicious. In this, the treaty works as designed.

In 2004, Mohamed ElBaradei, the then Director General of the International Atomic Energy Agency (IAEA), said that by some estimates thirty-five to forty states could have the knowledge to develop nuclear weapons.

Key Articles

Article I: Each nuclear-weapons state (NWS) undertakes not to transfer, to any recipient, nuclear weapons, or other nuclear explosive devices, and not to assist any non-nuclear weapon state to manufacture or acquire such weapons or devices.

Article II: Each non-NWS party undertakes not to receive, from any source, nuclear weapons, or other nuclear explosive devices; not to manufacture or acquire such weapons or devices; and not to receive any assistance in their manufacture.

Article III: Each non-NWS party undertakes to conclude an agreement with the IAEA for the application of its safeguards to all nuclear material in all of the state's peaceful nuclear activities and to prevent diversion of such material to nuclear weapons or other nuclear explosive devices.

Article IV: 1. Nothing in this Treaty shall be interpreted as affecting the inalienable right of all the Parties to the Treaty to develop research, production and use of nuclear energy for peaceful purposes without discrimination and in conformity with Articles I and II of this Treaty.

2. All the Parties to the Treaty undertake to facilitate, and have the right to participate in, the fullest possible exchange of equipment, materials and scientific and technological information for the peaceful uses of nuclear energy. Parties to the Treaty in a position to do so shall also co-operate in contributing alone or together with other States or international organizations to the further development of the applications of nuclear energy for peaceful purposes, especially in the territories of non-nuclear-weapon States Party to the Treaty, with due consideration for the needs of the developing areas of the world.

Article VI. The states undertake to pursue "negotiations in good faith on effective measures relating to cessation of the nuclear arms race at an early date and to nuclear disarmament", and towards a "Treaty on general and complete disarmament under strict and effective international control".

Article X. Establishes the right to withdraw from the Treaty giving 3 months' notice. It also establishes the duration of the Treaty (25 years before 1995 Extension Initiative).

History

The impetus behind the NPT was concern for the safety of a world with many nuclear weapon states. It was recognized that the cold war deterrent relationship between just the United States and Soviet Union was fragile. More nuclear players reduced security for all, multiplying the risks of miscalculation, accident or unauthorized use, or through the escalation of a small nuclear conflict.

The NPT process was launched by Frank Aiken, Irish Minister for External Affairs, in 1958. It was opened for signature in 1968, with Finland the first State to sign. By 1992 all five then-declared nuclear powers had signed the treaty, and the treaty was renewed in 1995 (and followed by the Comprehensive Test Ban Treaty in 1996). Several NPT signatories have given up nuclear weapons or nuclear weapons programs. South Africa undertook a nuclear weapons program, allegedly with the assistance of Israel in the 1970s, and may have conducted a nuclear test in the Atlantic ocean in 1979, but has since renounced its nuclear program and signed the treaty in 1991 after destroying its small nuclear arsenal. Several former Soviet Republics destroyed or transferred to Russia the nuclear weapons inherited from the Soviet Union.

United States-NATO Nuclear Weapons Sharing

At the time the treaty was being negotiated, NATO had in place secret nuclear weapons sharing agreements whereby the United States provided nuclear weapons to be deployed by, and stored in, other NATO states. Some argue this is an act of proliferation violating Articles I and II of the treaty. A counter-argument is that the U.S. controlled the weapons in storage within the NATO states, and that no transfer of the weapons or control over them was intended "unless and until a decision were made to go to war, at which the treaty would no longer be controlling", so there is no breach of the NPT. These agreements were disclosed to a few of the states, including the Soviet Union, negotiating the treaty, but most of the states that signed the NPT in 1968 would not have known about these agreements and interpretations at that time.

As of 2005, it is estimated that the United States still provides about 180 tactical B61 nuclear bombs for use by Belgium, Germany, Italy, the Netherlands and Turkey under these NATO agreements. Many states, and the Non-Aligned Movement, now argue this violates Articles I and II of the treaty, and are applying diplomatic pressure to terminate these agreements. They point out that the pilots and other staff of the "non-nuclear" NATO states practice handling and delivering the U.S. nuclear bombs, and non-U.S. warplanes have been adapted to deliver U.S. nuclear bombs which must have involved the transfer of some technical nuclear weapons information. NATO believes its "nuclear forces continue to play an essential role in war prevention, but their role is now more fundamentally political". NATO officials also point out that no nuclear weapons have ever been given over to non-U.S. control by the United States, so therefore there cannot have been a violation of Article I (which prohibits transferring "nuclear weapons or other nuclear explosive devices or control over such weapons or explosive devices") or Article II (which bars "receiv[ing] the transfer from any transferor whatsoever of nuclear weapons or other nuclear explosive devices or of control over such weapons or explosive devices").

U.S. nuclear sharing policies were originally designed to help prevent the proliferation of nuclear weapons—not least by persuading the then West Germany not to develop an independent nuclear capability by assuring it that West Germany would be able, in the event of war with the Warsaw Pact, to wield (U.S.) nuclear weapons in self-defence. (Until that point of all-out war, however, the weapons themselves would remain "safely" in U.S. hands.) The point was to limit the spread of countries having their own nuclear weapons programs, helping ensure that NATO allies would not choose to go down the proliferation route. (West Germany was discussed in U.S. intelligence estimates for a number of years as being a country with the potential to develop nuclear weapons capabilities of its own if officials in Bonn were not convinced that their defence against the Soviet Union and its allies could otherwise be met.)

India, Israel and Pakistan

Three states—India, Israel, and Pakistan—have declined to sign the treaty. India and Pakistan are confirmed nuclear powers, and Israel has a long-standing policy of deliberate ambiguity. These countries argue that the NPT creates a club of "nuclear haves" and a larger group of "nuclear have-nots" by restricting the legal possession of nuclear weapons to those states that tested them before 1967, but the treaty never explains on what ethical grounds such a distinction is valid.

India and Pakistan have publicly announced possession of nuclear weapons and have detonated nuclear devices in tests, India having first done so in 1974 and Pakistan following suit in 1998 in response to another Indian test. India is estimated to have enough fissile material for more than 150 warheads. Pakistan reportedly has between 80 and 120 warheads according to the former head of its strategic arms division. India is one of the few countries to have a no first use policy, a pledge not to use nuclear weapons unless first attacked by an adversary using nuclear weapons. The main reason India cites for not signing the NPT and for possessing nuclear weapons is that China is one of the "nuclear haves." India's External Affairs Minister Pranab Mukherjee said during a visit to Tokyo in 2007: "If India did not sign the NPT, it is not because of its lack of commitment for non-proliferation, but because we consider NPT as a flawed treaty and it did not recognise the need for universal, non-discriminatory verification and treatment." China and India have a longstanding border dispute, including a border war in 1962.

According to leaked intelligence, Israel has been developing nuclear weapons at its Dimona site in the Negev since 1958, and many nonproliferation analysts like David Albright estimate that Israel may have stockpiled between 100 to 200 warheads using the plutonium reprocessed from Dimona. The Israeli government refuses to confirm or deny possession of nuclear weapons, although this is now regarded as an open secret after Israeli low level nuclear technician Mordechai Vanunu—later abducted and jailed by Israel—revealed the program to the British *Sunday Times* in 1986. In early March 2006, India and the United States finalized a deal, having critics in both countries, to provide India with US civilian nuclear technology. Under the deal India has committed to classify 14 of its 22 nuclear power plants as being for civilian use and to place them under IAEA safeguards. Mohamed ElBaradei, the Director General of the IAEA, welcomed the deal by calling India "an important partner in the non-proliferation regime."

In December 2006, United States Congress approved the United States-India Peaceful Atomic Energy Cooperation Act that was cemented during President Bush's visit to India earlier in the year. The legislation allows for the transfer of civilian nuclear material to India. Despite its status outside the Nuclear Non-Proliferation Treaty, India was granted these transactions on the basis of its clean non-proliferation record, and India's unusually high need for energy fueled by its rapid industrialization and a billion-plus population.

On August 1, 2008, the IAEA approved the India Safeguards Agreement and on September 6, 2008, India was granted the waiver at the Nuclear Suppliers Group (NSG) meeting held in Vienna, Austria. The consensus was arrived after overcoming misgivings expressed by Austria, Ireland and New Zealand and is an unprecedented step in giving exemption to a country, which has not signed the NPT and the Comprehensive Test Ban Treaty (CTBT). While India could commence nuclear trade with other willing countries. The U.S. Congress approved this agreement and the President signed it on 8 October 2008.

The NSG Guidelines currently rule out nuclear exports by all major suppliers to Pakistan and Israel, with very narrow exceptions, since neither has full-scope IAEA safeguards (i.e. safeguards on all its nuclear activities). Attempts by Pakistan to reach a similar agreement have been rebuffed by the United States and other NSG members. The argument put forth is that not only does Pakistan lack the same energy requirements but that the track record of Pakistan as a nuclear proliferator makes it impossible for it to have any sort of nuclear deal in the near future.

On September 18, 2009 the General Conference of the International Atomic Energy Agency called on Israel to open its nuclear facilities to IAEA inspection and adhere to the non-proliferation treaty as part of a resolution on "Israeli nuclear capabilities," which passed by a narrow margin of 49-45 with 16 abstentions. The chief Israeli delegate stated that "Israel will not co-operate in any matter with this resolution."

North Korea

North Korea ratified the treaty on December 12, 1985, but gave notice of withdrawal from the treaty on January 10, 2003 following U.S. allegations that it had started an illegal enriched uranium weapons program, and the U.S. subsequently stopping fuel oil shipments under the Agreed Framework which had resolved plutonium weapons issues in 1994. The withdrawal became effective April 10, 2003 making North Korea the first state ever to withdraw from the treaty. North Korea had once before announced withdrawal, on March 12, 1993, but suspended that notice before it came into effect.

On February 10, 2005, North Korea publicly declared that it possessed nuclear weapons and pulled out of the six-party talks hosted by China to find a diplomatic solution to the issue. "We had already taken the resolute action of pulling out of the Nuclear Non-Proliferation Treaty and have manufactured nuclear arms for self-defence to cope with the Bush administration's evermore undisguised policy to isolate and stifle the DPRK," a North Korean Foreign Ministry statement said regarding the issue. Six-party talks resumed in July 2005. On September 19, 2005, North Korea announced that it would agree to a preliminary accord. Under the accord, North Korea would scrap all of its existing nuclear weapons and nuclear production facilities, rejoin the NPT, and readmit IAEA inspectors. The difficult issue of the supply of light water reactors to replace North Korea's indigenous nuclear power plant program, as per the 1994 Agreed Framework, was left to be resolved in future discussions. On the next day North Korea reiterated its known view that until it is supplied with a light water reactor it will not dismantle its nuclear arsenal or rejoin the NPT.

On October 2, 2006, the North Korean foreign minister announced that his country was planning to conduct a nuclear test "in the future", although it did not state when. On Monday, October 9, 2006 at 01:35:27 (UTC) the United States Geological Survey detected a magnitude 4.2 seismic event 70 km (45 miles) north of Kimchaek, North Korea indicating a nuclear test. The North Korean government announced shortly afterward that they had completed a successful underground test of a nuclear fission device.

In 2007, reports from Washington suggested that the 2002 CIA reports stating that North Korea was developing an enriched uranium weapons program, which led to North Korea leaving the NPT, had overstated or misread the intelligence. On the other hand, even apart from these press allegations—which some critics worry could have been planted in order to justify the United States giving up trying to verify the dismantlement of Pyongyang's uranium program in the face of North Korean intransigence—there remains some information in the public record indicating the existence of a uranium effort. Quite apart from the fact that North Korean First Vice Minister Kang Sok Ju at one point admitted the existence of a uranium enrichment program, Pakistan's then-President Musharraf revealed that the A.Q. Khan proliferation network had provided North Korea with a number of gas centrifuges designed for uranium enrichment. Additionally, press reports have cited U.S. officials to the effect that evidence obtained in dismantling Libya's WMD programs points toward North Korea as the source for Libya's uranium hexafluoride (UF_6) — which, if true, would mean that North Korea has a uranium conversion facility for producing feedstock for centrifuge enrichment.

Iran

Iran is a party to the NPT, but was found in non-compliance with its NPT safeguards agreement and the status of its nuclear program remains in dispute. In November 2003 IAEA Director General Mohamed ElBaradei reported that Iran had repeatedly and over an extended period failed to meet its safeguards obligations, including by failing to declare its uranium enrichment program. After about two years of EU3-led diplomatic efforts and Iran temporarily suspending its enrichment program, the IAEA Board of Governors, acting under Article XII.C of the IAEA Statute, found in a rare non-consensus decision with 12 abstentions that these failures constituted non-compliance with the IAEA safeguards agreement. This was reported to the UN Security Council in 2006, after which the Security Council passed a resolution demanding that Iran suspend its enrichment. Instead, Iran resumed its enrichment program.

The IAEA has been able to verify the non-diversion of declared nuclear material in Iran, and is continuing its work on verifying the absence of undeclared activities. In February 2008, the IAEA also reported that it was working to address "alleged studies" of weaponization, based on documents provided by certain Member States, which those states claimed originated from Iran. Iran rejected the allegations as "baseless" and the documents as "fabrications." In June 2009, the IAEA reported that Iran had not "cooperated with the Agency in connection with the remaining issues... which need to be clarified to exclude the possibility of military dimensions to Iran's nuclear program."

The United States concluded that Iran violated its Article III NPT safeguards obligations, and further argued based on circumstantial evidence that Iran's enrichment program was for weapons purposes and therefore violated Iran's Article II nonproliferation obligations. The November 2007 US National Intelligence Estimate (NIE) later concluded that Iran had halted an active nuclear weapons program in the fall of 2003 and that it had remained halted as of mid-2007. The NIE's "Key Judgments," however, also made clear that what Iran had actually stopped in 2003 was only "nuclear weapon design and weaponization work and covert uranium conversion-related and uranium enrichment-related work"-namely, those aspects of Iran's nuclear weapons effort that had not by that point already been leaked to the press and become the subject of IAEA investigations. Since Iran's uranium enrichment program at Natanz—and its continuing work on a heavy water reactor at Arak that would be ideal for plutonium production—began secretly years before in conjunction with the very weaponization work the NIE discussed and for the purpose of developing nuclear weapons, many observers find Iran's continued development of fissile material production capabilities distinctly worrying. Particularly because fissile material availability has long been understood to be the principal obstacle to nuclear weapons development and the primary "pacing element" for a weapons program, the fact that Iran has reportedly suspended weaponization work may not mean very much. As U.S. Director of National Intelligence Mike McConnell has put it, the aspects of its work that Iran allegedly suspended were thus "probably the least significant part of the program."

Iran states it has a legal right to enrich uranium for peaceful purposes under the NPT, and further says that it "has constantly complied with its obligations under the NPT and the Statute of the International Atomic Energy Agency". Iran also states that its enrichment program is part of its civilian nuclear energy program, which is allowed under Article IV of the NPT. The Non-Aligned Movement has welcomed the continuing cooperation of Iran with the IAEA and reaffirmed Iran's right to the peaceful uses of nuclear technology. UN Secretary General Ban Ki-moon has welcomed the continued dialogue between Iran and the IAEA, and has called for a peaceful resolution to the issue.

South Africa

South Africa also deserves a special mention as the only country that developed nuclear weapons by itself and later dismantled them-unlike the former Soviet states Ukraine, Belarus and Kazakhstan, which inherited nuclear weapons from the former USSR, and also acceded to the NPT as non-nuclear weapon states. During the days of apartheid, the white South African government developed a deep fear of both a black uprising and the threat of communism. This led to the development of a secret nuclear weapons program as an ultimate deterrent. South Africa has a large supply of uranium, which is mined in the country's gold mines. The government built a nuclear research facility at Pelindaba near Pretoria where uranium was enriched to fuel grade for the nuclear power plant at Koeberg as well as weapon grade for bomb production.

In 1991, after international pressure and when a change of government was imminent, South African Ambassador to the United States Harry Schwarz signed the Nuclear Non-Proliferation Treaty. In 1993, the then president Frederik Willem de Klerk openly admitted that the country had developed a limited nuclear weapon capability. These weapons were subsequently dismantled prior to accession to the NPT. South Africa then opened itself up to IAEA for inspection. In 1994 the IAEA completed its work and declared that the country had fully dismantled its nuclear weapons program.

Libya

Libya had signed and ratified the Nuclear Non-Proliferation Treaty and was subject to IAEA nuclear safeguards inspections, but undertook a secret nuclear weapons development program in violation of its NPT obligations, using material and technology provided by the A.Q. Khan proliferation network—including actual nuclear weapons designed allegedly originating in China. Libya began secret negotiations with the United States and the United Kingdom in March 2003 over potentially eliminating its WMD programs. In October 2003, Libya was embarrassed by the interdiction of a shipment of Pakistani-designed centrifuge parts sent from Malaysia, also as part of A. Q. Khan's proliferation ring. In December 2003, Libya announced that it had agreed to eliminate all its WMD programs, and permitted U.S. and British teams (as well as IAEA inspectors) into the country to assist this process and verify its completion. The nuclear weapons designs, gas centrifuges for uranium enrichment, and other equipment—including prototypes for improved SCUD ballistic missiles—were removed from Libya by the United States. (Libyan chemical weapons stocks and chemical bombs were also destroyed on site with international verification, with Libya joining the Chemical Weapons Convention.) Libya's noncompliance with its IAEA safeguards was reported to the U.N. Security Council, but with no action taken, as Libya's return to compliance with safeguards and Article II of the NPT was welcomed.

Leaving the Treaty

Article X allows a state to leave the treaty if "extraordinary events, related to the subject matter of this Treaty, have jeopardized the supreme interests of its country", giving three months' (ninety days') notice. The state is required to give reasons for leaving the NPT in this notice. NATO states argue that when there is a state of "general war" the treaty no longer applies, effectively allowing the states involved to leave the treaty with no notice. This is a necessary argument to support the NATO nuclear weapons sharing policy, but a troubling one for the logic of the treaty. NATO's argument is based on the phrase "the consequent need to make every effort to avert the danger of such a war" in the treaty preamble, inserted at the behest of U.S. diplomats, arguing that the treaty would at that point have failed to fulfil its function of prohibiting a general war and thus no longer be binding. Many states do not accept this argument.

North Korea has also caused an uproar by its use of this provision of the treaty. Article X.1 only requires a state to give three months' notice in total, and does not provide for other states to question a state's interpretation of "supreme interests of its country". In 1993, North Korea gave notice to withdraw from the NPT. However, after 89 days, North Korea reached agreement with the United States to freeze its nuclear program under the Agreed Framework and "suspended" its withdrawal notice. In October 2002, the United States accused North Korea of violating the Agreed Framework by pursuing a secret uranium enrichment program, and suspended shipments of heavy fuel oil under that agreement. In response, North Korea expelled IAEA inspectors, disabled IAEA equipment, and, on January 10, 2003, announced that it was ending the suspension of its previous NPT withdrawal notification. North Korea said that only one more day's notice was sufficient for withdrawal from the NPT, as it had given 89 days before. The IAEA Board of Governors rejected this interpretation.. Most countries held that a new three-months withdrawal notice was required, and some questioned whether North Korea's notification met the "extraordinary events" and "supreme interests" requirements of the Treaty. The Joint Statement of September 19, 2005 at the end of the Fourth Round of the Six-Party Talks called for North Korea to "return" to the NPT, implicitly acknowledging that it had withdrawn.

Future

The 2000 Review Conference had as main outcome the definition in practical terms of the nuclear weapons states' disarmament obligations, summarized in the so called Thirteen Points.

The inclusion of (civilian) nuclear power in the July 2005 Asia-Pacific Partnership for Clean Development and Climate was politically sensitive, as India, which tested its first atomic bomb in 1974, refused to sign the NPT. Prior to the announcement of the Asia-Pacific Partnership, on 18 July 2005, US President George W. Bush had met Indian Prime Minister Manmohan Singh and declared that he would work to change US law and international rules to permit trade in US civilian nuclear technology with India. Some, such as British columnist George Monbiot, argue that the U.S.-India nuclear deal, in combination with US attempts to deny Iran (an NPT signatory) civilian nuclear fuel-making technology, may destroy the NPT regime, while others contend that such a move will likely bring India, an NPT non-signatory, under closer international scrutiny. At the Seventh Review Conference in May 2005, there were stark differences between the United States, which wanted the conference to focus on non-proliferation, especially on its allegations against Iran, and most other countries, who emphasized the lack of serious nuclear disarmament by the nuclear powers. The non-aligned countries reiterated their position. that NATO's nuclear sharing arrangement violates the treaty.

The next Review Conference which will be held in May 2010 is seen as critical to consolidate the nuclear nonproliferation regime, based on the treaty. The 2009 Session of the NPT Preparatory Committee, held in May, failed to deliver an agreed recommendation for the upcoming Review Conference, but even so, it has been considered successful to define the main issues to be discussed during the meeting. The forthcoming "Global Summit on Nuclear Security" will be held in March, 2010. The summit was proposed by President Obama in Prague and is intended to strengthen the Nuclear Non-Proliferation Treaty in conjunction with the Proliferation Security Initiative and the Global Initiative to Combat Nuclear Terrorism.

Criticism and Responses

Gamal Abdel Nasser once said "basically they did whatever they wanted to do before the introduction of NPT and then devised it to prevent others from doing what they had themselves been doing before". In addition, some argue that the NWS have not fully complied, in practice, with their commitments mentioned in NPT. Article VI of the treaty requires NPT parties to "pursue negotiations" on an end to the arms race, "nuclear disarmament, and on a treaty on general and complete disarmament." Yet thousands of nuclear weapons remain, some on high alert, long after the end of the cold war. In January 2002, a report by the Defence Department following the U.S. Nuclear Posture Review recommended the development of nuclear weapons designed to destroy hardened and deeply-buried targets, but the resulting Robust Nuclear Earth Penetrator never gained full Congressional support and was canceled in 2005. The representative of Ghana, on behalf of the Non-Aligned Movement and the African Group said disarmament and non-proliferation were complementary and mutually reinforcing and that, "Without tangible progress in disarmament, the current emphasis on non-proliferation cannot be sustained."

The United States responds to criticism of its disarmament record by pointing out that since the end of the Cold War it has eliminated over 13,000 nuclear weapons and eliminated over 80% of its deployed strategic warheads and 90% of non-strategic warheads deployed to NATO, in the processing eliminating whole categories of warheads and delivery systems and reducing its reliance on nuclear weapons. U.S. officials have also pointed out the United States' ongoing—and, throughout 2007, sharply accelerating—work to dismantle nuclear warheads. When current accelerated dismantlement efforts ordered by President George W. Bush have been completed, the U.S. arsenal will be less than a quarter of its size at the end of the Cold War, and smaller than it has been at any point since the Eisenhower administration, well before the drafting of the NPT. The United States has also purchased many thousands of weapons' worth of uranium formerly in Soviet nuclear weapons for conversion into reactor fuel. (As a consequence of this latter effort, it has been estimated that the equivalent of one lightbulb in every ten in the United States is powered by nuclear fuel removed from warheads previously targeted at the United States and its allies during the Cold War.) The U.S. Special Representative for Nuclear Nonproliferation agreed that nonproliferation and disarmament are linked, noting that they can be mutually reinforcing but also that growing proliferation risks create an environment that makes disarmament more difficult. The United Kingdom,, France and Russia likewise defend their nuclear disarmament records, and the five NPT NWS issued a joint statement in 2008 reaffirming their Article VI disarmament commitments. As discussed above, the precise nature of nuclear weapons state obligations, if any, under Article VI of the Treaty is sharply contested.

8

Potential Threat of Nuclear Terrorism

Introduction

Nuclear terrorism denotes the use, or threat of the use, of nuclear weapons or radiological weapons in acts of terrorism, including attacks against facilities where radioactive materials are present. In legal terms, nuclear terrorism is an offense committed if a person unlawfully and intentionally "uses in any way radioactive material ... with the intent to cause death or serious bodily injury", according to 2005 United Nations International Convention for the Suppression of Acts of Nuclear Terrorism.

The notion of terrorist organizations using nuclear weapons (especially very small ones, such as suitcase nukes) has been a threat in American rhetoric and culture. It is plausible that terrorists could acquire a nuclear weapon.

Overview

Two of the main dangers associated with nuclear reactors are nuclear proliferation and nuclear terrorism. Terrorism involving nuclear weapons or radioactive materials could take a variety of forms. Terrorists could:

- Attack a nuclear reactor.
- Disrupt critical inputs (eg., water supply) for the safe running of a nuclear reactor.
- Steal nuclear fuel or waste.
- Acquire fissile material and fabricate a nuclear bomb.

- Acquire a ready-made nuclear weapon or take over a nuclear-armed submarine, plane or base.

History

Discussions of non-state nuclear terrorism among experts go back at least to the 1970s. In 1975 The Economist warned that "You can make a bomb with a few pounds of plutonium. By the mid-1980s the power stations may easily be turning out 200,000 lb of the stuff each year. And each year, unless present methods are drastically changed, many thousands of pounds of it will be transferred from one plant to another as it proceeds through the fuel cycle. The dangers of robbery in transit are evident.... Vigorous co-operation between governments and the International Atomic Energy Agency could, even at this late stage, make the looming perils loom a good deal smaller." And the New York Times commented in 1981 that The Nuclear Emergency Search Team's "origins go back to the aftershocks of the Munich Olympic massacre in mid-1972.

Until that time, no one in the United States Government had thought seriously about the menace of organized, international terrorism, much less nuclear terrorism. There was a perception in Washington that the value of what is called 'special nuclear material'-plutonium or highly enriched uranium-was so enormous that the strict financial accountability of the private contractors who dealt with it would be enough to protect it from falling into the wrong hands. But it has since been revealed that the physical safeguarding of bomb-grade material against theft was almost scandalously neglected."

This discussion took on a larger public character in the 1980s after NBC aired Special Bulletin, a television dramatization of a nuclear terrorist attack on the United States. In 1986 a private panel of experts known as the International Task Force on the Prevention of Terrorism released a report urging all nuclear-armed states to beware the dangers of terrorism and work on equipping their nuclear arsenals with permissive action links. "The probability of nuclear terrorism," the experts warned, "is increasing and the consequences for urban and industrial societies could be catastrophic."

Radiological Weapons

It is possible for a terrorist group to detonate a radiological or 'dirty bomb'. A 'dirty bomb' is composed of any radioactive source and a conventional explosive. The radioactive material is dispersed by the detonation of the explosive.

Detonation of such a weapon is not as powerful as a nuclear blast, but can produce considerable radioactive fallout. There are other radiological weapons called radiological dispersal devices where an explosive is not necessary. A radiological weapon may be very appealing to terrorist groups as it is highly successful in instilling fear and panic amongst a population (particularly because of the threat of radiation poisoning), and would contaminate the immediate area for some period of time, disrupting attempts to repair the damage. The economic losses could be enormous-easily reaching into the tens of billions of dollars.

Alleged Nuclear Terrorism Attempts and Plans

In June 2002, U.S. citizen Jose Padilla was arrested for allegedly planning a radiological attack on the city of Chicago; however, he was never charged with such conduct. He was instead convicted of charges that he conspired to "murder, kidnap and maim" people overseas. In November 2006, MI5 warned that al-Qaida were planning on using nuclear weapons against cities in the United Kingdom by obtaining the bombs via clandestine means.

In June 2007, the FBI released to the press the name of Adnan Gulshair el Shukrijumah, allegedly the operations leader for developing tactical plans for detonating nuclear bombs in several American cities simultaneously. The Alexander Litvinenko poisoning with radioactive polonium "represents an ominous landmark: the beginning of an era of nuclear terrorism," according to Andrew J. Patterson.

Security specialist Shaun Gregory argued in an article that terrorists have attacked Pakistani nuclear facilities three times in the recent past; twice in 2007 and once in 2008.

Obama Administration

Nuclear weapons materials on the black market are a global concern, and there is concern about the possible detonation of a small, crude nuclear weapon by a terrorist group, in a major U.S. city, with significant loss of life and property. The Obama administration says they will focus on reducing the risk of such nuclear threats and aims to strengthen homeland nuclear security.".

Pakistan

After several incidents in Pakistan in which terrorists attacked three of its military nuclear facilities it became clear that there emerged a serious danger that they would gain access to the country's nuclear arsenal, according to a journal published by the US Military Academy at West Point. In January 2010 it was revealed that the US army was training a specialised unit *"to seal off and snatch back"* Pakistani nuclear weapons in the event that militants would obtain a nuclear device or materials that could make one. Pakistan supposedly possesses about 80 nuclear warheads. US officials refused to speak on the record about the American safety plans.

Recovering Lost Weapons & Material

In August 2002, the United States launched a program to track and secure enriched uranium from 24 Soviet-style reactors in 16 countries, in order to reduce the risk of the materials falling into the hands of terrorists or "rogue states".

The first such operation was *Project Vinca*, "a multinational, public-private effort to remove nuclear material from a poorly secured Yugoslav research institute." The project has been hailed as "a nonproliferation success story" with the "potential to inform broader 'global cleanout' efforts to address one of the weakest links in the nuclear nonproliferation chain: insufficiently secured civilian nuclear research facilities."

In order to reduce the danger of attacks using nuclear waste material, European Union Commissioner Loyola de Palacio suggested in November 2002 the creation of common standards in the European Union, especially in the new member states operating Soviet-era reactors, for subterranean nuclear waste disposal. In November 2007, burglars with unknown intentions infiltrated the Pelindaba nuclear research facility near Pretoria, South Africa. The burglars escaped without acquiring any of the uranium held at the facility.

Nuclear Proliferation and the Potential Threat of Nuclear Terrorism

For many centuries, security strategies have been based on boundaries: the strategic placement of cities and borders to take advantage of natural barriers; defences that relied on walls, trenches and armadas; and the use of ethnic and religious groupings or other categories to distinguish friend from foe. In the 20th Century, the advent of airplanes, submarines, ballistic missiles and weapons of mass destruction began to undermine this approach to security — by making borders increasingly porous, and by enabling the remote delivery of destruction on a scale previously not envisioned. But the forcing factor — the change that has altered the international security landscape so drastically that it has compelled a fundamental reevaluation of security strategies — is, in fact, globalization. The global community has become interdependent, with the constant movement of people, ideas and goods. Many aspects of modern life — global warming, Internet communication, the global marketplace, and yes, the rise in international terrorism — point to the fact that the human race has walked through a door that cannot be re-entered. Our approaches to national and international security must be in keeping with this reality.

Today, our focus is on nuclear proliferation and the potential threat of nuclear terrorism in Asia and the Pacific — and I am pleased at the opportunity to share with you my perspectives on the challenges we face, and how the IAEA is working to strengthen nuclear security and the nuclear non-proliferation regime. But I would emphasize at the outset that, while much of our work must begin locally and regionally, we must not forget to think globally, because ultimately the existence of a nuclear threat anywhere is a threat everywhere, and as a global community, we will win or lose this battle together.

Nuclear Proliferation and Nuclear Verification

Turning first to the threat of nuclear weapons proliferation: the *Treaty on the Non-Proliferation of Nuclear Weapons (NPT)* remains the global anchor for nuclear non-proliferation and nuclear disarmament. Despite flaws in the system, implementation of the NPT continues to provide important security benefits — by providing assurance that, in the great majority of non-nuclear-weapon States, nuclear energy is not being misused for weapon purposes. Although the NPT is sometimes perceived as a project of the industrialized world, its benefits extend across any geopolitical divide. Still, it is clear that the events of the past few years have placed the NPT and the regime supporting it under unprecedented stress, exposing some of its limitations and pointing to areas that need to be adjusted. A number of conspicuous lessons and insights can be gained from the recent experience of the IAEA in verifying undeclared nuclear programmes in Iraq, Iran, Libya and North Korea.

Perhaps the most important lesson is that verification and diplomacy, used in conjunction, can be effective. The Iraq experience demonstrated that the nuclear inspection process — while requiring time and patience — can be effective even when the country under inspection is providing less than active cooperation. When international inspectors are provided adequate authority, aided by all available information, backed by a credible compliance mechanism, and supported by international consensus, the verification system works. The report recently issued by the Iraq Survey Group confirmed the conclusions the IAEA was providing to the United Nations Security Council before the war, when we said we had found no evidence to suggest that Iraq had reconstituted any element of its former nuclear weapon programme — a conclusion that clearly came as a relief to all concerned.

Looking more broadly at recent IAEA experience in other countries, it is clear that, for nuclear verification to be successful, IAEA inspectors must have adequate authority. The "any time, any place" authority granted by the Security Council in the case of Iraq was extraordinary, and it is not likely that countries would voluntarily grant the IAEA such blanket rights of inspection.

Nonetheless, within the NPT framework, adequate authority can be achieved in those countries that accept the so-called "additional protocol" as a supplement to their NPT safeguards agreement. The additional protocol provides the Agency with significant additional authority with regard to both information and physical access. As illustrated by the IAEA's experience in Iraq before the first Gulf War, without the authority provided by the protocol, our ability to verify nuclear activities is mostly limited to the nuclear material already declared — with little authority to verify the absence of undeclared, or clandestine, nuclear material or activities. By contrast, our recent efforts in Iran and elsewhere have made clear how much can be uncovered when the protocol is applied. Perhaps the most disturbing lesson to emerge from our work in Iran and Libya is the existence of an extensive illicit market for the supply of nuclear items, which clearly thrived on demand. The relative ease with which a multinational illicit network could be set up and operated demonstrates clearly the inadequacy of the present export control system. The fact that so many companies and individuals could be involved (more than two dozen, by last count) — and that, in most cases, this could occur apparently without the knowledge of their own governments — points to the shortcomings of national systems for oversight of sensitive equipment and technology. It also points to the limitations of existing international cooperation on export controls, which relies on informal arrangements, does not include many countries with growing industrial capacity, and does not include sufficient sharing of export information with the IAEA.

Clearly, it is time to change our assumptions regarding the inaccessibility of nuclear technology. In a modern society characterized by electronic information exchange, interlinked financial systems, and global trade, the control of access to nuclear weapons technology has grown increasingly difficult. The technical barriers to mastering the essential steps of uranium enrichment — and to designing weapons — have eroded over time. Much of the hardware in question is 'dual use', and the sheer diversity of technology has made it much more difficult to control or even track procurement and sales.

The only reasonable conclusion is that the control of technology is not, in itself, a sufficient barrier against further proliferation. For an increasing number of countries with a highly developed industrial infrastructure — and in some cases access to high enriched uranium or plutonium — the international community must rely primarily on a continuing sense of security as the basis for the adherence of these countries to their non-proliferation commitments. And security perceptions can rapidly change. This leads to the important conclusion that ways and means should be found to better control the sensitive parts of the fuel cycle — namely, the production of enriched uranium and the reprocessing of plutonium.

The concept of multilateral control or oversight over proliferation sensitive parts of the nuclear fuel cycle has been the subject of many studies and initiatives over the years. Recent non-proliferation and security challenges make it important and appropriate that we revisit this subject. Several months ago, I appointed a group of senior experts to look into various options for multilateral control. I also asked the group to look into how to guarantee the supply of reactor technology and fuel, and the possibility of setting up an international scheme for the management and disposal of spent nuclear fuel. The group plans to submit a report next March, before the NPT Review Conference, on the results of its study.

The evolution of the North Korean situation over the past 18 months also carries an important lesson — that is, that the international community cannot afford not to act in a timely manner in cases of non-compliance, and before available options are narrowed. Beginning in the mid-1980s, the Democratic People's Republic of Korea (DPRK) took seven years to fulfil its obligations under the NPT to conclude a safeguards agreement with the Agency. In 1992, shortly after this agreement was concluded and the IAEA began inspections, we sounded the alarm that the DPRK had not reported its total production of plutonium. From that time forward, the DPRK has been in continuous non-compliance with its NPT obligations, and has not allowed the IAEA to fully verify its nuclear programme. At the end of 2002, the DPRK capped that non-compliance by ordering IAEA inspectors out of the country, dismantling the monitoring cameras, breaking IAEA seals and, a few weeks later, declaring its withdrawal from the NPT.

Naturally, all of these actions were promptly reported by the Agency to the Security Council — but with little to no response. This lack of timely action may have complicated finding a solution, and may have conveyed the message that breaking the non-proliferation norms with impunity is a doable proposition — or, worse, that acquiring a nuclear deterrent will bring with it a special treatment.

The final lesson, an insight that has been demonstrated repeatedly, is that insecurity breeds proliferation. It is instructive that nearly all nuclear proliferation concerns arise in regions of longstanding tension. In other words, nuclear proliferation is a symptom, and the patient cannot ultimately be cured as long as we leave unaddressed the underlying causes of insecurity and instability — such as chronic disputes, the persistent lack of good governance and basic freedoms, the growing divide between rich and poor, and newly perceived schisms based on ethnic or religious differences.

It is in this context that I have begun to stress not only the value but also the limitations of the IAEA´s role. While the Agency can use verification effectively to bring to closure questions of compliance with legal and technical requirements, the long term value of these efforts can only be realized to the extent that they are reinforced by all other components of the non-proliferation regime, and followed by the necessary political dialogue among concerned States to address underlying issues of insecurity, and to build confidence and trust. I should note that verification, supported by diplomacy, has been an important part of the efforts so far in Iran and Libya, and in that sense I can only hope that the continuation of the six-party talks on the DPRK nuclear programme will yield results that will include, inter alia, full IAEA verification.

Nuclear Security and the Protection Against Nuclear Terrorism

With nuclear proliferation concerns as a backdrop, the security of nuclear and other radioactive material has taken on dramatically heightened significance in recent years. The IAEA has been active in the field of nuclear security for many years, but as you are all aware, the events of September 2001 propelled the rapid and dramatic re-evaluation of the risks of terrorism in all its forms — whether related to the security of urban centres, sports arenas, industrial complexes, harbors and waterways, oil refineries, air and rail travel, or nuclear and radiological activities. For those of us in the nuclear sphere, it became rapidly apparent that "the lesson of Chernobyl", in the safety sphere, should be applied to security as well: that is, that nuclear security should be urgently strengthened, without waiting for a "watershed" nuclear security event to provide the impetus for needed security upgrades. International cooperation has become the hallmark of these security efforts. While nuclear security is and should remain a national responsibility, some countries still lack the programmes and the resources to respond properly to the threat of nuclear and radiological terrorism. International efforts are focused both on assisting these countries in strengthening their programmes, and on building regional and global networks for combating transnational threats.

Understanding the Threats

The IAEA has categorized four potential nuclear security threats (or, more accurately, nuclear security risks): the acquisition of nuclear weapons by theft; the creation of nuclear explosive devices using stolen nuclear materials; the use of radioactive sources in radiological dispersal devices (RDDs); and the radiological hazards caused by an attack on, or sabotage of, a facility or a transport vehicle.

The threat of nuclear terrorism is real and current. Some experts share the view of the Director General of the United Kingdom Security Service, who said in August 2003: "It will only be a matter of time before a crude version of a [chemical, biological, radiological or nuclear] attack is launched at a major Western city." To date, the IAEA's own database on illicit trafficking has recorded, since 1993, approximately 630 confirmed incidents of trafficking in nuclear or other radioactive material. Sixty incidents were reported in 2003, and it is clear that the total for this year will be even higher. While the majority of trafficking incidents do not involve nuclear material, and while most of the radioactive sources involved are of limited radiological concern, the number of incidents shows that the measures to control and secure nuclear and other radioactive materials need to be improved. They also show that measures to detect and respond to illicit trafficking are essential.

A strategy to counter the potential threats needs to be comprehensive. It must encompass not only power and research reactors and their related fuel cycle facilities; not only waste storage sites and vehicles used in domestic and international transport; but also relevant research and academic institutions; and agricultural, industrial and medical institutions and applications where nuclear or radioactive materials are involved. This is a tall order.

Asia and the Pacific Region

In Asia and the Pacific region, interest has been expanding in a broad range of nuclear technologies. The reliance on nuclear power as a source of electricity is already substantial, with well established programmes in China (including Taiwan, China), Japan, the Republic of Korea, India and Pakistan — and when compared to any region in the world, Asia holds the strongest current growth market for nuclear power.

In addition, more than 50 research reactors and accelerators are operating in 15 Asian countries. Nuclear applications are also playing a strong role in development. Nuclear and isotopic techniques are being used, inter alia: to diagnose and treat cancer patients; to study and improve child nutrition; to produce higher yielding, disease resistant crops; to manage drinking water supplies; to eradicate disease-bearing pests; to increase industrial productivity; and to help address many other development issues.

Effective and credible national and regional approaches to security are therefore essential — not only for nuclear power plants, but also for research reactors, accelerators, and the ubiquitous array of radioactive sources that support these nuclear applications. To optimize the effectiveness of these efforts, it will be important for efforts to be prioritized by focusing on those facilities where the risk is greatest — and to maintain a balance between security needs and the many peaceful applications of nuclear technology.

For example, the recent increase in the denial of shipments of radioactive material, while driven by perceived security issues, can be a matter of significant humanitarian concern — particularly when such shipments involve radionuclides intended for use in medical applications. While we should be strongly focused on ensuring the security of nuclear and other radioactive materials globally, we should equally seek solutions that will ensure the continued delivery of the benefits that these materials and related applications provide.

For nuclear installations such as nuclear power plants and fuel cycle facilities, it is also important to understand how safety and security aspects come together in the identification and protection of vulnerabilities. The IAEA has increasingly been asked to provide guidance on how to reconcile the need for transparency, in matters of nuclear and radiation safety, with the need for confidentiality, from a security perspective. Effective risk management requires striking a balance that protects the security of sensitive information while ensuring that safety concerns are addressed in a transparent manner, and that lessons learned, relating to both safety and security, are shared for the benefit of the entire nuclear community.

Focus of Future Efforts

Looking to the future, it is clear that the imperatives that first led to the development of the IAEA's nuclear security plan have not diminished. We are now beginning a major review of our nuclear security activities. The main elements of a revised plan of activities are already emerging. One aspect of the new plan is to complete the international infrastructure of legal instruments, as well as relevant recommendations and guidelines.

One such legal instrument is the *Convention on Physical Protection of Nuclear Material (CPPNM)*. For a number of years, work has been progressing on a draft amendment to the CPPNM that would expand its scope and strengthen existing provisions. In July, at the request of the Government of Austria and 24 co-sponsoring States, I circulated proposed amendments to the *CPPNM* to all States Parties. The aim of these amendments, as proposed, is to extend the scope of the Convention to cover nuclear material used for peaceful purposes not only in international transport and storage, but also in domestic transport, storage and use, as well as the protection of nuclear material and facilities used for peaceful purposes from sabotage. While consultations are ongoing to resolve a few outstanding issues, it is my hope that we can convene a diplomatic conference early next year to amend the *Convention* and expand its scope.

A second aspect of the new plan will be to accelerate a shift in emphasis from evaluation to action. While we will continue to deliver advisory and needs assessment services, the work of the past three years have given us a much better understanding of

Member State needs, and we will be working with States to give more emphasis to security upgrades and technical assistance.

A third point of focus will be to enhance the sustainability and self-reliance of nuclear security programmes in Member States. This will include helping States establish the needed regulatory frameworks, assisting in the implementation of international guidelines, and addressing continued training needs. For example, major security enhancements are expected as we assist States in implementing the revised Code of Conduct on source safety and security. More than 60 States have already begun working towards implementation of the Code. The Agency is also developing Integrated Nuclear Security Support Plans with individual Member States, as frameworks for helping to address their nuclear security needs over the longer term.

The Importance of Regional Efforts

It is clear that the benefits of IAEA assistance — and the reach of our limited resources — can be maximized by coordinating our activities with other international and regional organizations and through the use of regional partnerships. The Australian Government has established a regional project on the Security of Radioactive Sources, and the IAEA hopes to contribute to the success of that project, using funds designated by the US Department of Energy for assistance in establishing Regional Radiological Security Partnerships. Australia, the IAEA, and the USA, together with other States in the region — notably, Indonesia, Malaysia, Thailand and Vietnam — are already in the process of developing a work plan.

9

Nuclear Arms Race, Power and Fission

Nuclear Power

The nuclear arms race was a competition for supremacy in nuclear warfare between the United States, the Soviet Union, and their respective allies during the Cold War. During the Cold War, in addition to the American and Soviet nuclear stockpiles, other countries also developed nuclear weapons, though none engaged in warhead production on nearly the same scale as the two superpowers.

World War II

The first nuclear weapon was created by the American Manhattan Project during the Second World War and was developed for use against the Axis powers. Scientists in the Soviet Union, then an ally of the United States, were aware of the possibility of nuclear weapons and had been doing some work in that direction.

The Soviet Union was not officially informed of the American experiments until Stalin was informed at the Potsdam Conference on July 24, 1945. The Americans did not trust the Soviets enough to keep the information from German spies; there was also deep distrust of the Soviets and their intentions, despite the wartime partnership. Even during the war many government and military figures in the USA saw the USSR as a potential enemy in the future. Despite this, the Soviets were well aware of the program due to a spy ring operating within the American nuclear program.

The atomic spies (including Klaus Fuchs and Theodore Hall) kept Stalin well informed of American developments. When U.S. President Harry S. Truman informed Stalin of the weapons, he was surprised at how calmly Stalin took the news and thought that Stalin had not understood what he had told him. In fact Stalin had long been aware of the program. The American program had been so secret that even Truman did not know about the weapons until he became president; Stalin had thus known about the Manhattan Project before Truman himself did.

In August of 1945, atomic bombs were dropped per Truman's order on designated Japanese cities. The first bomb was dropped on Hiroshima, and then another bomb was dropped on Nagasaki by the B-29 bombers *Enola Gay* and *Bock's Car* respectively.

Early Cold War

In the years immediately after the Second World War, the United States had a nuclear monopoly on both specific knowledge and, most importantly, raw materials. Initially, it was thought that uranium was relatively rare in the world, but this was discovered to be incorrect. While American leaders hoped that their exclusivity would be able to draw concessions from the Soviet Union, this proved ineffective. Behind the scenes the Soviet regime was working furiously to build their own atomic weapons. During the war Soviet efforts had been limited by a lack of uranium, but new supplies in Eastern Europe were taken and provided a steady supply while the Soviets developed a domestic source. While American thinkers had predicted that the USSR would not have nuclear weapons until the mid-1950s, the first Soviet bomb was detonated on August 29 of 1949, shocking the entire world. The weapon (called "Joe One" by the West) was more or less a copy of the weapon which the United States had dropped on Japan ("Fat Man").

Governments devoted massive amounts of resources to increasing the quality and quantity of their nuclear arsenal. Both nations quickly began work on hydrogen bombs and the United States detonated the first such device on November 1, 1952. Again the Soviets surprised the Americans by exploding a deployable thermonuclear device of their own the next August, though it was not actually a "true" multi-stage hydrogen bomb (that would wait until 1955). The Soviet H-bomb was almost completely a product of domestic research, as their espionage sources in the USA had only worked on very preliminary (and incorrect) versions of the hydrogen bomb.

The most important development in terms of delivery in the 1950s was the introduction of ICBMs. Missiles had long been seen as the ideal platform for nuclear weapons, and were potentially a more effective delivery system than strategic bombers, which was the primary delivery method at the beginning of the Cold War. In 1957 on the 4th of October with the launch of Sputnik the Soviet Union showed the world that they had missiles that could hit anywhere in the world. The United States launched their own on the 31 October 1959. The Space Race showcased technology that was critical to nuclear weapons delivery (the ICBM boosters) while maintaining the benign appearance of being done for the purpose of science and exploration.

This period also saw attempts begin to defend against nuclear weapons. Both powers built large radar arrays to detect incoming bombers and missiles. Fighters to use against bombers and anti-ballistic missiles to use against ICBMs were also developed. Large underground bunkers were constructed to save the leadership of the superpowers, and individuals were told to build fallout shelters and taught how to react to a nuclear attack (civil defence). These bombs could kill millions in the event of an attack by either side.

Mutually Assured Destruction (MAD)

All of these defensive measures were far from foolproof and by the 1950s both the United States and Soviet Union had the power to obliterate the other side. Both sides developed a "second-strike" capability, i.e. they could launch a devastating attack even after sustaining a full assault from the other side (especially by means of submarines). This policy was part of what became known as Mutually Assured Destruction: both sides knew that any attack upon the other would be suicide for themselves as well, and thus would (in theory) refrain from attacking one another.

Both Soviet and American thinkers hoped to use nuclear weapons to extract concessions from the other side, or from other powers such as China, but the risk of any use of these weapons was so large that both sides refrained from what John Foster Dulles referred to as brinkmanship. While some like General Douglas MacArthur argued nuclear weapons should be used during the Korean War both Truman and Eisenhower disagreed.

Both sides were also unaware of how their relative arsenals compared. The Americans tended to be lacking in confidence, in the 1950s they believed in a non-existent "bomber gap" (aerial photography later discovered that the Soviets had been playing a sort of Potemkin village game with their bombers in their military parades, flying them in large circles to make it appear they had far more than they truly did), and the 1960 American presidential election saw accusations of a wholly spurious "missile gap" between the Soviets and the Americans. The Soviet government structure tended to exaggerate the power of Soviet weapons to the leadership and Nikita Khrushchev.

An additional controversy formed in the United States during the early-1960s over whether or not it was known if their weapons would work *at all* if it came down to it. All of the individual components of nuclear missiles had been tested separately (warheads, navigation systems, rockets), but it had been infeasible to test them all *as a whole*. Critics charged that it was not really known how a warhead would function in the gravity forces and temperature differences encountered in the upper atmosphere and outer space, and Kennedy was unwilling to run a risky test of an ICBM with a live warhead. The closest thing to an actual test, 1962's Operation Frigate Bird, in which the submarine USS *Ethan Allen* launched a Polaris A1 missile over 1,000 miles to the nuclear test site at Christmas Island, was challenged by critics (including Curtis LeMay, who used doubt over missile accuracy to encourage the development of new bombers) on the grounds that it was a single test (and could therefore be an anomaly), was a lower-altitude SLBM (and therefore was subject to different conditions than an ICBM), and that significant modifications had been made to its warhead before testing.

Initial Nuclear Proliferation

In addition to the United States and the Soviet Union, three other nations, the United Kingdom, People's Republic of China, and France also developed far smaller nuclear stockpiles. In 1952, the United Kingdom became the third nation to possess nuclear weapons when it detonated an atomic bomb in Operation Hurricane in Australia on October 3, 1952. During the Cold War, British nuclear deterrence came from submarines and nuclear-armed aircraft. The Resolution class ballistic missile submarines armed with the American-built Polaris missile provided the sea deterrent, while aircraft such as the Avro Vulcan, SEPECAT Jaguar, Panavia Tornado and several other Royal Air Force strike aircraft carrying WE.177 gravity bomb provided the air deterrent.

France became the fourth nation to possess nuclear weapons on February 13, 1960, when the atomic bomb Gerboise Bleue was detonated in Algeria, then still a French colony. During the Cold War, the French nuclear deterrent was centered around the Force de frappe, a nuclear triad consisting of Dassault Mirage IV bombers carrying such nuclear weapons as the AN-22 gravity bomb and the ASMP stand-off attack missile, Pluton and Hades ballistic missiles, and the Redoutable class submarine armed with strategic nuclear missiles.

The People's Republic of China became the fifth nuclear power on October 16, 1964, when it detonated a uranium-235 bomb in a test codenamed 596. Due to Soviet/Chinese tensions, the Chinese might have used nuclear weapons against either the United States or the Soviet Union in the event of a nuclear war between the United States and the Soviet Union. During the Cold War, the Chinese nuclear deterrent consisted of gravity bombs carried aboard H-6 bomber aircraft, missile systems such as the DF-2, DF-3, and DF-4, and in the later stages of the Cold War, the Type 092 ballistic missile submarine.

Détente

Economic problems caused by the arms race in both powers, combined with China's new role and the ability to verify disarmament led to a number of arms control agreements beginning in the 1970s. This period known as détente allowed both states to reduce their spending on weapons systems. SALT I and SALT II and all limited the size of the states arsenals. Bans on nuclear testing, anti-ballistic missile systems, and weapons in space all attempted to limit the expansion of the arms race through the Partial Test Ban Treaty.

These treaties were only partially successful. Both states continued building massive numbers of nuclear weapons, and new technologies such as *multiple independently targetable reentry vehicles* (also known as MIRVs) limited the effectiveness of the treaties. Both superpowers retained the ability to destroy each other many times over.

Reagan and the Strategic Defence Initiative

Towards the end of Jimmy Carter's presidency, and continued strongly through the subsequent presidency of Ronald Reagan, the United States rejected disarmament and tried to restart the arms race through the production of new weapons and anti-weapons systems. The central part of this strategy was the Strategic Defence Initiative, a space based anti-ballistic missile system derided as "Star Wars" by its critics. During the second part of 1980s, the Soviet economy was teetering towards collapse and was unable to match American arms spending. Numerous negotiations by Mikhail Gorbachev attempted to come to agreements on reducing nuclear stockpiles, but the most radical were rejected by Reagan as they would also prohibit his SDI program.

Post-Cold War

With the end of the Cold War the United States, and especially Russia, cut down on nuclear weapons spending. Fewer new systems were developed and both arsenals have shrunk. But both countries still maintain stocks of nuclear missiles numbering in the thousands. In the USA, stockpile stewardship programs have taken over the role of maintaining the aging arsenal.

After the Cold War ended, a large amount of resources and money which was once spent on developing nuclear weapons in USSR was then spent on repairing the environmental damage produced by the nuclear arms race, and almost all former production sites are now major cleanup sites. In the USA, the plutonium production facility at Hanford, Washington and the plutonium pit fabrication facility at Rocky Flats, Colorado are among the most polluted sites. United States policy and strategy regarding nuclear proliferation was outlined in 1995 in the document "Essentials of Post-Cold War Deterrence". Despite efforts made in cleaning up uranium sites, significant problems stemming from the legacy of uranium development still exist today on the Navajo Nation in the states of Utah, Colorado, New Mexico, and Arizona. Hundreds of abandoned mines have not been cleaned up and present environmental and health risks in many Navajo communities.

India and Pakistan

The South-Asian states of India and Pakistan have also engaged in a nuclear arms race. India detonated what it called a "peaceful nuclear device" in 1974 ("Smiling Buddha") much to the surprise and alarm of the world who had been giving India nuclear technology for civilian, energy producing and peaceful purposes. The test generated great concern in Pakistan, which feared that it would be at the mercy of its long-time arch rival and quickly responded by pursuing its own nuclear weapons program. In the last few decades of the 20th century, Pakistan and India began to develop nuclear-capable rockets, and Pakistan had its own covert bomb program with Chinese proliferation which extended over many years since the first Indian weapon was detonated. In 1998 India, under Atal Bihari Vajpayee government, test detonated 5 more nuclear weapons. While the international response to the detonation was muted, domestic pressure within Pakistan began to build steam and Prime Minister Mian Muhammad Nawaz Sharif ordered the test, detonated 6 nuclear war weapons in a tit-for-tat fashion and to act as a deterrent.

Israel

Israel is widely believed to possess a substantial arsenal of nuclear weapons and maintains intermediate-range ballistic missiles to deliver them. The Israeli government refuses to officially confirm or deny that it has a nuclear weapon program, and has an unofficial but rigidly enforced policy of deliberate ambiguity, saying only that it would not be the first to "introduce nuclear weapons in the Middle East". Israel is widely believed to be one of the nuclear-armed nation-states not within the Nuclear Non-Proliferation Treaty (NPT), the other three being India, Pakistan and North Korea.In a December 2006 interview, Israeli Prime Minister Ehud Olmert said Iran aspires "to have a nuclear weapon as America, France, Israel and Russia." Olmert's office later said that the quote was taken out of context, in other parts of the interview, Olmert refused to confirm or deny Israel's nuclear weapon status. According to The Nuclear Threat Initiative, based on Vanunu's information, Israel had approximately 200 nuclear explosive devices by 1980 and a Jericho missile delivery system.

Milestone nuclear explosions

The following list is of milestone nuclear explosions. In addition to the atomic bombings of Hiroshima and Nagasaki, the first nuclear test of a given weapon type for a country is included, and tests which were otherwise notable (such as the largest test ever). All yields (explosive power) are given in their estimated energy equivalents in kilotons of TNT. Putative tests have not been included.

"Staging" refers to whether it was a "true" hydrogen bomb of the so-called Teller-Ulam configuration or simply a form of a boosted fission weapon. For a more complete list of nuclear test series, see List of nuclear tests. Some exact yield estimates, such as that of the Tsar Bomba and the tests by India and Pakistan in 1998, are somewhat contested among specialists.

Nuclear Power

Nuclear power is power (generally electrical) produced from controlled (i.e., non-explosive) nuclear reactions. Commercial plants in use to date use nuclear fission reactions. Electric utility reactors heat water to produce steam, which is then used to generate electricity. In 2009, 15% of the world's electricity came from nuclear power. More than 150 naval vessels using nuclear propulsion have been built.

Nuclear fusion reactions are widely believed to be safer than fission and appear potentially viable, though technically quite difficult and have yet to be created on a scale that could be used in a functional power plant. Fusion power has been under intense theoretical and experimental investigation since the 1950s.

Both fission and fusion appear promising for space propulsion applications, generating higher mission velocities with less reaction mass. This is due to the much higher energy density of nuclear reactions: some 7 orders of magnitude (10,000,000 times) more support of a hydrogen economy), for desalinating sea water, and for use in district heating systems.

History

Origins

As the father of nuclear physics, Ernest Rutherford is credited with splitting the atom in 1917. His team in England bombarded nitrogen with naturally occurring alpha particles from radioactive material and observed a proton emitted with energy higher than the alpha particle. In 1932 two of his students John Cockcroft and Ernest Walton, working under Rutherford's direction, attempted to split the atomic nucleus by entirely artificial means, using a particle accelerator to bombard lithium with protons, thereby producing two helium nuclei.

After James Chadwick discovered the neutron in 1932, nuclear fission was first experimentally achieved by Enrico Fermi in 1934 in Rome, when his team bombarded uranium with neutrons. In 1938, German chemists Otto Hahn and Fritz Strassmann, along with Austrian physicists Lise Meitner and Meitner's nephew, Otto Robert Frisch, conducted experiments with the products of neutron-bombarded uranium. They determined that the relatively tiny neutron split the nucleus of the massive uranium atoms into two roughly equal pieces, which was a surprising result. Numerous scientists, including Leo Szilard who was one of the first, recognized that if fission reactions released additional neutrons, a self-sustaining nuclear chain reaction could result. This spurred scientists in many countries (including the United States, the United Kingdom, France, Germany, and the Soviet Union) to petition their governments for support of nuclear fission research.

In the United States, where Fermi and Szilard had both emigrated, this led to the creation of the first man-made reactor, known as Chicago Pile-1, which achieved criticality on December 2, 1942. This work became part of the Manhattan Project, which built large reactors at the Hanford Site (formerly the town of Hanford, Washington) to breed plutonium for use in the first nuclear weapons, which were used on the cities of Hiroshima and Nagasaki. A parallel uranium enrichment effort also was pursued.

energetic than the chemical reactions which power the c
generation of rockets. Radioactive decay has been used
relatively small (few kW) scale, mostly to power space mi
and experiments.

Use

As of 2005, nuclear power provided 2.1% of the world's
and 15% of the world's electricity, with the U.S., France, an
together accounting for 56.5% of nuclear generated electr
2007, the IAEA reported there were 439 nuclear power re
operation in the world, operating in 31 countries.

In 2007, nuclear power's share of global electricity ge
dropped to 14%. According to the International Atomi
Agency, the main reason for this was an earthquake in
Japan on 16 July 2007, which shut down all seven react
Kashiwazaki-Kariwa Nuclear Power Plant. There were al
other reductions and "unusual outages" experienced in I
Germany. Also, increases in the load factor for the cu
of reactors appear to have plateaued.

The United States produces the most nuclear en
nuclear power providing 19% of the electricity it consu
France produces the highest percentage of its electri
from nuclear reactors—80% as of 2006. In the Europea
a whole, nuclear energy provides 30% of the electrici
energy policy differs between European Union cou
some, such as Austria, Estonia, and Ireland, have no ac
power stations. In comparison, France has a large num
plants, with 16 multi-unit stations in current use.

In the US, while the Coal and Gas Electricity
projected to be worth $85 billion by 2013, Nuclear Pow
are forecast to be worth $18 billion.

Many military and some civilian (such as som
ships use nuclear marine propulsion, a form of nuclea
A few space vehicles have been launched using full-fle
reactors: the Soviet RORSAT series and the America

International research is continuing into safety i
such as passively safe plants, the use of nuclea
additional uses of process heat such as hydrogen

After World War II, the fear that reactor research would encourage the rapid spread of nuclear weapons and technology, combined with what many scientists thought would be a long road of development, created a situation in which the government attempted to keep reactor research under strict government control and classification. In addition, most reactor research centered on purely military purposes. There was an immediate arms and development race when the United States military refused to follow the advice of its own scientific community to form an international cooperative to share information and control nuclear materials. By 2006, things have come full circle with the Global Nuclear Energy Partnership.

Electricity was generated for the first time by a nuclear reactor on December 20, 1951, at the EBR-I experimental station near Arco, Idaho, which initially produced about 100 kW (the Arco Reactor was also the first to experience partial meltdown, in 1955). In 1952, a report by the Paley Commission (*The President's Materials Policy Commission*) for President Harry Truman made a "relatively pessimistic" assessment of nuclear power, and called for "aggressive research in the whole field of solar energy." A December 1953 speech by President Dwight Eisenhower, "Atoms for Peace," emphasized the useful harnessing of the atom and set the U.S. on a course of strong government support for international use of nuclear power.

Early Years

On June 27, 1954, the USSR's Obninsk Nuclear Power Plant became the world's first nuclear power plant to generate electricity for a power grid, and produced around 5 megawatts of electric power.

Later in 1954, Lewis Strauss, then chairman of the United States Atomic Energy Commission (U.S. AEC, forerunner of the U.S. Nuclear Regulatory Commission and the United States Department of Energy) spoke of electricity in the future being "too cheap to meter." Strauss was referring to hydrogen fusion-which was secretly being developed as part of Project Sherwood at the time-but Strauss's statement was interpreted as a promise of very cheap energy from nuclear fission. The U.S. AEC itself had issued far more conservative testimony regarding nuclear fission to the

U.S. Congress only months before, projecting that "costs can be brought down... [to]... about the same as the cost of electricity from conventional sources..." Significant disappointment would develop later on, when the new nuclear plants did not provide energy "too cheap to meter."

In 1955 the United Nations' "First Geneva Conference", then the world's largest gathering of scientists and engineers, met to explore the technology. In 1957 EURATOM was launched alongside the European Economic Community (the latter is now the European Union). The same year also saw the launch of the International Atomic Energy Agency (IAEA). The world's first commercial nuclear power station, Calder Hall in Sellafield, England was opened in 1956 with an initial capacity of 50 MW (later 200 MW). The first commercial nuclear generator to become operational in the United States was the Shippingport Reactor (Pennsylvania, December, 1957).

One of the first organizations to develop nuclear power was the U.S. Navy, for the purpose of propelling submarines and aircraft carriers. It has a good record in nuclear safety, perhaps because of the stringent demands of Admiral Hyman G. Rickover, who was the driving force behind nuclear marine propulsion as well as the Shippingport Reactor (Alvin Radkowsky was chief scientist at the U.S. Navy nuclear propulsion division, and was involved with the latter). The U.S. Navy has operated more nuclear reactors than any other entity, including the Soviet Navy, with no publicly known major incidents. The first nuclear-powered submarine, USS *Nautilus* (SSN-571), was put to sea in December 1954. Two U.S. nuclear submarines, USS *Scorpion* and USS *Thresher*, have been lost at sea. These vessels were both lost due to malfunctions in systems not related to the reactor plants. Also, the sites are monitored and no known leakage has occurred from the onboard reactors.

The United States Army also had a nuclear power program, beginning in 1954. The SM-1 Nuclear Power Plant, at Ft. Belvoir, Va., was the first power reactor in the US to supply electrical energy to a commercial grid (VEPCO), in April 1957, *before* Shippingport. Enrico Fermi and Leó Szilárd in 1955 shared U.S. Patent 2,708,656 for the nuclear reactor, belatedly granted for the work they had done during the Manhattan Project.

Development

Installed nuclear capacity initially rose relatively quickly, rising from less than 1 gigawatt (GW) in 1960 to 100 GW in the late 1970s, and 300 GW in the late 1980s. Since the late 1980s worldwide capacity has risen much more slowly, reaching 366 GW in 2005. Between around 1970 and 1990, more than 50 GW of capacity was under construction (peaking at over 150 GW in the late 70s and early 80s) — in 2005, around 25 GW of new capacity was planned. More than two-thirds of all nuclear plants ordered after January 1970 were eventually cancelled. A total of 63 nuclear units were canceled in the USA between 1975 and 1980.

During the 1970s and 1980s rising economic costs (related to extended construction times largely due to regulatory changes and pressure-group litigation) and falling fossil fuel prices made nuclear power plants then under construction less attractive. In the 1980s (U.S.) and 1990s (Europe), flat load growth and electricity liberalization also made the addition of large new baseload capacity unattractive.

The 1973 oil crisis had a significant effect on countries, such as France and Japan, which had relied more heavily on oil for electric generation (39% and 73% respectively) to invest in nuclear power. Today, nuclear power supplies about 80% and 30% of the electricity in those countries, respectively.

A general movement against nuclear power arose during the last third of the 20th century, based on the fear of a possible nuclear accident as well as the history of accidents, fears of radiation as well as the history of radiation of the public, nuclear proliferation, and on the opposition to nuclear waste production, transport and lack of any final storage plans. Perceived risks on the citizens' health and safety, the 1979 accident at Three Mile Island and the 1986 Chernobyl disaster played a part in stopping new plant construction in many countries, although the public policy organization Brookings Institution suggests that new nuclear units have not been ordered in the U.S. because the Institution's research concludes they cost 15–30% more over their lifetime than conventional coal and natural gas fired plants.

Unlike the Three Mile Island accident, the much more serious Chernobyl accident did not increase regulations affecting Western reactors since the Chernobyl reactors were of the problematic RBMK design only used in the Soviet Union, for example lacking "robust" containment buildings. Many of these reactors are still in use today. However, changes were made in both the reactors themselves (use of low enriched uranium) and in the control system (prevention of disabling safety systems) to reduce the possibility of a duplicate accident.

An international organization to promote safety awareness and professional development on operators in nuclear facilities was created: WANO; World Association of Nuclear Operators.

Opposition in Ireland, and Poland prevented nuclear programs there, while Austria (1978), Sweden (1980) and Italy (1987) (influenced by Chernobyl) voted in referendums to oppose or phase out nuclear power. In July 2009, the Italian Parliament passed a law that canceled the results of an earlier referendum and allowed the immediate start of the Italian nuclear program.

Flexibility of Nuclear Power Plants

It is often claimed that nuclear stations are inflexible in their output, implying that other, typically fossil stations would be used to meet peak demand. Whilst it may have been true for certain reactors, this is not longer true of at least some modern designs. Nuclear plants are routinely used in load following mode on a large scale in France.

Economics

The economics of nuclear power plants are primarily influenced by the high initial investment necessary to construct a plant. In 2009, estimates for the cost of a new plant in the U.S. ranged from $6 to $10 billion. It is therefore usually more economical to run them as long as possible, or construct additional reactor blocks in existing facilities. In 2008, new nuclear power plant construction costs were rising faster than the costs of other types of power plants.. A prestigious panel assembled for a 2003 MIT study of the industry found the following: In deregulated markets, nuclear power is not now cost competitive with coal and natural gas. However, plausible reductions by industry in capital cost, operation and maintenance costs, and construction time could reduce the gap. Carbon emission credits, if enacted by government, can give nuclear power a cost advantage. —The Future of Nuclear Power Comparative economics with other power sources are also discussed in the Main article above and in nuclear power debate.

Future of the Industry

As of 2007, Watts Bar 1, which came on-line in February 7, 1996, was the last U.S. commercial nuclear reactor to go on-line. This is often quoted as evidence of a successful worldwide campaign for nuclear power phase-out. However, even in the U.S. and throughout Europe, investment in research and in the nuclear fuel cycle has continued, and some nuclear industry experts predict electricity shortages, fossil fuel price increases, global warming and heavy metal emissions from fossil fuel use, new technology such as passively safe plants, and national energy security will renew the demand for nuclear power plants. According to the World Nuclear Association, globally during the 1980s one new nuclear reactor started up every 17 days on average, and by the year 2015 this rate could increase to one every 5 days.

Many countries remain active in developing nuclear power, including China, India, Japan and Pakistan. all actively developing both fast and thermal technology, South Korea and the United States, developing thermal technology only, and South Africa and China, developing versions of the Pebble Bed Modular Reactor (PBMR). Several EU member states actively pursue nuclear programs, while some other member states continue to have a ban for the nuclear energy use. Japan has an active nuclear construction program with new units brought on-line in 2005. In the U.S., three consortia responded in 2004 to the U.S. Department of Energy's solicitation under the Nuclear Power 2010 Program and were awarded matching funds—the Energy Policy Act of 2005 authorized loan guarantees for up to six new reactors, and authorized the Department of Energy to build a reactor based on the Generation IV Very-High-Temperature Reactor concept to produce both electricity and hydrogen. As of the early 21st century, nuclear power is of particular interest to both China and India to serve their rapidly growing economies—both are developing fast breeder reactors.. In the energy policy of the United Kingdom it is recognized that there is a likely future energy supply shortfall, which may have to be filled by either new nuclear plant construction or maintaining existing plants beyond their programmed lifetime. There is a possible impediment to production of nuclear power plants as only a few companies worldwide have the capacity to forge single-piece reactor pressure vessels, which are necessary in most reactor designs.

Utilities across the world are submitting orders years in advance of any actual need for these vessels. Other manufacturers are examining various options, including making the component themselves, or finding ways to make a similar item using alternate methods. Other solutions include using designs that do not require single-piece forged pressure vessels such as Canada's Advanced CANDU Reactors or Sodium-cooled Fast Reactors.

The World Nuclear Industry Status Report 2009 states that "even if Finland and France each builds a reactor or two, China goes for an additional 20 plants and Japan, Korea or Eastern Europe add a few units, the overall worldwide trend will most likely be downwards over the next two decades". With long lead times of 10 years or more, it will be difficult to maintain or increase the number of operating nuclear power plants over the next 20 years. The one exception to this outcome would be if operating lifetimes could be substantially increased beyond 40 years *on average*. This seems unlikely since the present average age of the operating nuclear power plant fleet in the world is 25 years.

However, China plans to build more than 100 plants, while in the US the licenses of almost half its reactors have already been extended to 60 years, and plans to build more than 30 new ones are under consideration. Further, the U.S. NRC and the U.S. Department of Energy have initiated research into Light water reactor sustainability which is hoped will lead to allowing extensions of reactor licenses beyond 60 years, in increments of 20 years, provided that safety can be maintained, as the loss in non-CO_2-emitting generation capacity by retiring reactors "may serve to challenge U.S. energy security, potentially resulting in increased greenhouse gas emissions, and contributing to an imbalance between electric supply and demand." In 2008, the International Atomic Energy Agency (IAEA) predicted that nuclear power capacity could double by 2030, though that would not be enough to increase nuclear's share of electricity generation.

Nuclear Reactor Technology

Just as many conventional thermal power stations generate electricity by harnessing the thermal energy released from burning fossil fuels, nuclear power plants convert the energy released from the nucleus of an atom, typically via nuclear fission. When a relatively large fissile atomic nucleus (usually uranium-235 or plutonium-239) absorbs a neutron, a fission of the atom often results. Fission splits the atom into two or more smaller nuclei with kinetic energy (known as fission products) and also releases gamma radiation and free neutrons. A portion of these neutrons may later be absorbed by other fissile atoms and create more fissions, which release more neutrons, and so on.

This nuclear chain reaction can be controlled by using neutron poisons and neutron moderators to change the portion of neutrons that will go on to cause more fissions. Nuclear reactors generally have automatic and manual systems to shut the fission reaction down if unsafe conditions are detected. A cooling system removes heat from the reactor core and transports it to another area of the plant, where the thermal energy can be harnessed to produce electricity or to do other useful work. Typically the hot coolant will be used as a heat source for a boiler, and the pressurized steam from that boiler will power one or more steam turbine driven electrical generators.

There are many different reactor designs, utilizing different fuels and coolants and incorporating different control schemes. Some of these designs have been engineered to meet a specific need. Reactors for nuclear submarines and large naval ships, for example, commonly use highly enriched uranium as a fuel. This fuel choice increases the reactor's power density and extends the usable life of the nuclear fuel load, but is more expensive and a greater risk to nuclear proliferation than some of the other nuclear fuels. A number of new designs for nuclear power generation, collectively known as the Generation IV reactors, are the subject of active research and may be used for practical power generation in the future. Many of these new designs specifically attempt to make fission reactors cleaner, safer and/or less of a risk to the proliferation of nuclear weapons. Passively safe plants (such as the ESBWR) are available to be built and other designs that are believed to be nearly fool-proof are being pursued. Fusion reactors, which may be viable in the future, diminish or eliminate many of the risks associated with nuclear fission.

Life Cycle

A nuclear reactor is only part of the life-cycle for nuclear power. The process starts with mining. Uranium mines are underground, open-pit, or in-situ leach mines. In any case, the uranium ore is extracted, usually converted into a stable and compact form such as yellowcake, and then transported to a processing facility. Here, the yellowcake is converted to uranium hexafluoride, which is then enriched using various techniques. At this point, the enriched uranium, containing more than the natural 0.7% U-235, is used to make rods of the proper composition and geometry for the particular reactor that the fuel is destined for. The fuel rods will spend about 3 operational cycles (typically 6 years total now) inside the reactor, generally until about 3% of their uranium has been fissioned, then they will be moved to a spent fuel pool where the short lived isotopes generated by fission can decay away. After about 5 years in a cooling pond, the spent fuel is radioactively and thermally cool enough to handle, and it can be moved to dry storage casks or reprocessed.

Conventional Fuel Resources

Uranium is a fairly common element in the Earth's crust. Uranium is approximately as common as tin or germanium in Earth's crust, and is about 35 times more common than silver. Uranium is a constituent of most rocks, dirt, and of the oceans. The fact that uranium is so spread out is a problem because mining uranium is only economically feasible where there is a large concentration. Still, the world's present measured resources of uranium, economically recoverable at a price of 130 USD/kg, are enough to last for "at least a century" at current consumption rates. This represents a higher level of assured resources than is normal for most minerals. On the basis of analogies with other metallic minerals, a doubling of price from present levels could be expected to create about a tenfold increase in measured resources, over time. However, the cost of nuclear power lies for the most part in the construction of the power station. Therefore the fuel's contribution to the overall cost of the electricity produced is relatively small, so even a large fuel price escalation will have relatively little effect on final price. For instance, typically a doubling of the uranium market price would increase the fuel cost for a light water reactor by 26% and the electricity cost about 7%, whereas doubling the price of natural gas would typically add 70% to the price of electricity from that source. At high enough prices, eventually extraction from sources such as granite and seawater become economically feasible.

Current light water reactors make relatively inefficient use of nuclear fuel, fissioning only the very rare uranium-235 isotope. Nuclear reprocessing can make this waste reusable and more efficient reactor designs allow better use of the available resources.

Breeding

As opposed to current light water reactors which use uranium-235 (0.7% of all natural uranium), fast breeder reactors use uranium-238 (99.3% of all natural uranium). It has been estimated that there is up to five billion years' worth of uranium-238 for use in these power plants. Breeder technology has been used in several reactors, but the high cost of reprocessing fuel safely requires uranium prices of more than 200 USD/kg before becoming justified economically. As of December 2005, the only breeder reactor producing power is BN-600 in Beloyarsk, Russia. The electricity output of BN-600 is 600 MW — Russia has planned to build another unit, BN-800, at Beloyarsk nuclear power plant. Also, Japan's Monju reactor is planned for restart (having been shut down since 1995), and both China and India intend to build breeder reactors.

Another alternative would be to use uranium-233 bred from thorium as fission fuel in the thorium fuel cycle. Thorium is about 3.5 times as common as uranium in the Earth's crust, and has different geographic characteristics. This would extend the total practical fissionable resource base by 450%. Unlike the breeding of U-238 into plutonium, fast breeder reactors are not necessary—it can be performed satisfactorily in more conventional plants. India has looked into this technology, as it has abundant thorium reserves but little uranium.

Fusion

Fusion power advocates commonly propose the use of deuterium, or tritium, both isotopes of hydrogen, as fuel and in many current designs also lithium and boron. Assuming a fusion energy output equal to the current global output and that this does not increase in the future, then the known current lithium reserves would last 3000 years, lithium from sea water would last 60 million years, and a more complicated fusion process using only deuterium from sea water would have fuel for 150 billion years. Although this process has yet to be realized, many experts and civilians alike believe fusion to be a promising future energy source due to the short lived radioactivity of the produced waste, its low carbon emissions, and its prospective power output.

Water

Like all forms of power generation using steam turbines, nuclear power plants use large amounts of water for cooling. At Sellafield, which is no longer producing electricity, a maximum of 18,184.4 m^3 a day (over 4 million gallons) and 6,637,306 m^3 a year (figures from the Environment Agency) of fresh water from Wast Water is still abstracted to use on site for various processes. As with most power plants, two-thirds of the energy produced by a nuclear power plant goes into waste heat, and that heat is carried away from the plant in the water (which remains uncontaminated by radioactivity). The emitted water either is sent into cooling towers where it goes up and is emitted as water droplets (literally a cloud) or is discharged into large bodies of water — cooling ponds, lakes, rivers, or oceans. Droughts can pose a severe problem by causing the source of cooling water to run out. The Palo Verde Nuclear Generating Station near Phoenix, AZ is the only nuclear generating facility in the world that is not located adjacent to a large body of water. Instead, it uses treated sewage from several nearby municipalities to meet its cooling water needs, recycling 20 billion US gallons (76,000,000 m^3) of wastewater each year.

Like conventional power plants, nuclear power plants generate large quantities of waste heat which is expelled in the condenser, following the turbine. Colocation of plants that can take advantage of this thermal energy has been suggested by Oak Ridge National

Laboratory (ORNL) as a way to take advantage of process synergy for added energy efficiency. One example would be to use the power plant steam to produce hydrogen from water. (Separation of water into hydrogen and oxygen can use less energy if the water begins at a high temperature.)

Solid Waste

The safe storage and disposal of nuclear waste is a significant challenge and yet unresolved problem. The most important waste stream from nuclear power plants is spent fuel. A large nuclear reactor produces 3 cubic metres (25–30 tonnes) of spent fuel each year. It is primarily composed of unconverted uranium as well as significant quantities of transuranic actinides (plutonium and curium, mostly). In addition, about 3% of it is made of fission products. The actinides (uranium, plutonium, and curium) are responsible for the bulk of the long term radioactivity, whereas the fission products are responsible for the bulk of the short term radioactivity.

High-level Radioactive Waste

Spent fuel is highly radioactive and needs to be handled with great care and forethought. However, spent nuclear fuel becomes less radioactive over the course of thousands of years of time. After about 5 percent of the rod has reacted the rod is no longer able to be used. Today, scientists are experimenting on how to recycle these rods to reduce waste. In the meantime, after 40 years, the radiation flux is 99.9% lower than it was the moment the spent fuel was removed, although still dangerously radioactive. Spent fuel rods are stored in shielded basins of water (spent fuel pools), usually located on-site. The water provides both cooling for the still-decaying fission products, and shielding from the continuing radioactivity. After a few decades some on-site storage involves moving the now cooler, less radioactive fuel to a dry-storage facility or dry cask storage, where the fuel is stored in steel and concrete containers until its radioactivity decreases naturally ("decays") to levels safe enough for other processing. This interim stage spans years or decades or millennia, depending on the type of fuel. Most U.S. waste is currently stored in temporary storage sites requiring oversight, while suitable permanent disposal methods are discussed. As of 2007, the United States had accumulated more than 50,000 metric tons of spent nuclear fuel from nuclear reactors. Underground storage at Yucca Mountain nuclear waste repository in U.S. has been proposed as permanent storage. After 10,000 years of radioactive decay, according to United States Environmental Protection Agency standards, the spent nuclear fuel will no longer pose a threat to public health and safety. The amount of waste can be reduced in several ways, particularly reprocessing. Even so, the remaining waste will be substantially radioactive for at least 300 years even if the actinides are removed, and for up to thousands of years if the actinides are left in. Even with separation of all actinides, and using fast breeder reactors to destroy by transmutation some of the longer-lived non-actinides as well, the waste must be segregated from the environment for one to a few hundred years, and therefore this is properly categorized as a long-term problem. Subcritical reactors or fusion reactors could also reduce the time the waste has to be stored. It has been argued that the best solution for the nuclear waste is above ground temporary storage since technology is rapidly changing. There is hope that current waste may well become a valuable resource in the future.

Low-level Radioactive Waste

The nuclear industry also produces a huge volume of low-level radioactive waste in the form of contaminated items like clothing, hand tools, water purifier resins, and (upon decommissioning) the materials of which the reactor itself is built. In the United States, the Nuclear Regulatory Commission has repeatedly attempted to allow low-level materials to be handled as normal waste: landfilled, recycled into consumer items, et cetera. Most low-level waste releases very low levels of radioactivity and is only considered radioactive waste because of its history.

Comparing Radioactive Waste to Industrial Toxic Waste

In countries with nuclear power, radioactive wastes comprise less than 1% of total industrial toxic wastes, much of which remains hazardous indefinitely and some of which decomposes or is treated to make the waste less toxic. Overall, nuclear power produces far less waste material by volume than fossil-fuel based power plants.

Coal-burning plants are particularly noted for producing large amounts of toxic and mildly radioactive ash due to concentrating naturally occurring metals and mildly radioactive material from the coal. On the other hand, coal plants do not produce the large amounts of highly-radioactive nuclear waste that nuclear power plants do.

A recent report from Oak Ridge National Laboratory claims that coal power actually results in more radioactive waste being released into the environment than nuclear power operation, and that the population effective dose equivalent from radiation from coal plants is 100 times as much as from ideal operation of nuclear plants. Indeed, coal ash is much less radioactive than nuclear waste, but nuclear plants use shielding to protect the environment from the irradiated reactor vessel, fuel rods, and any radioactive waste on site. However, these claims of lower radiation emissions do not include the radiation released from nuclear power plants during accidents like the Three Mile Island accident or the Chernobyl disaster, or from leakage of nuclear waste during storage.

Reprocessing

Reprocessing can potentially recover up to 95% of the remaining uranium and plutonium in spent nuclear fuel, putting it into new mixed oxide fuel. This produces a reduction in long term radioactivity within the remaining waste, since this is largely short-lived fission products, and reduces its volume by over 90%. Reprocessing of civilian fuel from power reactors is currently done on large scale in Britain, France and (formerly) Russia, soon will be done in China and perhaps India, and is being done on an expanding scale in Japan. The full potential of reprocessing has not been achieved because it requires breeder reactors, which are not yet commercially available. France is generally cited as the most successful reprocessor, but it presently only recycles 28% (by mass) of the yearly fuel use, 7% within France and another 21% in Russia.

Unlike other countries, the US stopped civilian reprocessing from 1976 to 1981 as one part of US non-proliferation policy, since reprocessed material such as plutonium could be used in nuclear weapons: however, reprocessing is now allowed in the U.S. Even so, in the U.S. spent nuclear fuel is currently all treated as waste.

In February, 2006, a new U.S. initiative, the Global Nuclear Energy Partnership was announced. It would be an international effort to reprocess fuel in a manner making nuclear proliferation unfeasible, while making nuclear power available to developing countries.

Depleted Uranium

Uranium enrichment produces many tons of depleted uranium (DU) which consists of U-238 with most of the easily fissile U-235 isotope removed. U-238 is a tough metal with several commercial uses—for example, aircraft production, radiation shielding, and armor—as it has a higher density than lead. Depleted uranium is also useful in munitions as DU penetrators (bullets or APFSDS tips) "self sharpen", due to uranium's tendency to fracture along shear bands. There are concerns that U-238 may lead to health problems in groups exposed to this material excessively, such as tank crews and civilians living in areas where large quantities of DU ammunition have been used in shielding, bombs, missile warheads, and bullets. In January 2003 the World Health Organization released a report finding that contamination from DU munitions were localized to a few tens of meters from the impact sites and contamination of local vegetation and water was 'extremely low'. The report also states that approximately 70% of ingested DU will leave the body after twenty four hours and 90% after a few days.

Debate on Nuclear Power

The nuclear power debate is about the controversy which has surrounded the deployment and use of nuclear fission reactors to generate electricity from nuclear fuel for civilian purposes. The debate about nuclear power peaked during the 1970s and 1980s, when it "reached an intensity unprecedented in the history of technology controversies", in some countries.

Proponents of nuclear energy contend that nuclear power is a sustainable energy source that reduces carbon emissions and increases energy security by decreasing dependence on foreign oil. Proponents claim that nuclear power produces virtually no conventional air pollution, such as greenhouse gases and smog, in contrast to the chief viable alternative of fossil fuel. Proponents also believe that nuclear power is the only viable course to achieve energy independence for most Western countries. Proponents claim that the risks of storing waste are small and can be further reduced by using the latest technology in newer reactors, and the operational safety record in the Western world is excellent when compared to the other major kinds of power plants.

Opponents believe that nuclear power poses many threats to people and the environment. These threats include the unsolved problem of processing, transport and storage of radioactive nuclear waste, the risk of nuclear weapons proliferation and terrorism, as well as health risks and environmental damage from uranium mining. They also contend that reactors themselves are enormously complex machines where many things can and do go wrong, and there have been many serious nuclear accidents. Critics do not believe that the risks of using nuclear fission as a power source can be offset through the development of new technology. They also argue that when all the energy-intensive stages of the nuclear fuel chain are considered, from uranium mining to nuclear decommissioning, nuclear power is not a low-carbon electricity source.

Nuclear Fission

In nuclear physics and nuclear chemistry, nuclear fission is a nuclear reaction in which the nucleus of an atom splits into smaller parts, often producing free neutrons and lighter nuclei, which may eventually produce photons (in the form of gamma rays). Fission of heavy elements is an exothermic reaction which can release large amounts of energy both as electromagnetic radiation and as kinetic energy of the fragments (heating the bulk material where fission takes place). For fission to produce energy, the total binding energy of the resulting elements has to be higher than that of the starting element. Fission is a form of nuclear transmutation because the resulting fragments are not the same element as the original atom.

Nuclear fission produces energy for nuclear power and to drive the explosion of nuclear weapons. Both uses are made possible because certain substances called nuclear fuels undergo fission when struck by free neutrons and in turn generate neutrons when they break apart. This makes possible a self-sustaining chain reaction that releases energy at a controlled rate in a nuclear reactor or at a very rapid uncontrolled rate in a nuclear weapon. The amount of free energy contained in nuclear fuel is millions of times the amount of free energy contained in a similar mass of chemical fuel such as gasoline, making nuclear fission a very tempting source of energy; however, the products of nuclear fission are radioactive and remain so for significant amounts of time, giving rise to a nuclear waste problem. Concerns over nuclear waste accumulation and over the destructive potential of nuclear weapons may counterbalance the desirable qualities of fission as an energy source, and give rise to ongoing political debate over nuclear power.

Physical Overview

Mechanics

Nuclear fission can occur without neutron bombardment, as a type of radioactive decay. This type of fission (called spontaneous fission) is rare except in a few heavy isotopes. In engineered nuclear devices, essentially all nuclear fission occurs as a "nuclear reaction"—a bombardment-driven process that results from the collision of two subatomic particles. In nuclear reactions, a subatomic particle collides with an atomic nucleus and causes changes to it. Nuclear reactions are thus driven by the mechanics of bombardment, not by the relatively constant exponential decay and half-life characteristic of spontaneous radioactive processes. A great amount of nuclear reactions is known. Nuclear fission differs importantly from other types of nuclear reactions in that it can be amplified and sometimes controlled via a nuclear chain reaction. In such a reaction, free neutrons released by each fission event can trigger yet more events, which in turn release more neutrons and cause more fissions.

The chemical element isotopes that can sustain a fission chain reaction are called nuclear fuels, and are said to be fissile. The most common nuclear fuels are ^{235}U (the isotope of uranium with an atomic mass of 235 and of use in nuclear reactors) and ^{239}Pu (the isotope of plutonium with an atomic mass of 239). These fuels break apart into a bimodal range of chemical elements with atomic masses centering near 95 and 135 u (fission products). Most nuclear fuels undergo spontaneous fission only very slowly, decaying instead mainly via an alpha/beta decay chain over periods of millennia to eons. In a nuclear reactor or nuclear weapon, the overwhelming majority of fission events are induced by bombardment with another particle, a neutron, which is itself produced by prior fission events.

Energetics

Typical fission events release about two hundred million eV of energy for each fission event. By contrast, most chemical oxidation reactions (such as burning coal or TNT) release at most a few eV per event, so nuclear fuel contains at least ten million times more usable energy than does chemical fuel. The energy of nuclear fission is released as kinetic energy of the fission products and fragments, and as electromagnetic radiation in the form of gamma rays; in a nuclear reactor, the energy is converted to heat as the particles and gamma rays collide with the atoms that make up the reactor and its working fluid, usually water or occasionally heavy water.

When a uranium nucleus fissions into two daughter nuclei fragments, an energy of ~200 MeV is released. For uranium-235 (total mean fission energy 202.5 MeV), typically ~169 MeV appears as the kinetic energy of the daughter nuclei, which fly apart at about 3% of the speed of light, due to Coulomb repulsion. Also, an average of 2.5 neutrons are emitted with a kinetic energy of ~2 MeV each (total of 4.8 MeV). The fission reaction also releases ~7 MeV in prompt gamma ray photons. The latter figure means that a nuclear explosion or criticality accident emits about 3.5% of its energy as gamma rays, less than 2.5% of its energy as fast neutrons, and the rest as kinetic energy of fission fragments ("heat"). In an atomic bomb, this heat may serve to raise the temperature of the bomb core to 100 million kelvins and cause secondary emission of soft X-rays, which convert some of this energy to ionizing radiation. However, in nuclear reactors, the fission fragment kinetic energy remains as low-temperature heat which causes little or no ionization. The total prompt fission energy amounts to about 181 MeV, or ~ 89% of the total energy. The remaining ~ 11% is released in beta decays which have various half-lives, but begin as a process in the fission products immediately; and in delayed gamma emissions associated with these beta decays. For example, in uranium-235 this delayed energy is divided into about 6.5 MeV in betas, 8.8 MeV in antineutrinos (released at the same time as the betas), and finally, an additional 6.3 MeV in delayed gamma emission from the excited beta-decay products (for a mean total of ~ 10 gamma ray emissions per fission, in all).

The 8.8 MeV/202.5 MeV = 4.3% of the energy which is released as antineutrinos is not captured by the reactor material as heat, and escapes directly through all materials (including the Earth) at nearly the speed of light, and into interplanetary space. Almost all of the remaining radiation is converted to heat, either in the reactor core or its shielding.

Some processes involving neutrons are notable for absorbing or finally yielding energy—for example neutron kinetic energy does not yield heat immediately if the neutron is captured by a uranium-238 atom to breed plutonium-239, but this energy is emitted if the plutonium-239 is later fissioned. On the other hand, so called "delayed neutrons" emitted as radioactive decay products with half-lives up to a minute, from fission-daughters, are very important to reactor control because they give a characteristic "reaction" time for the total nuclear reaction to double in size, if the reaction is run in a "delayed-critical" zone which deliberately relies on these neutrons for a supercritical chain-reaction (one in which each fission cycle yields more neutrons than it absorbs). Without their existence, the nuclear chain-reaction would be prompt critical and increase in size faster than it could be controlled by human intervention. In this case, the first experimental atomic reactors would have run away to a dangerous and messy "prompt critical reaction" before their operators could have manually shut them down (for this reason, designer Enrico Fermi included radiation-counter-triggered control rods, suspended by electromagnets, which could automatically drop into the center of Chicago Pile-1). If these delayed neutrons are captured without producing fissions, they produce heat as well.

Product Nuclei and Binding Energy

In fission there is a preference to yield fragments with even proton numbers, which is called the odd-even effect on the fragments charge distribution. However, no odd-even effect is observed on fragment mass number distribution. This result is attributed to nucleon pair breaking.

In nuclear fission events the nuclei may break into any combination of lighter nuclei, but the most common event is not fission to equal mass nuclei of about mass 120; the most common event (depending on isotope and process) is a slightly unequal fission in which one daughter nucleus has a mass of about 90 to 100 u and the other the remaining 130 to 140 u. Unequal fissions are energetically more favorable because this allows one product to be closer to the energetic minimum near mass 60 u (only a quarter of the average fissionable mass), while the other nucleus with mass 135 u is still not far out of the range of the most tightly bound nuclei (another statement of this, is that the atomic binding energy curve is slightly steeper to the left of mass 120 u than to the right of it).

Origin of the Active Energy and the Curve of Binding Energy

Nuclear fission of heavy elements produces energy because the specific binding energy (binding energy per mass) of intermediate-mass nuclei with atomic numbers and atomic masses close to ^{62}Ni and ^{56}Fe is greater than the nucleon-specific binding energy of very heavy nuclei, so that energy is released when heavy nuclei are broken apart.

The total rest masses of the fission products (Mp) from a single reaction is less than the mass of the original fuel nucleus (M). The excess mass Äm = M – Mp is the invariant mass of the energy that is released as photons (gamma rays) and kinetic energy of the fission fragments, according to the mass-energy equivalence formula $E = mc^2$. The variation in specific binding energy with atomic number is due to the interplay of the two fundamental forces acting on the component nucleons (protons and neutrons) that make up the nucleus. Nuclei are bound by an attractive nuclear force between nucleons, which overcomes the electrostatic repulsion between protons. However, the nuclear force acts only over relatively short ranges (a few nucleon diameters), since it follows an exponentially decaying Yukawa potential which makes it insignificant at longer distances. The electrostatic repulsion is of longer range, since it decays by an inverse-square rule, so that nuclei larger than about 12 nucleons in diameter reach a point that the total electrostatic repulsion overcomes the nuclear force and causes them to be spontaneously unstable. For the same reason, larger nuclei (more than about eight nucleons in diameter) are less tightly bound per unit mass than are smaller nuclei; breaking a large nucleus into two or more intermediate-sized nuclei, releases energy. The origin of this energy is the nuclear force, which intermediate-sized nuclei allows to act more efficiently, because each nucleon has more neighbours which are within the short range attraction of this force.

Also because of the short range of the strong binding force, large stable nuclei must contain proportionally more neutrons than do the lightest elements, which are most stable with a 1 to 1 ratio of protons and neutrons. Nuclei which have more than 20 protons cannot be stable unless they have more than an equal number of neutrons.

Extra neutrons stabilize heavy elements because they add to strong-force binding (which acts between all nucleons), without adding to proton-proton repulsion. Fission products have, on average, about the same ratio of neutrons and protons as their parent nucleus, and are therefore usually unstable to beta decay (which changes neutrons to protons) because they have proportionally too many neutrons compared to stable isotopes of similar mass. This tendency for fission product nuclei to beta-decay is the fundamental cause of the problem of radioactive high level waste from nuclear reactors. Fission products tend to be beta emitters, emitting fast-moving electrons to conserve electric charge, as excess neutrons convert to protons in the fission-product atoms.

Nuclear or "Fissile" Fuels

The most common nuclear fuels, ^{235}U and ^{239}Pu, are not major radiological hazards by themselves: ^{235}U has a half-life of approximately 700 million years, and although ^{239}Pu has a half-life of only about 24,000 years, it is a pure alpha particle emitter and hence not particularly dangerous unless ingested. Once a fuel element has been used, the remaining fuel material is intimately mixed with highly radioactive fission products that emit energetic beta particles and gamma rays. Some fission products have half-lives as short as seconds; others have half-lives of tens of thousands of years, requiring long-term storage in facilities such as Yucca

Mountain nuclear waste repository until the fission products decay into non-radioactive stable isotopes.

Chain Reactions

Several heavy elements, such as uranium, thorium, and plutonium, undergo both spontaneous fission, a form of radioactive decay and *induced fission,* a form of nuclear reaction. Elemental isotopes that undergo induced fission when struck by a free neutron are called fissionable; isotopes that undergo fission when struck by a thermal, slow moving neutron are also called fissile. A few particularly fissile and readily obtainable isotopes (notably ^{235}U and ^{239}Pu) are called nuclear fuels because they can sustain a chain reaction and can be obtained in large enough quantities to be useful.

All fissionable and fissile isotopes undergo a small amount of spontaneous fission which releases a few free neutrons into any sample of nuclear fuel. Such neutrons would escape rapidly from the fuel and become a free neutron, with a mean lifetime of about 15 minutes before decaying to protons and beta particles. However, neutrons almost invariably impact and are absorbed by other nuclei in the vicinity long before this happens (newly-created fission neutrons move at about 7% of the speed of light, and even moderated neutrons move at about 8 times the speed of sound). Some neutrons will impact fuel nuclei and induce further fissions, releasing yet more neutrons. If enough nuclear fuel is assembled in one place, or if the escaping neutrons are sufficiently contained, then these freshly generated neutrons outnumber the neutrons that escape from the assembly, and a *sustained nuclear chain reaction* will take place.

An assembly that supports a sustained nuclear chain reaction is called a critical assembly or, if the assembly is almost entirely made of a nuclear fuel, a critical mass. The word "critical" refers to a cusp in the behavior of the differential equation that governs the number of free neutrons present in the fuel: if less than a critical mass is present, then the amount of neutrons is determined by radioactive decay, but if a critical mass or more is present, then the amount of neutrons is controlled instead by the physics of the chain reaction. The actual mass of a *critical mass* of nuclear fuel depends strongly on the geometry and surrounding materials.

Not all fissionable isotopes can sustain a chain reaction. For example, ^{238}U, the most abundant form of uranium, is fissionable but not fissile: it undergoes induced fission when impacted by an energetic neutron with over 1 MeV of kinetic energy. But too few of the neutrons produced by ^{238}U fission are energetic enough to induce further fissions in ^{238}U, so no chain reaction is possible with this isotope. Instead, bombarding ^{238}U with slow neutrons causes it to absorb them (becoming ^{239}U) and decay by beta emission to ^{239}Np which then decays again by the same process to ^{239}Pu; that process is used to manufacture ^{239}Pu in breeder reactors. In-situ plutonium production also contributes to the neutron chain reaction in other types of reactors after sufficient plutonium-239 has been produced, since plutonium-239 is also a fissile element which serves as fuel. It is estimated that up to half of the power produced by a standard "non-breeder" reactor is produced by the fission of plutonium-239 produced in place, over the total life-cycle of a fuel load.

Fissionable, non-fissile isotopes can be used as fission energy source even without a chain reaction. Bombarding ^{238}U with fast neutrons induces fissions, releasing energy as long as the external neutron source is present. This is an important effect in all reactors where fast neutrons from the fissile isotope can cause the fission of nearby ^{238}U nuclei, which means that some small part of the ^{238}U is "burned-up" in all nuclear fuels, especially in fast breeder reactors that operate with higher-energy neutrons. That same fast-fission effect is used to augment the energy released by modern thermonuclear weapons, by jacketing the weapon with ^{238}U to react with neutrons released by nuclear fusion at the center of the device.

Fission Reactors

Critical fission reactors are the most common type of nuclear reactor. In a critical fission reactor, neutrons produced by fission of fuel atoms are used to induce yet more fissions, to sustain a controllable amount of energy release. Devices that produce engineered but non-self-sustaining fission reactions are subcritical fission reactors. Such devices use radioactive decay or particle accelerators to trigger fissions. Critical fission reactors are built for three primary purposes, which typically involve different engineering trade-offs to take advantage of either the heat or the neutrons produced by the fission chain reaction:

- *power reactors* are intended to produce heat for nuclear power, either as part of a generating station or a local power system such as a nuclear submarine.
- *research reactors* are intended to produce neutrons and/or activate radioactive sources for scientific, medical, engineering, or other research purposes.
- *breeder reactors* are intended to produce nuclear fuels in bulk from more abundant isotopes. The better known fast breeder reactor makes ^{239}Pu (a nuclear fuel) from the naturally very abundant ^{238}U (not a nuclear fuel). Thermal breeder reactors previously tested using ^{232}Th to breed the fissile isotope ^{233}U continue to be studied and developed.

While, in principle, all fission reactors can act in all three capacities, in practice the tasks lead to conflicting engineering goals and most reactors have been built with only one of the above tasks in mind. (There are several early counter-examples, such as the Hanford N reactor, now decommissioned). Power reactors generally convert the kinetic energy of fission products into heat, which is used to heat a working fluid and drive a heat engine that generates mechanical or electrical power. The working fluid is usually water with a steam turbine, but some designs use other materials such as gaseous helium. Research reactors produce neutrons that are used in various ways, with the heat of fission being treated as an unavoidable waste product. Breeder reactors are a specialized form of research reactor, with the caveat that the sample being irradiated is usually the fuel itself, a mixture of ^{238}U and ^{235}U.

Fission Bombs

One class of nuclear weapon, a *fission bomb* (not to be confused with the *fusion bomb*), otherwise known as an *atomic bomb* or *atom bomb*, is a fission reactor designed to liberate as much energy as possible as rapidly as possible, before the released energy causes the reactor to explode (and the chain reaction to stop). Development of nuclear weapons was the motivation behind early research into nuclear fission: the Manhattan Project of the U.S. military during

World War II carried out most of the early scientific work on fission chain reactions, culminating in the Trinity test bomb and the Little Boy and Fat Man bombs that were exploded over the cities Hiroshima, and Nagasaki, Japan in August 1945.

Even the first fission bombs were thousands of times more explosive than a comparable mass of chemical explosive. For example, Little Boy weighed a total of about four tons (of which 60 kg was nuclear fuel) and was 11 feet (3.4 m) long; it also yielded an explosion equivalent to about 15 kilotons of TNT, destroying a large part of the city of Hiroshima. Modern nuclear weapons (which include a thermonuclear *fusion* as well as one or more fission stages) are literally hundreds of times more energetic for their weight than the first pure fission atomic bombs, so that a modern single missile warhead bomb weighing less than 1/8th as much as Little Boy has a yield of 475,000 tons of TNT, and could bring destruction to 10 times the city area.

While the fundamental physics of the fission chain reaction in a nuclear weapon is similar to the physics of a controlled nuclear reactor, the two types of device must be engineered quite differently. It is impossible to convert a nuclear reactor to cause a true nuclear explosion, or for a nuclear reactor to explode the way a nuclear explosive does, (though partial fuel meltdowns and steam explosions have occurred). It is also difficult to extract useful power from a nuclear explosive, although at least one rocket propulsion system, Project Orion, is intended to work by exploding fission bombs behind a massively-padded and shielded vehicle. The strategic importance of nuclear weapons is a major reason why the technology of nuclear fission is politically sensitive. Viable fission bomb designs are, arguably, within the capabilities of bright undergraduates being relatively simple from an engineering viewpoint. However, the difficulty of obtaining fissile nuclear material to realize the designs, is the key to the relative unavailability of nuclear weapons to all but modern industrialized governments with special programs to produce fissile materials.

History— Natural Fission Chain-reactors on Earth

Criticality in nature is uncommon. At three ore deposits at Oklo in Gabon, sixteen sites (the so-called Oklo Fossil Reactors) have been discovered at which self-sustaining nuclear fission took place approximately 2 billion years ago. Unknown until 1972 (but postulated by Paul Kuroda in 1956), when French physicist Francis Perrin discovered the Oklo Fossil Reactors, it was realized that nature had beaten humans to the punch. Large-scale natural uranium fission chain reactions, moderated by normal water, had occurred far in the past and would not be possible now. This ancient process was able to use normal water as a moderator only because 2 billion years before the present, natural uranium was richer in the shorter-lived fissile isotope ^{235}U (about 3%), than natural uranium available today (which is only 0.7%, and must be enriched to 3% to be usable in light-water reactors).

Artificial Nuclear Fission

New Zealander, Ernest Rutherford is credited with splitting the atom in 1917. His team in Manchester, England bombarded nitrogen with naturally occurring alpha particles from radioactive material and observed a proton emitted with energy higher than the alpha particle. In 1932 his students John Cockcroft and Ernest Walton, working under Rutherford's direction, attempted to split the nucleus by entirely artificial means, using a particle accelerator to bombard lithium with protons, thereby producing two helium nuclei. After English physicist James Chadwick discovered the neutron in 1932, Enrico Fermi and his colleagues in Rome studied the results of bombarding uranium with neutrons in 1934. The first person who mentioned the idea of nuclear fission in 1934 was Ida Noddack.

After the Fermi publication, Lise Meitner, Otto Hahn and Fritz Strassmann began performing similar experiments in Germany. Meitner, an Austrian Jew, lost her citizenship with the Anschluss in 1938. She fled and wound up in Sweden, but continued to collaborate by mail and through meetings with Hahn in Sweden. By coincidence her nephew Otto Robert Frisch, also a refugee, was also in Sweden when Meitner received a letter from Hahn describing his chemical proof that some of the product of the bombardment of uranium with neutrons, was barium and not barium's much heavier chemical sister element radium (barium's atomic weight is about 60% that of uranium). Frisch was skeptical, but Meitner trusted Hahn's ability as a chemist. Marie Curie had been separating barium from radium for many years, and the techniques were well-known. According to Frisch: Was it a mistake? No, said Lise Meitner; Hahn was too good a chemist for that. But how could barium be formed from uranium? No larger fragments than protons or helium nuclei (alpha particles) had ever been chipped away from nuclei, and to chip off a large number not nearly enough energy was available. Nor was it possible that the uranium nucleus could have been cleaved right across. A nucleus was not like a brittle solid that can be cleaved or broken; George Gamow had suggested early on, and Bohr had given good arguments that a nucleus was much more like a liquid drop. Perhaps a drop could divide itself into two smaller drops in a more gradual manner, by first becoming elongated, then constricted, and finally being torn rather than broken in two? We knew that there were strong forces that would resist such a process, just as the surface tension of an ordinary liquid drop tends to resist its division into two smaller ones. But nuclei differed from ordinary drops in one important way: they were electrically charged, and that was known to counteract the surface tension.

The charge of a uranium nucleus, we found, was indeed large enough to overcome the effect of the surface tension almost completely; so the uranium nucleus might indeed resemble a very wobbly unstable drop, ready to divide itself at the slightest provocation, such as the impact of a single neutron. But there was another problem. After separation, the two drops would be driven apart by their mutual electric repulsion and would acquire high speed and hence a very large energy, about 200 MeV in all; where could that energy come from?...Lise Meitner... worked out that the two nuclei formed by the division of a uranium nucleus together would be lighter than the original uranium nucleus by about one-fifth the mass of a proton. Now whenever mass disappears energy is created, according to Einstein's formula E=mc2, and one-fifth of a proton mass was just equivalent to 200MeV. So here was the source for that energy; it all fitted!

In December 1938, the German chemists Otto Hahn and Fritz Strassmann sent a manuscript to *Naturwissenschaften* reporting they had detected the element barium after bombarding uranium with neutrons; simultaneously, they communicated these results to Lise Meitner. Meitner, and her nephew Otto Robert Frisch, correctly interpreted these results as being nuclear fission. Frisch confirmed this experimentally on 13 January 1939. In 1944, Hahn received the Nobel Prize for Chemistry for the discovery of nuclear fission. Some historians who have documented the history of the discovery of nuclear fission believe Meitner should have been awarded the Nobel Prize with Hahn.

Meitner's and Frisch's interpretation of the work of Hahn and Strassmann crossed the Atlantic Ocean with Niels Bohr, who was to lecture at Princeton University. Isidor Isaac Rabi and Willis Lamb, two Columbia University physicists working at Princeton, heard the news and carried it back to Columbia. Rabi said he told Enrico Fermi; Fermi gave credit to Lamb. Bohr soon thereafter went from Princeton to Columbia to see Fermi. Not finding Fermi in his office, Bohr went down to the cyclotron area and found Herbert L. Anderson. Bohr grabbed him by the shoulder and said: "Young man, let me explain to you about something new and exciting in physics." It was clear to a number of scientists at Columbia that they should try to detect the energy released in the nuclear fission of uranium from neutron bombardment. On 25 January 1939, a Columbia University team conducted the first nuclear fission experiment in the United States, which was done in the basement of Pupin Hall; the members of the team were Herbert L. Anderson, Eugene T. Booth, John R. Dunning, Enrico Fermi, G. Norris Glasoe, and Francis G. Slack. The next day, the Fifth Washington Conference on Theoretical Physics began in Washington, D.C. under the joint auspices of the George Washington University and the Carnegie Institution of Washington. There, the news on nuclear fission was spread even further, which fostered many more experimental demonstrations. Frédéric Joliot-Curie's team in Paris discovered that secondary neutrons are released during uranium fission, thus making a nuclear chain-reaction feasible. The figure of about two neutrons being emitted with nuclear fission of uranium was verified independently by Leo Szilárd and Walter Henry Zinn. The number of neutrons emitted with nuclear fission of U was then reported at 3.5/fission, and later corrected to 2.6/fission by Frédéric Joliot-Curie, Hans von Halban and Lew Kowarski.

Bibliography

Ackland, Len. Making a Real Killing: Rocky Flats and the Nuclear West. Albuquerque: The University of New Mexico Press, 1999.

Bradley, John. Learning to Glow: A Nuclear Reader. Tucson: University of Arizona Press, 2000.

Cochran, Thomas B. Nuclear Weapons Databook. Cambridge, MA: Ballinger Publishing Company, 1987.

Duncan, Francis. Rickover and the Nuclear Navy: The Discipline of Technology. Annapolis: Naval Institute Press, 1990.

Freedman, Lawrence. The Evolution of Nuclear Strategy. Studies in International Security, #20. New York: St. Martin's Press, 1981.

Gerstell, Richard. How to Survive an Atomic Bomb. Washington, D.C.: Combat Forces Press, 1950.

Herken, Gregg. The Winning Weapon: The Atomic Bomb in the Cold War, 1945-1950. Princeton: Princeton University Press, 1988.

Kaufmann, Albert R. Nuclear Reactor Fuel Elements: Metallurgy and Fabrication. New York: Interscience Publishers, Inc., 1962.

Lifton, Robert Jay, and Mitchell, Greg. Hiroshima in America: A Half Century of Denial. New York: Avon Books, 1995.

McPhee, John. The Curve of Binding Energy. New York: The Noonday Press, 1992.

Nininger, Robert D. Minerals for Atomic Energy. New York: D. Van Nostrand Company, Inc., 1954.

Pash, Boris T. The Alsos Mission. New York: Award House, 1969.

Sherwin, Martin J. A World Destroyed: The Atomic Bomb and the Grand Alliance. New York: Vintage Books, 1977.

Teller, Edward. The Legacy of Hiroshima. New York: Doubleday, 1962.

Winkler, Allan M. Life Under A Cloud: American Anxiety About the Atom. New York: Oxford University Press, 1993.

Index

□□□